Advance Praise for
All-American: 45 American Men on Being

"These are essential stories, each one a world, taken together a cosmos. America is a nation rejuvenated by immigrants. Islam is a tradition at its best when it travels. These pieces show that the hyphen between American and Muslim is a bridge not a barrier, that this young nation and that ancient tradition can be mutually enriching rather than mutually exclusive."

—Eboo Patel, Founder and President, Interfaith Youth Core, author of *Sacred Ground: Pluralism, Prejudice and the Promise of America*

"Filled with insight, humor and candid self-awareness, the stories in *All-American* are at once deeply personal and eminently relatable. Each one is a reminder of the unique dilemma of American identity: we are a nation of individualists striving to form a more perfect union. This book is a must-read for anyone who wants to learn more about their Muslim neighbors and about the wonderful diversity of our nation."

—G. Willow Wilson, author of *The Butterfly Mosque*

"The incredible variety of voices here will combat the pervasive and bigoted idea that all Muslim men share monolithic values and worldviews. This is an essential collection at a crucial time."

—Dave Eggers, author of *Zeitun* and *A Heartbreaking Work of Staggering Genius*

"Important, necessary, eloquent and humane, *All-American* is an eye-opening, heartfelt journey through the stupendous diversity of the American Muslim experience. Superb."

—Junot Dìaz, Pulitzer Prize recipient for Fiction for *The Brief Wondrous Life of Oscar Wao*

"I'm not Muslim. (For the record, I am not much of anything, religiously speaking—a lapsed Unitarian married to a lapsed Catholic who figures he may someday become a quasi-Buddhist.) But I am definitely, proudly American, and I found myself intrigued, surprised and moved by many of these fellow Americans' stories and voices—as well as unsettled, of course, that this book needs to exist at all."

—Kurt Andersen, novelist and host of Public Radio's *Studio 360*

"Over a decade after 9/11, the stereotypes, prejudices, and sometimes plain ignorance around Islam still, alas, remain. That is why the editors of and contributors to this collection are to be applauded. They not only present an alternative, more realistic, and accurate picture of Muslims in America, but they remind the reader of what America at its best stands for—a pluralistic, tolerant, just and open society."

—Akbar Ahmed, Ibn Khaldun Chair of Islamic Studies, School of International Service, American University

"Islam is the fastest growing religion in American and also the most misunderstood, All-American will help correct that imbalance. This book deserves the widest possible readership, especially among the young."

—Ahmed Rashid, author of *Taliban* and *Descent into Chaos*

"As W. H. Auden wrote, 'We must love one another or die.' And in order to love one another, we must know one another. Nothing could be more important to knit together American community life than sharing the stories of Muslim Americans. And no one is better suited to pull the best stories together than Wajahat Ali, a masterful storyteller himself."

—Macky Alston, documentary filmmaker and director of Auburn Media, Auburn Theological Seminary

All-American

A Note about the *I Speak for Myself* series:

I Speak for Myself is an inclusive platform through which people can make themselves heard and where everyone's voice has a place. ISFM's mission focuses on delivering one core product, a "narrative collection," that is mindset-altering, inspiring, relatable, and teachable. We aim to deliver interfaith, intercultural titles that are narrow in scope but rich in diversity.

Please be sure to check out our website, www.ISpeakforMyself.com, to learn more about the series, join the conversation, and even create an *I Speak for Myself* book of your own!

Sincerely,
Zahra T. Suratwala and Maria M. Ebrahimji
Co-Founders, *I Speak for Myself*

BOOKS IN THE SERIES

Volume 1: *I Speak for Myself: American Women on Being Muslim*

Volume 2: *American Men on Being Muslim: 45 American Men on Being Muslim*

Forthcoming:

Volume 3: *Demanding Dignity: Young Voices from the Front Lines of the Arab Revolutions*

All-American

45 AMERICAN MEN
ON BEING MUSLIM

edited by Wajahat M. Ali & Zahra T. Suratwala
Foreword by Congressman Keith Ellison

WHITE CLOUD PRESS
ASHLAND, OREGON

The views and opinions expressed by each contributing writer in this book are theirs alone and do not necessarily represent those of the series' editors or I Speak for Myself, Inc.

White Cloud Press books may be purchased for educational, business, or sales promotional use. For information, please write: Special Market Department, White Cloud Press, PO Box 3400, Ashland, OR 97520
Website: www.whitecloudpress.com

Design by Confluence Book Services

First edition: 2012

Printed in the United States of America

Library of Congress Cataloging-in-Publication Data

All-American : 45 American men on being Muslim / co-editors Wajahat M. Ali and Zahra T. Suratwala ; foreword by Congressman Keith Ellison.
  p. cm. -- (I speak for myself series)
  ISBN 978-1-935952-59-6 (pbk.)
1. Muslim men--United States--Biography. I. Ali, Wajahat. II. Suratwala, Zahra T.
  E184.M88A46 2012
  297.092'2--dc23
                              2012014744

Table of Contents

Note on Transcriptions

In transcribing Arabic, Persian, Urdu and other foreign words and names, we have chosen not to use diacritical marks and the like as found in scholarly literature. On first usage, a foreign word will be italicized with a short translation in parenthesis. A Glossary at the back of the book provides more complete definitions of terms.

Foreword

"It's not what you call me, but what I answer to."
—African proverb

Although a decade has passed since September 11, 2001, and the world has been abuzz about Islam and what it means since then, it is clear Muslim-Americans must tell their own stories.

Many have attempted to define Islam and the people who adhere to the faith. Islam in America is not something new. Islam has been practiced in America for fourteen generations, but our beliefs, our practices, and even our daily lives remain woefully misunderstood.

As a Member of the United States Congress I can assure you that I have been well treated, well received, and well respected by my colleagues. But because I get to discuss policy matters and be part of the public conversation every day, I can admit that misconceptions still exist.

What is regrettable is that in the past decade American Muslims have been associated with individuals who claim to practice the faith but actually use it as a means to establish their identity. These individuals have been willing to kill others and to die because of the identity they've *associated* with the religion—not because of the faith *inherent* in the religion. I must repeat something I've said before: If you use your religion as an identity as opposed to a path to divine inspirations and guidance, then you are no different than street gangs such as the Crips and the Bloods.

This is why the book you are now holding is so important. Readers of *All-American: 45 American Men on Being Muslim* will find within stories of faith that reveal a beautiful variety found among Muslims and that emphasize the "Americanness" of each writer.

Those who seek the divine want to make this world a better place, which first requires that we communicate. And I must say that each writer in *All-American* is communicating—connecting with readers in an honest, intimate, and effective way.

It's my hope that each of us will emulate these writers. If you can make a movie, make one. If you can sing a song, sing it. If you can write a play, write it. If you want to run for office, run. But do something to make this world a better place. For if each of us follows this example we won't have to worry about which religion we follow because we will all be united in what we *believe*, which is service to humanity.

Keith M. Ellison
Member, Congress of the United States

Introduction
by Wajahat M. Ali

A merican and Muslim.

To some, this might seem like the greatest oxymoron since military intelligence, or affordable housing, or…American Muslim.

According to the essays compiled in this book, however, there at least forty-five men whose narratives prove that individuals can live and identify fully as both Muslim and American—without conflict.

And apparently they're not that rare.

An incorrect perception nonetheless persists that Islam and America are inherently incompatible, at perpetual loggerheads, and doomed for an epic civilization clash. Some preach that all Muslims should be viewed through a lens of suspicion and fear, due to criminal deeds of a perverse few who misuse a religion to rationalize their hate.

Words like "stealth jihadists," "creeping Shariah," "violent extremists," and "radical Islam" have been mainstreamed and are rhetorically handcuffed to 1.5 billion diverse followers worldwide.

Islam is the most negatively viewed religion in America, with its lowest favorability rating since 2001. Nearly 60 percent of Americans say they do not know a Muslim, a third believe Muslims should not be eligible to sit on the US Supreme Court, and a similar number hold that Muslims should be barred from running for President.

The reality of American Muslims, however, paints a far more nuanced, complex, colorful and optimistic picture. Currently there are

2.6 million Muslims in the US, comprising nearly one percent of the population. A 2011 Gallup poll found the vast majority of Muslim Americans are loyal and optimistic about America's future. They are mostly middle class, mainstream, and well integrated into American society. Also, the Muslim American community is by far the most diverse US religious group in terms of ethnic diversity, socio-economic status, education levels and political affiliation.

The American Muslim men profiled within these pages eradicate antiquated assumptions of what it means to be "Muslim," "American," and even a "man." This may be a book of essays, but it is most simply a gathering of voices who are telling stories. It is fitting that the protagonists of these tales are American Muslim men who finally get the chance to tell their story to us, instead of having their story told to them by others with a political agenda, a well-intentioned yet naïve myopia, or sensationalistic headlines willing to exploit stereotypes for the sake of selling papers or gaining Facebook likes and re-tweets.

In traditional times in Muslim lands, the storyteller was more valuable than the swordsman.

The storyteller was responsible for sharing the tribe's history and narrating tales that reminded them of their shared values, identity and legacy.

In the seventh century, a merchant from Saudi Arabia was given a revelation in the Qur'an, Islam's Holy Book: "Oh those who believe, we have made you of different nations and tribes, so that you may know one another."

And how do we get to *know* a people, really?

Even in America, we often say, "Hey man, tell me your story." So, here are forty-five American Muslims telling their story.

But, are they American Muslims or Muslim Americans?

Sunni or Shiite?

Indigenous or Immigrant?

Conservative or Liberal?

Traditionally Conservative with Liberal leanings or Progressively Liberal with Traditional leanings?

Practicing Muslims with respect for Secularism or Secular Muslims with respect for Spirituality?

Can they be all of the above? None of the above? Some of the above?

Are there more options?

We love labeling in America.

We are a nation that thrives on lumping people into distinct, clean, tidy categories that can easily be checked on a ballot box. Yet America and her people can never be confined within the suffocating entrapments of a single box, label, category, stereotype or caricature. We must take into consideration the nation's rich bouillabaisse of languages, religions and ethnicities that intersect and circumambulate one another endlessly, on a daily basis.

It's this vibrancy, this piggybacking of cultures, this ever-evolving, messy, smorgasbord of various people and communities that continues to define and re-define the American mosaic.

We're a bunch of Whirling Dervishes constantly in motion—with ecstasy, love, fear, panic, hope, and energy in no short supply.

As this anthology proves, American Muslim is a multi-hyphenated identity that not only exists, but rather flourishes in the multicultural laboratory that is America.

For too long the stories of Muslim men have been inelegantly colored by tawdry stereotypes and weighed down by the narrative anchors of violence, fundamentalism, fear, and hysteria. The stories of princes and kings of our communities, past and present, are never mentioned nor remembered.

Apparently, there are no more Muhammad Alis and no more Hakeem the Dreams. We Muslim men have been replaced by the Osama Bin Ladens and Anwar Awlakis; the Rage Boys and the Underwear Bombers.

Some might think Muslim men want to drape a burqa over the Statute of Liberty and transform our mosques into stealth Trojan horses instead of constitutionally protected religious houses of worship where communities have been praying for decades.

There are those who fear we want to replace PB&J sandwiches in schools with falafel and hummus—although that would make for a healthier alternative. (Just saying.)

There are some who believe that all Muslim men are like the Borg, the cybernetic alien entity from *Star Trek,* that all share one dour, lifeless personality, and one oppressive, collective consciousness.

The contributors within this anthology prove those fears are unfounded, wrong, and just plain silly.

Instead of focusing on the outrageous and sensationalistic, these stories, through their honesty, personality, and humor, remind us of the commonality of human experiences that bind all stories and storytellers, regardless of our cultural idiosyncrasies and differences.

In essence, these stories *are* America.

The American Muslims within these pages are all unique protagonists of their universal narratives who proudly claim both Islam and America as core foundations of their identity. From an Iranian American breakdancer and a white convert who embraced Islam through Hip Hop and *The Autobiography of Malcolm X*, to South Asian Americans who found their calling through stand-up comedy and others who discovered a passion for politics. Presented here are poets, scientists, a US soldier, and a teacher. These men run the gamut from married, divorced, straight, and gay, to single and ready to mingle (or Facebook poke).

Remember, the storyteller was once more valued than the swordsman.

In today's world, we have enough swords and bombs and hate and fear.

We need more storytellers to share their tales of love, hope, pain, resilience, and understanding.

We need stories that are by us, but for everyone. And maybe even new stories about the tastiness of peanut butter and hummus sandwiches.

The Faith That
Faith Produced
by Haroon Moghul

Haroon Moghul is a doctoral candidate at Columbia University, a Fellow at the Institute for Social Policy and Understanding, and an Associate Editor at Religion Dispatches. He speaks frequently at mosques, universities, and conferences across the country and internationally. His first novel, *The Order of Light* (Penguin, 2006), was an eerie forecasting of the Arab Spring, featuring angry young men and women lighting themselves on fire to protest the injustices of an authoritarian Middle East. He has given a number of lectures explaining the Arab Spring through the metaphor of *Star Wars*. Born in New England, Haroon has lived in New York City for much of the last decade and is a lifelong Lakers fan. He recently led almost fifty North American Muslims on a tour of the Muslim heritage of Spain, which he plans to expand to Bosnia and Turkey in the coming year.

I was washing dishes in the kitchen when I stopped believing in God. Years later, I'm often unsettled at how much of my life I'd spent in that kitchen and how little of it I can recall, except for that one moment. Overwhelmed by constant desperation, I turned suddenly courageous, pondered what might happen if He didn't exist, decided that He didn't, and then He was gone. I think the rapid departure hit me the hardest. How had I been so easily taken in?

1

I was raised to believe I should be Muslim, before everything and after everything. My brain bought into this priority and everywhere reproduced it, till I'd spawned a deranged monster running wild in my head, condemning everything I came across as insufficiently Islamic. And not just other people; I was the harshest judge of my disappointingly un-Muslim self. In that kitchen, that life of forced and faux piety reached its theological dénouement. It popped up as I pivoted from the sink to the dishwasher: What if I could sin, because sin wasn't sin? And then—what if He didn't care what I did, because He wasn't?

If there was no God, my caustic monster could be driven into a corner, and then pummeled bloodied and helpless. My frustration, late night breakdowns, and everyday desolation would leave me be. And so I did it. I did what even the pagan Arabs around Muhammad, (peace be upon him), refused to do: I rejected God altogether. And on ceasing to be a Muslim, it occurred to me that perhaps this was not only a good thing, but also a reasonable thing. If with sudsy hands and slippery dishes I could just let God go, then it seemed— almost inevitably—that I'd never really believed in Him, anyway.

So what happened after I renounced Allah? There was that sense that I'd perhaps never believed. There was, of course, the awkward flinch. The waiting, looking behind my back and all around me, with the faucet still at full blast while I listened to the sound of a world absent of divinity. There was even some disbelief in the efficacy of my disbelief, an uncertainty of what I had just accomplished. Just because I chose not to believe in God, how could that mean He didn't exist? And then, more worryingly—could I really get away with this?

I was so taken by the sense of Him—impossibly demanding, relentlessly censorious—that I feared He'd still punish me even from non-existence. Not too different from how, even when you're a little bit grown up, you still check for monsters under the bed. Perhaps the dishwasher would explode or I'd somehow drown in a never-before clogged kitchen sink, and the police would only find my bloated body days later. Such was the depth of my Islam.

We call them dark nights of the soul. The idea is ascribed to a Spanish Muslim, Ibn 'Abbad ar-Rundi, though at the time I had no idea what was happening to me. It would've been nice to have known that my spiritual anguish didn't mean I was rejecting faith, or being rejected by the object of my faith. Such anguish might be a purging; God nudging us to reject something in ourselves, an error in our acts or our aspirations. But I was never taught Islam as a journey, even though I came from a religious family.

I grew up in an environment where religion and religious ideas frequently circulated. Much of the time they just squatted there, competing with the oxygen. The study of Arabic was facilitated. Going to the masjid was beyond routine; it was habit. I found myself convinced, or made myself convinced, by what we called orthodoxy. But it wasn't my faith—or my practice. My knowledge of Islam did worse than paralyze me—it defeated me. I mean altogether wrecked me.

How could I, (1) complete all of the endless tasks Islam assigned, (2) make sure I was doing them for the right reasons, and (3) keep on the watch, the straight and narrow, not for weeks or months, but for *decades*, to satisfy this God into not burning me alive? I might live Islamically, but just for a few days, and thereafter I'd give in to temptations my Islam had no room for, my religious education gave me no means to comprehend, and my sense of the divine gave me no slack to grapple with.

Islam left me crumpled in otherworldly exhaustion, the spiritual effort to be Muslim wearying me like no physical exertion ever could. Beyond those occasional days filled with a passion for God—there was nothing. Not the least inclination to have anything to do with Him. And, after enough of that, I wanted out. Out of the guilt and endless hand-wringing; a way to throttle that judgmental monster of my mind, to tell him to take a life-long time-out in the corner, euthanize him or expel him, deport or detain him—anything to give me some peace.

I'd had enough of the questions, the doubts, the self-incrimination, the endless feelings of unworthiness, the inability to find myself in the desperate hatred of myself for my own weakness. I was sick of asking which of these feelings were legitimate and which illegitimate, which were epiphenomenal and which inevitable—the distinctions between which seem stupidly petty unless you're trying so damn hard to figure out why the prayer rug seems to take over the room and chase you from it.

In a Muslim tradition, we read that God told Muhammad, "I am as My servant thinks of Me." If we think of Him as angry, He'll be angry with us. Soon my rage at an implacable God bounced off of Him and stuck to me. Anger. Envy. Frustration. A hatred of myself and my desires, and a flood of negative energy that, religiously and psychologically speaking, I could only direct against my God or myself. If I couldn't meet the challenge He'd set for me, then why was I even alive? And, of course, when faith leads one to turn on oneself, then not surprisingly it becomes easier to choose deicide over suicide.

The Qur'an says God created humankind to piously serve Him. And He tests us in this, to see if we'll live up to our purpose. But He never asked us if we *wanted* to go along. And despite our lack of choice, we're still expected to perform. On the few occasions I managed to bring this up to some Muslims for their advice, I got this response: God knows us better than we know ourselves. When He gave us Islam, it's like a doctor prescribing medication. (Figures a community of medical professionals would think that made sense.) But I didn't see why the doctor who created us, created us sick, and more than that, held us to account for a failure to take His medicine. No other doctor throws you in hell if you dispute his prescription.

Many who question God's existence are more concerned with His relevance to them than any metaphysics. We can only be free if we remove the shackles of faith, these self-ruining feelings of incompleteness, prudery and debasement, and accept the inevitability of our random lives. I don't mean to be flippant. This is how it seemed to me, and I'd be lying if I said it didn't knock me off my feet. Why spend my existence fighting myself, when I was doing a pretty crap job of it anyway, suffer a personally unsatisfying and intellectually marginal existence, and then burn in hell?

I wanted so badly for the absence of Him to free me—from moral failures, from rigid standards I could not live within, and from a life of lonely denial. I wanted to stop being angry at the world and stop hating myself. And so there I was, washing dishes. Even now, it amazes me how suddenly the idea popped into my mind, how audacious it was, and yet how quickly I embraced it. That absence of belief felt like a physical absence, like remembering the house you grew up in only to realize you'd been alone all your life, and none of the people you recalled filling up the other rooms even when you couldn't see them had ever really been there.

And now, years later, why tell a story whose very point constitutes Islam's gravest sin? Only because we need to be honest, as we used to be. Once, our mentors and scholars, our music and literature, and even our architecture, were devoted to the admission of Islam as a journey, throughout which we needed every support we could have. We've lately become so enraptured by Islam's simplicity, portability, and rationality, that we've confused the accessibility of a tradition with the mastery of the destination it sets before us.

Islam's deceptively easy declaration of itself—there is no God but God, and Muhammad is the messenger of that God—is a testimony (*shahadah*) whose only realization is existential. For I was taught the *shahadah*, and I still despaired of God. Just to speak these words, and to mean them, may take all of a lifetime, and it is for this reason that, for Islam to work, God must be both Infinitely Merciful and Endlessly Just.

And so we see the journey so many Muslims of our times have taken, from ideologies and identities to the fatal exhaustion and inadequacy of the mind to determine things on its own. A spiritual revolution, often beginning in pain, the desolate pain of separation, failure, and defeat. That is my journey, too—one that's taken me many years to even realize I was on, and for all its ecstasies and disappointments, it is a journey to faith that began with the loss of it.

Pop Culture Matters
by Svend White

Svend White is an Information Technology consultant and occasional Muslim activist. He currently lives with his wife and daughter in Oklahoma. He was raised a Muslim in Boston and has lived
and worked in Europe, South Asia, and the Persian Gulf. He has
a Master's Degree in Religion (Islamic Studies) from the University of Georgia, Athens. His work has been published in several
scholarly journals and he has contributed chapters and encyclo-
pedia entries to scholarly volumes on Islam and Muslims. He has
also written for some prominent related online and print media,
including *Q-News*, *Islamica Magazine*, ReligionDispatches.com,
openDemocracy.net, and altmuslim.com.

A s a teen in Boston in the late 1980s, I was once browsing the record bins to pounding house music, when the music suddenly
morphed into a funky, Middle Eastern rhythm. My ears perked up
and, to my delight, the singer soon exclaimed, "Insha'Allah!" *Finally*,
I thought, *something to listen to that I can relate to*, and I eagerly bought
the cassette. I ripped off its plastic wrapping and examined its liner
to discover the identity of this cool Muslim group, only to discover
Hebrew instead of Arabic. The singer was Ofra Haza, a Yemeni Jew
sometimes called "the Madonna of the Middle East." I was crest-
fallen, though less because she was Jewish than because the cosmos

seemed to be taunting me. My status as a cultural island had been reaffirmed by a Jewish woman speaking an Islamic prayer.

I am an American-born Muslim of Danish, English and French-Canadian descent, but I never converted to Islam. My brother Erik and I were raised in a Muslim family in Boston. Some find this fact shocking, but while that's admittedly an atypical background, a white Muslim is hardly an exotic bird today. Over the years, I've met many Muslims born of the union of two converts, but only one that was white *and* born in the early 1970s. So my background distinguishes itself mainly by its historical timing—my coming of age in the late 1980s as opposed to the 1990s or 2000s—as opposed to its ethno-cultural particulars.

My father was raised a staunch Catholic in Boston. He planned to become a Jesuit until, as a teenager, he came across Thomas Paine's *The Age of Reason* and brought the deist manifesto's rationalistic critiques of the Bible to his priest.[1] He explored other religions on his own for a time, including Islam, without finding much that he liked. Then he made the acquaintance of a thoughtful gentleman in California from the then-young nation of Pakistan. Liking what he learned about Islam through this new friend, he converted in 1957, just before shipping out to Korea with the Marines. A decade later in Copenhagen, my Lutheran-raised Danish mother likewise discovered and embraced Islam through a friendship with a Pakistani coworker. These two Pakistanis happened to be kin; a trans-Atlantic courtship by mail ensued and culminated in my future parents' unlikely marriage in 1971. I was born in Boston in 1972, and my brother arrived five years later. So, despite my deathly pallor and red hair, I was raised a Muslim,[2] and until

---

[1] Ironically, I now find many of Paine's objections wanting. But I am grateful that book wasn't checked out from the library that fateful day in 1956.

[2] Nonetheless, I'm ultimately not sure what category—convert or "born" Muslim—applies more to my background, as important dynamics of both resonate for me. I was raised a Muslim, but I had infrequent contact with the broader Muslim community in Boston before my college years and usually found myself the sole Muslim in my class or circle.

the age of five had the unexpected first name of "Muhammad Akram."[3]

Getting back to cultural matters, it is easy for adults to forget the power of pop culture in the lives of children. It's the barest of exaggerations to say that I would have *killed* to have a hip, pious Muslim singer like the international sensation—and *nasheed* (Islamic devotional song) sensation—Sami Yusuf when I was a kid. Poets, Percy Bysshe Shelley famously noted, are the "unacknowledged legislators of the world." As a parent of a young girl, I struggle to conceive of a metaphor grandiose enough to convey the influence of "poets"—that is, artists, writers and other producers of culture—today, a century and a half later. However ephemeral and trite most of its manifestations may be, a society's culture and its accompanying aesthetic sensibilities are powerful and inexorable components of children's sense of themselves.

Putting on my father's hat for a moment, I think that Muslim parents can and should strive to counter or at least mitigate the often superficial (and sometimes downright harmful) values peddled by American popular culture today, but they must also choose their battles wisely and realize the stark limitations on their influence in some critical domains. However different their parents' tastes might be, a child's aesthetic sensibilities are to a great extent osmotically absorbed from the surrounding society and, I suspect, practically impervious to preaching or parental dictates.

I don't think that importing "authentic" religious culture from abroad is a viable solution for meeting the needs of Muslim children in this position. It behooves community leaders to support efforts to

---

[3] Being idealistic and eager to be "authentic"—as I suspect converts to all religions often are—my parents uncritically accepted the hoary myth that a person must adopt an "Islamic" name upon conversion. Thus, Barry Quentin White spent much of the 1960s going by "Muhammad Sadiq Abyad"—the final word meaning "white" in Arabic——and Jette often went by "Aisha." However, after observing the highly negative reactions among Bostonians to their little red—haired son named Muhammad, they tacked on a more ethnically appropriate first name. I still got teased, but at least I didn't spend my childhood enduring "Float like a butterfly, sting like a bee" jokes.

promote or create alternatives to those aspects of the majority culture with which we disagree that are no less engaging to our children, but which remain consonant with our religious values. Otherwise, a cognitive gulf arises between our children's values and their cultural milieu. Nature, as the saying goes, abhors a vacuum, so something will ultimately fill that void and erode those cherished values—if not also the child's sense of belonging to their religious community.

As one might guess, this was no academic question for me when I was growing up in the '70s and '80s. I knew nothing of what sociologists call "identity formation," but I yearned for heroes and cultural points of references that affirmed my eclectic identity and made my religious community visible in American society. I was very conscious of my religious differences from my CCD—or *shul*-attending classmates.[4] And, thanks to various cultural differences, I often did feel not entirely conformable in the major Boston mosques, with their more upwardly-mobile congregations[5] and constant din of foreign languages.

This longing for community and its cultural trappings manifested itself in a variety of ways. Some now seem silly. What, I wondered, would a *Muslim* do if he got cornered by Dracula? It's easy enough to whip up a passable cross or perhaps even a rough approximation of a Star of David with random objects as you scramble to escape a bloodsucker, but you'd need a machine shop to produce a reasonable facsimile of a crescent and a star, which is hardly fair. Others were rather more serious; I hadn't heard of "Orientalism," either, but I knew there was something profoundly wrong with my religion consistently being represented to the masses on TV by the dastardly Iron Sheikh and his "camel clutch."

---

[4] CCD stands for "Confraternity of Christian Doctrine," a Catholic organization involved in educating Catholic children about their faith, often in after—school courses. *Shul* is Yiddish for "school."

[5] In retrospect, I see a touch of nativism on my part in this perception, perhaps as a defense mechanism. I did feel an abstract sense of kinship with these kids as fellow Muslims, but we didn't seem to have much in common, though my nascent class—warrior streak probably did not help me connect.

So I re-purposed what I could in my cultural toolbox to provide support for a non-Christian identity. I gobbled up hip-hop, with its scores of self-proclaimed Muslims—many of whom admittedly seemed far more influenced by Moorish Science Afrocentric mythology than the religion I knew. But non-Christians couldn't be very choosy in those far less multicultural times. I was instinctively offended from an early age by the Borg-like unchallenged sway enjoyed by the Yuletide season—I knew it wasn't fair that Christmas dominated my imagination every December while my classmates had barely heard of Hannukah, much less Ramadan—so for me, the Grinch and Ebenezer Scrooge weren't villains who eventually redeemed themselves. In my half-joking telling, they were multi-cultural freedom fighters holding the line against a Trojan horse, tragic heroes who, in the end, succumbed to the forces of conformism.

In any other situation, Ofra Haza's religion would have been an unalloyed good, as for me Judaism and Jewish culture were far from stigmatized. To the contrary, they enjoyed a privileged status in my eyes as a proven, unimpeachably authentic mode of being American that didn't require one to leave one's religion's various "archaic" rituals and behavioral taboos at the door. Until my college years—and in spite of Moustapha Akkad's legendary 1976 biopic of the Prophet Muhammad, *The Message*—had you asked me to name my favorite "Muslim" film, I probably would have answered, "Fiddler on the Roof," which was the first movie that I remember finding moving.

I even had a rather unlikely quasi-Zionist attachment as a teen. Before I became aware of the Holy Land's tortured modern history or the plight of my Palestinian coreligionists, I was instinctively fascinated by Israel—and a bit jealous of my Jewish friends for its existence—since I saw it as a modern, culturally-compatible place where my Jewish friends could practice their faith freely, without fear of ridicule from disapproving Goyim. I didn't have or know of anything comparable for me as an American Muslim. I no longer harbor such an idealized image of the Jewish State, but even so I suspect that I understand the appeal of *aliyah* (Hebrew for immigrating to Israel) more than most *goyim* (Yiddish for non-Jews).

When I transferred to an elementary school in Somerville in the early 1980s, I was encouraged by my new teacher, a former Red Sox pitcher, to explain to my classmates just what "the religion of Muzlum"[sic] was all about. I tried to keep it really simple, saying, "Well, we're just like Jews. We don't eat pork and we pray several times a day. We..." and then I noticed that much of the class had started to giggle and cease talking: I wondered what had triggered the snickers. Slowly, it dawned on me that it was my matter-of-fact declaration that Muslims are "like Jews" that had tickled their funny bone. To at least of some of them, "Jews" weren't representatives of an ancient, respected religious tradition—they were simply exotic stock characters in ethnic jokes. It blew my mind—to me, Jews were normal people, only a bit cooler and more interesting.[6]

In conclusion, it has to be said that in numerous respects conditions today are a quantum leap better than those of my childhood. Just as one need not travel to the ends of the Earth to obtain *halal* (permitted) meat or attend *jummah* (the weekly religious service, held early on Friday afternoon). In most major cities, there is a great variety of English-language books, movies, and even CDs that are designed to capture the imaginations of Muslim youngsters living in Western countries. More importantly, perhaps, some of the North American Muslim community's leading scholars have embraced the legitimacy of—and, indeed, the need for—new approaches to Islam that are both rooted in the

---

[6] I discovered that I wasn't the only person to be aware of my religious differences later that year when a classmate confronted me one morning before class, demanding, "Tell your people to let our boys go!" It eventually emerged, to my disbelief, that she was requesting that I put in a good word for the American hostages being held in Beirut at the time. The assumption seemed to be that all Muslims had a personal hotline to the Amal Militia in the Beqa Valley. (Interestingly, the girl was of Irish descent and very proud of it. Sadly, it never occurred to me to ask her about the Irish Republican Army.)

age-old principles of Islamic tradition but also aware of the tastes and specific needs of American society.[7]

While I would not presume to universalize the foibles and struggles of my own childhood, my experiences certainly seem to support the wisdom of this emerging new paradigm. Much important progress has undeniably been made, but I think it remains important for community leaders to reflect on the challenges faced by many American Muslims so that they know not to stifle cultural trends that may seem trivial to them, but which may, unbeknownst to them, be singularly important to their children. Having struggled with these issues as a child myself and now being the father of a young girl who will soon embark on this complex and increasingly perilous journey, I want all the tools I can get to keep her connected to the American Muslim community.

---

[7] For two analyses of this extremely important trend, see Umar Faruq Abd—Al-lah's seminal essay "Islam and the Cultural Imperative" (*Cross Currents*, 56:3, 2006) and Sherman Jackson's groundbreaking reevaluation of the Nation of Islam in light of its achievements in community building, *Islam and the Blackamerican: looking toward the third resurrection* (Oxford University Press, 2005).

Disable Your Cloaking Device
by Jason Moy

Jason W. Moy is an attorney working for the United States Army Judge Advocates General Corps. Born in San Francisco, California to non-Muslim parents, he converted to Islam while attending the University of Southern California on a Reserve Officer Training Corps Scholarship. Jason graduated with a degree in Political Science and a minor in military science and furthered his education by going to law school at the University of California at Davis. After law school, Jason was stationed in South Korea where he assisted Soldiers in civil and tax law matters. While in Korea, he became the de facto spiritual leader for several Muslim Soldiers stationed there. Following his assignment in Korea, Jason became a defense counsel for US soldiers and spent sixteen months in Afghanistan, earning a Bronze Star for his service. He is currently stationed at Fort Bragg, North Carolina and works as a legal advisor for the 95th Civil Affairs Brigade (Airborne).

"This is so embarrassing; God, why do I have to do this…why? Well, they don't have the Truth, so why should I care what they think? What do I care if they think I am odd? Let them think what they are going to think. This is something that I MUST do in order to obey Allah. I shouldn't be embarrassed; I should be proud."

Shortly before September 11, 2001, after spending a couple years researching religions on my own, I decided to embrace Islam as my way of life. At the time, I was studying political science at the University of Southern California on a US Army Reserve Officer Training Corps Scholarship.

After surveying the religious world, I found myself gravitating towards Islam due to its fierce monotheism, easily digestible definition of God, and compatibility with our understanding of science and human observation. After years of searching for an outfit, it was time to get out of the dressing room and put on my religion. However, the garment I was putting on came straight from the Emperor's new wardrobe—it was invisible.

There I was, a white boy on the outside, Muslim on the inside. So in the beginning, I proudly spread the word in order to fulfill my duties of *dawa* (inviting others to Islam). Others began to realize that I was Muslim, and to some non-Muslim Americans it was like I had caught an awful disease. They would typically ask, "How did that happen?" As if I had befallen some sort of terrible fate—doomed and contagious. And 9/11 didn't help either.

I wanted to express my newly found self, but soon learned that it may be best to keep my cloaking device on amongst non-Muslims. I felt many of them did not want to know what I discovered in Islam, but only wanted to learn how to avoid what I had caught, like a public service announcement on how to avoid catching the plague. Of course that was not always the case, but it was true enough of the time for me to feel defensive.

After joining the Army, I found myself, like many other soldiers, in Afghanistan. The average soldier had no idea I was Muslim unless I let them know, and usually I had no reason to do so. My colleagues knew because I would tell them I had to go pray, or I had to fast for Ramadan. However, there were a few times that I had to remove my cloaking device in order to perform certain ritual tasks amongst the general population of soldiers. One of those was *wudu* (ablutions).

Multiple times a day, I hiked across the chunky gravel, inhaling the dusty air, going towards the shower facility in Afghanistan to perform wudu. The shower facilities consisted of decommissioned, modified shipping containers polymerized into a modularized structure. On the bottom floor were the boilers powered by diesel fuel, and the toilets. The top floor contained the showers and a group of sinks. As I walked to these man-made oases in an otherwise slate-grey, monochromatic environment, I struggled with how I felt others perceived me, how easy it would be not to pray, but how I must continue on and fight the whispers in my head telling me to give up.

Making wudu to attain ritual purity for prayer in Afghanistan is a humbling experience. Each time I walked to the shower facility, the inner voices would come: "Why am I doing this; why do I have to put myself in this uncomfortable position?"

As I ascended the stairs to the top level, so did my anxiety: I continued my inner monologue, reinforcing the superiority of my decision, bashing the whispers of doubt as being from *Shaytan* (Satan). I would normally try to find the least occupied group of sinks and begin. Sometimes, to my delight, the place would be empty, but that was a rarity. Many times I had to grin and bear it.

The sinks were extraordinarily close, so that four could be crammed into the space that would typically be the amount of space for dual vanity sinks in an upscale master bedroom. It was badly cramped brushing your teeth in the morning when there was more than one other person there, so much so that, lots of times soldiers would stagger themselves to avoid rubbing elbows. Three average-sized soldiers would fill the space allegedly available for four. Wudu is a water intensive process where the tendency to splash or spread water is high, especially when you raise your feet to the sink. This increases the possibility of cross contamination, which is one of the most taboo things in deployed military shower culture. I had to be very careful while performing wudu, making sure not to offend anyone.

To make wudu, I had to put myself into a distinctly altered uniform. I first removed my Army Combat Uniform pattern coat, so that my arms were uncovered to the elbows. In doing so, I inadvertently hid my rank as Captain. Next, I completed a complex balancing act, untying one boot, taking the boot off, removing my mid-calf high green sock, placing that sock into my cargo pocket and then putting my bare foot back into my boot. God forbid that my foot would actually touch the disgusting floors in those showers. Then repeat for the other side. If I was noticed at this point, I got a lot of looks flashed my way. But I had to power through reminding myself—I have the Truth on my side and *maghrib* (sunset and time for evening prayer) is only moments away. Once the footwork was complete, it was go time. Wash the hands, normal; face, normal; rinse out the mouth, normal; then the nose—abnormal. Arms, hair, ears—mostly normal. Then the unsheathing of the foot—definitely abnormal.

Perhaps for an Afghani that walked into the same place wearing sandals, *shalwar* (loose pajama-like trousers), *khameez* (long shirt or tunic), and a big bushy beard, this would not have been all that interesting. Perhaps soldiers would even expect an unfamiliar hygiene routine. But from an American, a white dude, a captain—it was a shock.

Each time I performed wudu it was a struggle. I didn't want to be embarrassed. What if someone mentions something to me? I felt so small, but consoled myself by remembering—this is what God wants of me. Why should I care if they stare at me? If they want to talk, let them. Perhaps I can educate them. The process did get a bit easier once I got some leather *khuffs* (socks) that could be simply wiped over with water, versus putting my whole foot in the sink.

But for every nasty or disapproving look I received, I can think of a time when I was able to communicate to others the love I have for Islam. My colleagues knew of my faith and also realized that I was a normal dude who liked *Aqua Teen Hunger Force*, *Lost*, and video games. After a time, I invited them to come to the largest masjid on Bagram Air Field to enjoy a typical Afghani meal of Kabuli rice and rustic lamb curry. Some came to Jummah prayers with me, some decided to fast with me during a couple of days in Ramadan. We shared many late night discussions about theology. And then one of them wanted to learn make wudu.

During Ramadan, our legal office was being visited by several high-level officers for a conference. It was near *dhuhr* (mid-day, time for afternoon prayers), and food was being served. Rather than sit uncomfortably watching people eat, I told my boss I was going to run over to the mosque and pray. A colleague and good friend of mine stated that he was fasting as well and wanted to come with me. I figured that he just wanted to get away from the company and get a bit of fresh air.

As we went to the masjid, I needed to make a pit stop for wudu. Now, my friend had been to the masjid with me, he had been to Jummah, enjoyed Afghani food, and we had waxed and waned about religion; he had even prayed beside me previously. But I had never told him about wudu. There was no reason to do so—until this point.

When we got to the shower facilities, I mentioned that I needed to wash up for prayer. He inquired and I told him about the requirements for wudu. To my complete surprise he wanted to join me—not to watch, but to participate. What a gift from God! I felt like the tables were completely turned, that I was not being looked at with disgust and disapproval, but rather as a role model or a teacher. This validated my choices and I felt rewarded for all the times I hiked up those stairs fighting my doubts.

Throughout my journey of being a Muslim male in America I have had the experience of being a spy and being spied upon (I was once asked in law school by a fellow student if my allegiance to the United States is solid because I am a Muslim), being an educator and being educated, and struggling with my own thoughts and the perceived thoughts of others. I have learned that while it might be more comfortable to cover your Muslimness, putting yourself out there allows you to experience more—for better or for worse. I would rather gladly be stared at and experience twinges of embarrassment, than miss the joy of teaching someone the wonders of Islam and watch as they embrace it.

Lying to Myself
by Aman Ali

Aman Ali is an award-winning storyteller in New York City and one of the only young American Muslim voices in the public spotlight today. His passionate and animated style of storytelling draws heavily from his upbringing and travels and continues to gain buzz from people all around the world. He's made appearances on dozens of media outlets such as *CNN, HBO, ABC News* and *NPR* to talk about his upbringing as a twenty-something Muslim born and raised in America.

As a performer, he's traveled all over the world and regularly hits the road for shows at colleges and theaters all around the country. As a reporter, he's covered everything from Hurricane Katrina recovery efforts in New Orleans to Capitol Hill politics in Washington DC to hula festivals in Hawaii. He has received several awards for his reporting, including one from the Associated Press in 2010 for his breaking news coverage in New York. He is also recognized for being the co-creator of the social media phenomenon 30 Mosques in 30 Days, a 13,000-mile road trip he took with his friend with the mission of telling authentic and compelling stories about Muslims in America.

I've been detained and interrogated at airports at least a dozen times over the past few years. I'm on a no-fly list and get frisked by TSA agents almost every time I go to the airport. In fact, I've had my junk grabbed so many times you might as well give me the nickname "Antiques Roadshow."

That previous paragraph has potential to be a good standup bit for me to use on stage. I'm sure it would get some decent laughs. But as a standup comic going on five years now, at this point in my life I'd be ashamed to even think about doing that.

I'll explain.

I grew up as a scrawny Indian kid in a predominantly white farm town in Ohio. I tried out for sports teams in high school but got cut because I had the physique of an eight-year-old gymnast. I'd try to act suave with the ladies, but it would generate about as much interest as an Islamic bank. I was hopeless. But instead of feeling insecure about it, I often parlayed it into the delight of others and myself. I found by joining my friends in laughing at my problems, it often squashed the insecurities I had about myself and gave me a sense of confidence I wasn't able to get from other activities, such as sports. My problems were often shared by my peers, making my jokes a way for me to quickly bond with people. Eventually, it was hard to describe myself without talking about my love for jokes.

Towards the end of college, I stumbled into standup. There were very few Muslim comedians out there, so I had an untapped market to fill up my calendar with shows. I watched the other Muslim co-medians crack jokes about hassles at the airport and being profiled as a terrorist, and audiences gobbled it up with laughter. So I followed suit, cranking out joke after joke about post 9/11 racial profiling. It got laughs, but my career wasn't really going anywhere. I'd do a show thinking it went well and I wouldn't get asked to come back.

Then one day I realized something I was always doing after shows. I'd roll out to dinner with people after a gig and crack them up ten times harder than when I was on stage. I'd tell them my awkward stories about growing up in Ohio, like how I told my first grade teacher I didn't feel comfortable taking part in the winter hol-iday celebrations because I didn't celebrate Christmas or Hanukah.

When one of the students asked why I wasn't doing any singing, my teacher told the kid "Oh, that's because Aman celebrates Kwanzaa."

Instead of doing lame airport jokes, I started getting on stage and telling these stories of my upbringing. Tales like trying to explain to my mom, an endearing Indian immigrant who thinks the CD rom tray on computers are cup holders, what I was doing when she walked in on me while I was throwing money in the air and dancing to a rap video on BET. It was even harder to come up with an explanation when she found me gyrating with my pants sagged down, pretending to make it rain on the booty girls on the screen. It was goofy shenanigans like these that seemed to strike a chord with people much more than anything I had ever talked about on stage.

I wasn't exactly sure where all this was leading until recently. I co-created a social media phenomenon called "30 Mosques in 30 Days," where my friend and I traveled to a different state each day during the Islamic month of Ramadan and blogged about it. We humanized the Muslim American experience by telling ordinary stories of folks around the country. All this was going on as everyone on the news yapped their flaps about the Ground Zero mosque or the Florida pastor threatening to burn a Qur'an.

None of the Muslims I met as I was traveling were really talking about those stories in the news. Instead, they were sharing with me their own awkward tales. One girl I met in North Carolina told me how she learned about "the birds and the bees." She was a huge fan of Pokemon cartoons in middle school and got on a downloading service to snag some episodes. She started watching what she thought was Pokemon but it turned out to be Japanese anime porn. The twelve-year-old pristinely-behaved Pakistani girl's parents almost fainted when she asked them to explain why Pikachu was spanking Jigglypuff with a leather whip.

There are countless cases of stories even today about Muslims getting pulled off airplanes or Muslim women being fired from jobs for wearing headscarves. I don't want to downplay the severity of those issues, but to say that these issues of backlash are reflective of average, ordinary Muslim American life in this country is absurd.

As a Muslim man in my mid-twenties, I talk about issues that matter to me…women. And how I have no luck with them because I always seem to stumble upon the girls who have tons of drama in their lives. A lot of guys think Muslim girls want to marry guys that are wealthy doctors, lawyers, or engineers. I disagree. I think the best profession to attract a girl is a job at the airport. Because a girl wants a guy who knows how to handle baggage.

But I digress. When I finally found my voice on stage, the crowds became larger and larger. And the other musicians/poets/comedians who were only talking about 9/11 stuff found their audiences fizzling over time. I think people are sick of hearing it. Frankly, I can't blame them. 9/11 happened 10 years ago.

I think one of the reasons it seems like most people in this country haven't embraced Muslims to the extent they have with other groups, is because we're only perceived as two dimensional characters—beard-or scarf-wearing (sometimes both?) zealots who are always getting patted down at the airports. By talking about that subject, I feel like I'm not only reinforcing those stereotypes, but I'm also lying to myself. I fly around three to four times a month, but only a tiny fraction of those times do I really have problems flying.

There are many Muslim entertainers that talk about these profiling subjects and are successful at it. I don't want to criticize someone for being successful, but I wish there were more entertainers that would shy away from these boring and dated subjects. How are we, as Muslims, going to dissolve these terrorist stereotypes if that's what we keep talking about? For me, such topics are just not reflective of who I am. I am not a political victim of a Big Brother government. Instead, I'm a scrawny Muslim kid that bops his head at hip-hop shows while everyone else is getting down because I'm too self-conscious to join them. And I highly doubt I'm the only one.

On stage, for the first time in years, I finally feel like myself. I get the same joy that I got as a kid, cracking up my friends with my stories. I'm no longer doing anything in someone else's footsteps. Instead, I'm the exact same person on stage as I am off stage, and the joy I get from that is incredible.

One of my favorite movie scenes of all time is at the end of *Teenage Mutant Ninja Turtles*, the first movie in the franchise. Michaelangelo is in midst of a fight when a Foot Soldier tries to strike him in the head from behind with an axe. Michaelangelo ducks his head into a shell, kicks the guy, then pops his head out and yells "GOD, I LOVE BEING A TURTLE!" That's how I feel every time I walk off stage.

In this City by the Lake
by Amer Ahmad

Amer Ahmad was named City of Chicago Comptroller by Mayor Rahm Emanuel on May 16, 2011. As Comptroller, he is responsible for the City's revenue and finance functions including the billing and collection of city revenue, cash flow and debt management, processing vendor payments and payroll, preparing and maintaining official financial records, administration of employee and annuitant benefit programs, and internal audit and risk management.

Previously, Amer Ahmad served as a Senior Vice President and head of the public sector group at the Cleveland-based bank KeyCorp. He served as Deputy State Treasurer and Chief Financial Officer for the State of Ohio Treasury. In that capacity, he oversaw more than $11 billion in state investments, $9 billion in state debt obligations, and over $150 billion per year in custodial assets for Ohio's pension systems. Prior to becoming a public servant, Amer was a Vice President at the Chicago-based investment firm William Blair & Company. Amer received his MBA from Harvard Business School and his Bachelor's degree in political science from Columbia University. Amer is married to Samar Kaukab Ahmad and resides in Chicago's Hyde Park neighborhood.

December 12, 2006: The hospital Neonatal Intensive Care Unit was frenzied with activity—beeping alarms, nurses in colorful scrubs performing their regular duties, and a muffled kitten-like cry coming from another room. Life in the neonatal intensive care unit never stops—not even the brutal Chicago winter can bring it to a halt. But for me, time stood still as I desperately looked into the incubator at the tiny being in front of me, a human being that weighed just two pounds. This was my first child, my daughter, Safa. As I stood there, I thought about how remarkable it was that things could change so suddenly, from a quiet and comfortable state of being to absolute chaos.

Only a few hours earlier, I was sitting in my comfortable investment bank office in one of Chicago's famed architectural skyscrapers. I was living the good life—the life of a young and successful investment banker. I was happily married, had a lucrative job, and a great network of family and friends.

Raised by Pakistani immigrant parents who had settled in Northeastern Ohio, I had worked hard to get to where I was at the time. I excelled in high school and convinced my parents that an Ivy League education was the next step for me. I spent the next four years in New York City at Columbia University, where I pursued my interests in public service. With the guidance of an esteemed lawyer in New York, I traveled to Estonia and worked with the new nation's leadership as it rebuilt its infrastructure in a post-Soviet world. Soon after, I was selected as a semi-finalist for the prestigious Rhodes Scholarship. Each of these experiences was an early sign that pointed towards a life of public service.

Upon graduating from Columbia, I began a career in investment banking. I worked in fast paced environments—from New York City to Tokyo. Like many other Wall Street analysts, I headed back to school after a few years for my MBA at Harvard Business School. I continued carving my path in the investment banking world as I settled in Chicago and built a successful career in finance. I was living the life where I seemed to have it all.

Yet, I knew something was missing. Around this time, my wife and I learned that we were expecting our first child. Our days were full of excitement and anticipation as we eagerly awaited her birth. And then there came that fateful day—the day my eldest daughter, Safa, was born prematurely—fourteen weeks too early. That day I decided that I must act on the signs that were all around me.

Long before she was born, I had decided that if I were to have a daughter I wanted to name her Safa. There is a verse in the Qur'an (2:158) that says, "Surely, Safa and Marwa are among the signs appointed by God…" As Muslims, we are taught from an early age to bear witness to the signs all around us. We believe that God has placed these signs, like the mountains of Safa and Marwa, everywhere as a signal for humankind to constantly return to its true *fitra* (natural state or nature). Imbedded in this search for our natural disposition is the idea that in serving humanity, we, as Muslims, are serving God.

I now know that Safa's birth and survival were among His signs. But there had been other signs all along signaling to me that my talents and my blessings needed to be applied in a way that would benefit those around me. It seems that signs often arrive in packs. Or perhaps they are always there, lining the road that we travel, and it's just that when we actually open our eyes to them we are amazed by their multitude.

As I painstakingly watched my daughter grow healthy, ounce-by-ounce, America's counties, cities, and states were struggling to maintain their own financial health. It was then when I received a call from my home state of Ohio about an opportunity to serve in the Office of the Treasurer of State. The tumultuous trials of being a NICU parent allowed me to finally see the signs around me and understand what they were calling me to do. All along, I was being called to live a life of public service.

Soon after Safa's (emotional) first birthday, I accepted an offer to serve my home state of Ohio as its Deputy State Treasurer and CFO. Despite the nation's and Ohio's difficult economic situation, I was tasked with overseeing $15 billion in state investments, nearly $17 billion in tax and fee collection, and over $150 billion in pension fund custody. As an American Muslim serving the citizens of Ohio, I had never felt more satisfied or at peace with my day-to-day work.

The elections of 2010 turned out to be a reflective time for many Democrats, and I, too, stepped back to reevaluate how I could continue my life of service. After a very emotional campaign, full of politics, accusations and falsehoods, I was exhausted. The election results were yet another sign—this time I made a decision to exit the life of a public servant and return to the private sector. Returning to the private sector was an opportunity for me to take a step back and spend the time I needed to reenergize and rebuild myself.

After an energetic mayoral campaign and commanding victory, Chicago was on the cusp of a new future. One snowy day in March 2011, I received a call from Mayor Rahm Emanuel to return to my Second City to be a part of this historic opportunity and serve as the Comptroller and Director of Revenue for the City of Chicago. I had to make a decision: choose a life of comfort and personal financial ease, or live a life of public service. The signs that had always been around me were evident to me once again and with eyes wide open, I accepted the offer without hesitation.

In my new role, I help lead a team of financial experts that are charged with the goal of decreasing the city's deficit and putting Chicago back on the path of financial prosperity. The Mayor has tasked his team with this monumental undertaking—to renew, reinvigorate and rebuild this city. All this at a time when the world, the nation, states, and local economies are struggling financially and balancing budgets are seemingly insurmountable challenges for governments everywhere.

Indeed, if life can begin anew, where better than in the city of Chicago—a city that has constantly rebuilt itself; a city that has weathered economic downturns and urban flight; a city that has survived the Great Depression and the Great Fire. This is a city that always finds a way to come back to its true self and show the world that Chicago is a place where Bulls, Bears and Cubs roam, skyscrapers kiss the shores of Lake Michigan, and its hardworking Midwestern ideals are still maintained.

If 2.7 million Chicagoans can find a way to rebuild their great city yet again, then so too can a group of six million American Muslims be inspired to return to our true fitra and show the world that we are made up of diverse, culturally-rich, and storied communities that are proud of our American heritage. Yes, we are physicians and engineers, but we are also firefighters, teachers *and* public servants.

Returning to my fitra has been a challenging and winding road. Like the city of Chicago, I've been asked to constantly redefine myself and my role in order to stay consistent with my mission—that of a public servant who works to help my fellow citizens rebuild our states and cities in the toughest economic climate since the Great Depression. The efforts to rebuild our economically struggling cities, states and country inspire me to help my own American Muslim community to find its way in the great American narrative. And like our nation's public servants, we don't have a single minute to spare.

Now is the time for American Muslims to stand up to be counted and demand a role in all social and public policy areas. My own personal experiences attest to the fact that it won't be easy. Just when we think we've made inroads, something happens—Fort Hood, the Times Square attack, or some other eruption. Many of us feel like we have to start rebuilding our reputations from scratch, and so we dust off those standard talking points: "Yes, we are a peaceful people and religion." But rather than repeatedly defining what we are not, I feel that we must repeatedly challenge our critics and speak loudly and broadly about what we really are.

I believe the time has come to have Muslim names show up on fundraising invitations, diplomatic host committees, blue ribbon commissions, social advocacy panels, election ballots and in public policy debates. And not only relating to typically historic Muslim causes and foreign policy issues, but about education, transportation, healthcare, and, yes, finance and budgets. It's only then that we'll truly have a seat at the table—the big, important table.

Without these seats at the big, important tables, it is much harder to nurture compassionate communities in an effective and meaningful way. We will be able to still have nice social and fundraising events for natural disasters and for the geo-political tragedy of the month, but, without the development of this truly effective American Muslim civic participation paradigm, we will not likely see many changes in our representation in really senior level roles such as congress, state assemblies, cabinet offices, or Fortune 500 board rooms.

The birth of my eldest daughter, Safa, signified to me the urgency of pursuing my own path towards public service. It is time for each one of us to bear witness to the signs around us. Now is the time to go out there and really take a risk to become organizers of our communities and participants in civic matters.

As I work to help Mayor Emanuel renew this great city—I also work to renew myself, my faith, and my calling as a public servant. My story is like the story of many American Muslims striving to find their calling and return to their natural state of being, their fitra. And together, our collective story is like the story of this great American city by the Lake.

re: Location |
re: Definition
by Mark Gonzales

An HBO Def Poet with a Master's in Education, a Mexican and a Muslim, Mark Gonzales lives in the center of intersection. Living a line break of borders that resembles Kahlil Gibran and Pablo Neruda in a lyrical breakdance cypher, he is respected internationally for his creative approaches to suicide prevention, human rights, and human development via performance, photojournalism, and narrative therapy.

Mark is at the forefront of curriculum development, relationship building, and healing strategy sharing between historically traumatized communities. He is the first poet of the Hip Hop generation from the States to perform in Syria, and was an invited performer at TEDxRamallah, the first TEDx talks held in Palestine. He is currently serving as visiting professor and artist in residence for the Institute for Diversity in the Arts at Stanford University.

In a nation where even children's toys are stamped with country of origin, it does not astound me that a favorite question posed by American's is: *Where are you from?* (annoy, yes | astound, no). As a poet and educator, I am grateful that communities across the globe have trusted me in their schools and streets to facilitate a process to reclaim silenced stories and stolen land. Forgive me for not sharing what that process entails; that is a story to be told on another day, one of beauty, earth cracked palm people, and justice as a unicorn. What I will share is this: *Where are you from?* is one of the most widespread writing prompts across community, cultural, and educational spaces in the United States. A question that, even when asked innocently, is layered with implications. One need only be or ask a person who has ever walked through an urban war zone, or feared forced relocation due to lack of papers, to understand this. For even when offered from the warmest of hearts, *Where are you from?* implies the following: *You are not from here.*

Where are you from? My Family.

Ancestrally speaking, my people were a part of this continent before the borders I now live within were imagined in a Manifest Destiny wet dream. Some people party to Prince's "Like it was 1999"; I party like it was 1491. My family traces our ancestry to small villages north of Distrito Federal, Mexico. My *abuela* fled the capitol with her mother when the revolution broke out in 1910. She ended up as a worker on the field of my *abuelo* (grandfather). When he returned from Chicago, they married and left the country, spending the 1920s and '30s working mines and building railroads throughout the Southwest United States. My father was born in Wyoming in 1936, and when he was six, the entire family relocated to the Yakama Reservation in central Washington to work the fields as part of the first Bracero programs that began in 1941. (The reason for that relocation: the forced relocation of Japanese family farmers to concentration camps and the need for new labor. Never doubt that there is a whisper inside your family's trauma song that carries another culture's voice harmonizing.)

My mother was French, her body carrying a solid blood lineage from France. Her family, relocated as light-skinned Europeans called Sauve, arrived in the Yakama area in the late 1800s with a completely different experience and energy than that of the Indigenous side of my family.

Where are you from? My soul.

Enter a masjid on any given day and find a community who prays as if their forehead were lips longing to kiss the earth. Sujoot: the process of raising your soul by bowing your body. Amidst the insanity of crumbling economies and empire, I find serenity and protection in these moments of surrender. Yet salaat does not miraculously erase the racialized reality that I/you/we live in. *Where are you from?* follows me even here, into this space I call my soul song.

From dialogues to panels, I have shared with people of many faiths, even my own, what led me on this journey into Islam across continents and comets. For in the mathematics of identity economies "Mexican does not equal Muslim." Catholic, protestant, political ping-pong ball, custodian, street-corner fruit vendor entrepenuer—we have many identities in the sphere of popular culture, but Muslim is not one of them. Yet I cannot help but remind audiences that indigenous ancestors have lived life in balance with the universe since the beginning of time. At the cultural core of an indigenous system of values is respect to those who came before (ancestors), and surrender to the One whose name is described in many tongues. My spiritual and poetic path seeks to repair the soul wounds inflicted by centuries of others' supremacy, a global generation reclaiming what has been stolen. It is a commitment to correct an empire's resurrection of perverted interpretations of a history that is at odds with our lived experience. I have chosen this path called Islam to guide me in methods of listening to elders and sitting with the humble acknowledgement that energy exists eternally and this life is preparation for the next.

I believe our skin is tailor-made to our bones. No skin will fit onto my skeleton like the one I currently live in. Through that same lens, I believe spirituality is custom made to our souls. As a child I was raised in one design cut from a fabric of a cultural faith, but I later learned that it was not necessarily custom made. How much more vast could humanity be if we all wandered the planet in search of a womb warmth that wrapped souls and spanned eternity? The ending of essentializing our birth path, and the reclaiming of our first path: balance and submission.

Where are you from? Poems, Surahs, and HeartBeat language that line breaks borders.

How could a poet not be drawn to a path whose first command was, "*Iqra!*" We of stolen cultures have been raised on a narrative of our absence, accustomed to living in the shadows of the empire in silence. Yet I am one of many in a generation riding a rising vision to refuse any system that does not celebrate the beautiful resilience of a people an empire could not destroy.

I write not in the act of resistance, but in the spirit of affirmation that contextualizes resistance to the lies, deceit and destruction known as historical trauma within the arch of time that is the growth of our people. Each letter contains a roadmap for refugees of all tribes to remember and return to the homes burned and buried by "pioneers." Each story erases our erasure till grandparents no longer sleep at night unable to talk to their children because the genocide of language is another way to apartheid a tribe. I love that infinite Justice is an attribute of Allah, for shedding oppression is the purest form of prayer.

Salaat. Pray. Play in the intersections of crescent and Mayan moons here in between the threads of a rug and the threads of time.

Where are you from? Here, this moment.

Culturally (of the popular variety) and politically speaking, the indigenous people of Mexico are not celebrated inside the US; Muslims are not celebrated inside the US; and Hip Hop is not celebrated inside the US. As such, I recognize my cultural and spiritual identity causes those who are more supremacist-minded to ignore the details of my story even before they have read it. No matter: from the block to Iraq, I'll rock Kufis and Kangols regardless, speaking for myself and for my ancestors who were denied the platform. I write as I pray, as a conversation between the chaos of self and society and the perfection that IS.

What else can I do but speak in a language that resonates with my spine? What else am I OBLIGATED to do, but sing honor to ancestors and Allah while cultivating dignity for the breathing and the buried. Whether on oceans or continents, my tongue will even moonwalk on a comet with this simple answer to your obsessive question:

> *Where are you from?*   My mother's womb: no hyphen.
> *Where are you from?*   My ancestors: no hyphen.
>   Where am I from?
>   Allah. No hyphen.

On Baseball and Islam in America

by Shahzad Husain Abbas

Shahzad received his Bachelor's and Master's degree in English literature from the University of Pennsylvania. While there, he was awarded the Thouron Fellowship, which allowed him to continue his study of English Literature at the University of Cambridge in England. When Shahzad returned to America in the early 2000s, he pivoted his career path from academics to the Web. He has been helping online businesses connect with their customers through search and social media ever since. Shahzad is happily married with two wonderful, rambunctious children, and he and his wife are making every effort to expose them to the beauty of Islam. (Shahzad's also doing everything in his power to make sure they become lifelong Yankee fans).

It's 1:38 PM and as usual I'm late. I'm racing to the mosque—well, "racing" is a stretch, since I'm behind the wheel of my school-bus-like Toyota Sienna—to pick up my son Saifuddin from his Islamic school, which he attends every Saturday. My mom, who doubles as his teacher and also his best friend, is none too happy that I'm taking Saifuddin out early from his Islamic studies for a baseball game. My rationale is that he's only going to miss the last hour, and I'll ensure he makes up any lost lessons.

Prior to dropping him off at Islamic school, I told Saifuddin to be ready at 1:40 so we could make it to the two o'clock game on time. At the time, he nodded at me with such wide-eyed earnestness that I thought for sure that even though he's only six, he'd recognize and honor this pact between father and son. I should've known better. Saifuddin isn't ready in the mosque foyer, where I told him to be; instead he is engaging in a "bey blade" battle with his friends during their recess. When I go over to get him, Saifuddin turns around and I give him a look, to which he responds with a "what did I do now?" shrug. I hustle him out of the mosque and into the Sienna. Even though the baseball field is only a few minutes away, he still needs to change out of his clothes, and if we don't hurry he is going to miss the first pitch.

After driving into the parking lot of the baseball field, Saifuddin and I head into the backseat of the van to change out of his distinctively white Muslim attire and into his baseball uniform. Shielded from onlookers by the van's tinted windows, I unbutton his *kurtah* (long white shirt) and replace it with his Yankee shirt, remove his *topi* (Islamic cap) and put his baseball cap in its place, and take off his *hijar* (white drawstring pants) and quickly help him into his baseball pants. After tucking in his shirt, tying his pants tightly and lacing up his cleats, I look out at the field and see that his team has just headed into the dugout now prior to first pitch. Saifuddin's transformation from Islamic school student to baseball player complete, we make our way from the field to the diamond.

More than any other American sport, baseball is a generational game, passed down from fathers to sons. There's history and spirituality and sentiment in it; to appreciate baseball you have to become a student of its past. It's a game of memory: not only of iconic numbers like 61 and .406, but of historic players like Joe D and Jackie Robinson and standout champions like the '98 Yankees, the '04 Red Sox and the '86 Mets. It's also a game with its own language and rhythmic sounds, from the "Hey Batter Batter" chatter to the ping of the ball struck by the metal bat to esoteric acronyms and phrases tossed around like ERA and WHIP and "Baltimore Chop." To succeed in baseball requires singular individual focus—the only chance a batter has of making contact is to narrow his field of vision to the pitcher and the thrown ball, dimming out all other sounds and sights.

And yet baseball is also about community and teamwork. I love, for example, how my son's teammates in the dugout chant "Let's Go SAI-FUD-DIN" when he's up at bat, and how he joins in the chorus when it's their turn to hit. Baseball is also a struggle: you will strike out and you will make errors. The best teams in the major leagues lose sixty games a year, and the best hitters fail to get a hit seventy percent of the time. Yet despite the fact that it doesn't come easy—or maybe because of it—baseball teaches us never to waste an "at bat," never to give up on a play, and to savor and celebrate success because it is hard-earned. The history, the language, the focus needed to succeed, and the struggle to achieve excellence stand side by side with the power of community, teamwork and the importance of self-reliance and individual will: the lessons imparted by baseball are also the Islamic values I'm trying to impart to my American-born son.

I came to America from Pakistan when I was four years old, and since my entire family emigrated at once, I've had precious few reasons to ever go back. In that way, Pakistan is like a long-lost father to the four-year-old me: I'll always love it, but I'll never know it. The language, the tradition, the culture, the people are all passingly familiar to me, yet irrevocably foreign. The same goes for Pakistan's own bat-and-ball national pastime—cricket. Instead, as my family knows, I'm American through-and-through, majoring in English and mangling Urdu, collecting mp3s of alt-rock and Tupac instead of *ghazals* or Nusrat, and, when asked the fundamental question, "What's your favorite team?", proclaiming that I am a diehard follower of the quintessential American franchise in sports—the New York Yankees.

But while I'm estranged from Pakistan, through my parents' efforts, I'm not estranged from Islam. When they moved here, they were among the first members of our Muslim community. They took me to Islamic school every Saturday, where I forged lifelong friendships. They taught me the history and culture of my faith and spent countless hours shuttling back and forth between home and our community center. The brightest memories I have of my father involve him teaching me how to read Qur'an in the early morning, and before my mom was my son's Islamic teacher, she was mine. As a result I am quintessentially an American Muslim, two words I proudly use to describe myself with absolutely no contradiction.

So now I find myself thirty-five years old, married with two children, and my wife and I want to raise our children as American Muslims who love both of these aspects of themselves. Saifuddin has started to learn *namaaz* (daily prayers), and this is his first year in baseball. And in my efforts to teach him, I'm finding common challenges in both.

When I read namaaz, the daily prayers towards Mecca that Muslims are so well known for, I imagine a circle around my *massalla* (prayer-mat) that buffers me from the hustle and bustle of the outside world. If the kids are fighting or the phone is ringing; if email's buzzing or the TV's blaring; if my wife is calling or if the dishes need cleaning; namaaz is simply a moment in my day where everything else can just *wait*. Although Saifuddin is starting to learn namaaz in Islamic school, he'll quickly forget it if we don't reinforce those lessons at home, especially since Islamic school only occurs once a week. So every day at sunset, I have Saifuddin recite the *azaan* (call to prayer), and we read namaaz together as a family.

Because he's so fidgety, it's a challenge for me to teach him the importance of stillness. As a ritual prayer, namaaz of course has a spiritual component, but it's a *physical* task as well. Like most kids his age, he's got energy to burn, so his natural instinct when doing namaaz is to rock his arms up and down when they should be quiet by his side, to look in every direction but the Qibla, which is the only place on the massalla where his eyes should be fixated, and to shuffle his feet when they're not supposed to move.

He has had the same problems during batting in baseball, as well. He went through a stretch where he struck out six times in a row, and this is in a non-competitive league where coaches soft-toss pitches to their own players. He simply lost his focus and forgot everything we taught him: to stand with feet apart, elbow up, bat vertical and chin on shoulder in his batting stance, and to stride with his front foot and keep his eye on the ball in his swing-through. Instead, he was lunging forward, anxious and unbalanced, swinging and missing at every ball thrown his way.

During baseball season, if there is still some daylight left after dinner is done and his schoolwork is finished, we take advantage of the longer spring days by practicing his swing in our backyard. Before we start, I'll ask him to take a few practice cuts, and if his form is off, I'll go over and lift his elbow up or ask him to mimic me as I take a practice swing. We'll have time for fifteen or twenty pitches before my wife calls us in for namaaz. And when we stand side by side for our daily prayers, I find myself course-correcting his namaaz, just as I do his baseball stance: if he's swinging his hands, I'll remind him to steady them, if his gaze strays, I'll remind him to concentrate on the Qiblah, and if he's moving too fast, I'll nudge him to slow down.

Because of rainouts, this Saturday game is his first in two weeks, which has given us ample time to practice on our own. When the game starts, I take my seat on the bench with the other Yankee parents, but when it is his turn at bat, I can't help but nervously make my way down behind home plate. Separated from the field by the protective homeplate fence, I kneel down twenty feet behind Saifuddin as he strides to the plate. Above his teammates' chants of "Let's Go SAI-FUD-DIN!" I clap a couple of times and say, "C'mon *Beta*, remember how we practiced!" He looks at me and nods his head, then gets into his stance—knees shoulder-length apart, chin just above his front shoulder, and his hands back and choking up slightly on his bat. The coach says, "Ready Saifuddin?" and tosses the first pitch. It is outside and low, and he watches it sail by. This is the first time he doesn't swing at a pitch all season, and it is a hopeful sign. A few of the parents clap and say, "Good eye Saifuddin, good eye!" in encouragement.

The catcher tosses the ball back to the coach. As he starts his next delivery, Saifuddin freezes in anticipation. His focus on the pitch does away with all his habitual twitches. As the ball comes in, Saifuddin strides toward it purposefully, and his eyes see the ball meet the bat at the point of contact, just as we had practiced the day before, when Saifuddin kept his eye on the Qiblah for his whole namaaz.

The Imam: American Man, Muslim and Gay
by Daayiee Abdullah

Daayiee is a scholar, a former public interest lawyer and a specialist in Shariah Sciences/Quranic Interpretation. He frequently lectures internationally on progressive Muslim concepts, intra-faith and interfaith networking and the development of inclusive revisions of Islamic theological thought and interpretations of Shariah and fiqh. Daayiee has long been involved in actively promoting understanding and awareness of issues of racial, gender and sexual equality both within and beyond Muslim communities. He serves as the Director of LGBT Outreach for Muslims for Progressive Values, and Chapter Leader of MPV-Washington, DC Chapter, and is the Imam and Education Director of Masjid el-Tawhid An-Nur Al-Isslaah (Mosque for Enlightenment and Reformation), affiliated with the Toronto-based El-Tawhid Jum'ah Circle. Daayiee is a former Board member of Al-Fatiha Foundation, a GLBTQ Muslim organization, and is the author of the recently published book, *Questions and Answers for Queer Muslims*.

I credit my early home life with the fact that I am open about being a gay American Muslim man. I grew up in a family of mostly men: in the house were my father and six brothers, and we had close ties with my nine uncles and their numerous male children, as well as the masses of male friends and associates from school, work, prayer spaces, and my community as a whole. I learned quite early that men, not unlike women, are as diverse and plentiful as the stars are in the sky. I also learned that one cannot judge a man by outward appearances only—one has to look to the internal, intrinsic nature of the person to learn what type of character he exhibits.

As a young child, I knew that I was gay—I didn't know the words for it, but I knew very deeply what it meant to love someone of the same sex. And as I grew up I learned, from the men around me, that a man did not have to be someone who is a monolithic, cold, harsh, unfeeling and brutish being, but that a man could have feelings, show his humanity and humility, and depend upon his relatives, friends and companions to help him maintain his wholeness.

So, being very observant of how the men around me interacted and immersed themselves in the world, these men of gentle nature, great wisdom and uncompromising strength, expressed in their own way, gave me a blueprint or template by which I would live my life. Having this example gave me great strength and courage, and convinced me that no matter what challenges I faced as a man who loved a man, I would have the tenacity, inspiration and faith to meet each one of them without fear.

As I moved from childhood to my teenage years, I had my first love affair with a classmate who was a few years older. We were steadfast boyfriends for three years before he committed suicide. It was a great shock to me. Although I had dealt with death before, I did not know why my friend had chosen to end his life. However, I was able to avoid lingering on his death by focusing on school. That year, at the age of fifteen, I graduated from high school and, following a tradition established in my parents' home, I proffered my diploma to my father and in return he granted me full respect and the responsibility to be in control of my life.

As I headed off to college, exploring my life as a gay man, I learned that being gay was not so easy a road to travel, because society did not appreciate men like me. I knew then that I had to tell my parents that I was gay: I needed to be truthful with them and have their support as I weathered the ups and downs.

As I grew into adulthood, I decided to move to the gay mecca of San Francisco, and later to the black, gay Mecca of Washington, DC. In 1983, my life took a turn for the better when I learned about Islam through several of my Uigher (Chinese Muslims from Western China) classmates at Beijing University, where I was studying Mandarin Chinese. It was through my interactions with them that I learned that I could be gay and Muslim, and that put me on a spiritual road that has led me to my life today as an openly gay Imam.

When it comes to dialoging with gay and straight Muslim men, there is often a wave of misunderstanding that permeates their understanding—a misunderstanding that claims that Muslim men cannot be gay. Though Muslim men cover a wide range of phenotypes, being Muslim, male, American and gay is assumed to be an oxymoron and a complete impossibility. Yet when I first met other gay Muslim men at an Al-Fatiha conference, where there were a wide variety of nationalities represented, we freely discussed our negative and positive experiences with gay and straight Muslim men. Details such as our nationality, school of Islamic thought, or familial backgrounds did not matter. We were all able to respond affirmatively that there were non-gay Muslim men who accepted us as gay and Muslim, who loved us for who we were, and who did not judge us on what we did in our quest to find a mate—our "comfort and cloak" (Quranic term for spouse/partner).

Quite often, due to hostile homo-hatred, most gay Muslim men would never reveal themselves to the general Muslim public, particularly at the mosque. Having heard and seen some of the atrocious, mean spirited, ignorant and sometimes physical attacks on Muslim men when they were discovered to be gay, I had to question whether or not to embrace my Islamic faith and bear my truth in my early years as a Muslim, or choose to hide my true self beneath a façade of heterosexuality that was neither truthful nor enticing. I chose to be truthful before Allah and mankind, and there was no turning away from either.

Some gay Muslim men choose to hide their true sexual orientation from their coreligionists out of fear that they will lose family, friends, jobs and mutual respect. They fear that type of disclosure would ruin their lives. This has caused some gay Muslims to reject their faith. I never felt that I had to do that, because I was a full-fledged adult and comfortable with my sexuality some 15 years before I became Muslim. It wasn't necessary for me to live a life devoid of any religious connection to Muslims.

Of course, there are various ways a gay Muslim man navigates his religious life—whether it is man-to-man in the public sphere of the mosque, or face-to-face in the inner recesses of the bedroom. I give praise to and appreciate the respect and positivity that the vast majority of my straight brothers in the faith give to me. Happily, in most instances my interactions with straight Muslim men have led to friendship, camaraderie, companionship, and in several instances, mutual respect and unrequited passion that supersedes any physical attraction.

It is quite easy to find anti-gay rhetoric within Muslim media. Whether claims are made that being gay is affiliated with criminality, sinful intent, and abnormality of sexual proclivities, the majority of these commentaries are amateurishly derived based upon what some ill-informed mullah told them about some hadith. On several occasions in the past twelve years, I have challenged a number of imams at panel discussions and at the mosque, that their diatribes lack clearly derived scholarship from the Qur'an, and in fact, that they depend upon a mythology that supports a cultural expectation. As expected, they are unable to provide anything of substance, and the debate often turns into a one-way name-calling event that seeks to assassinate my character rather than my scholarship.

To some, I am the epitome of what they believe to be sinful sexual extravagance that demeans Muslim manhood. In some instances I have had Muslim brothers refuse to offer "salaams," or avoid shaking my hand, or even moving so that they are not in front of me when we pray. I have never taken offense to those men acting in this manner, but it is humorous, and I have to maintain my composure to prevent myself from laughing out loud at their foolishness. However, stupid is as stupid does.

Those early lessons about manhood, absorbed into my very core during childhood and adolescence, became the pillars upon which I am able to stand tall and claim my place among Muslim men. Whether in the ancient lands from which the Abrahamic faith sprung, or the recesses of the North American landscape—I stand proudly as an American Muslim who is gay. This has not always been an easy path to follow, for it has been laden with obstacles—physical, metaphorical, and spiritual—each one requiring extraordinary patience, kindness, and faith.

Needless to say, being an openly gay imam and spiritual leader, which is only possible in the West and particularly in America, I continue to encounter blatant anti-gay demonization. But thankfully, over the twelve years that I have provided spiritual leadership and performed religious and cultural rituals for both gay and non-gay Muslims (such as leading prayers, pastoral counseling, performing wedding rituals and marriage counseling for mixed faith and same-sex couples, as well as end-of-life arrangements and funeral rites), Muslims of all backgrounds have appreciated the work that I do. Far too often some are refused such services from other imams who fail miserably to recognize the *iman* (faith) of these believers seeking their services. This reveals and indicts the Muslim community in ways that are shameful, because so many Muslim men call themselves imams, yet reject believers in God. That is a judgment that is best resolved on the Day of Judgment.

In my twenty-eight years since converting to Islam, I am very proud to say that I have met numerous Muslim men for whom I have great respect and mutual admiration. As I look back over those years, it was never the nationality, place, or time that built our association, but it was the fine character of the person who trusted me with their friendship, as I trusted them with my truth. Not unlike the Qur'anic message found in verse 2:226 (that there is no compulsion in religion), it also stands very true that there is no compulsion in proffering platonic love between men. It has to be recognized and earned the old-fashioned way, through the meeting of the minds, the exposure and sharing of the heart, and reaping the blessings of sincere friendship through our love for Allah.

If All the Trees of the World were Pens
by Hussein Rashid

Hussein Rashid (www.husseinrashid.com) is a proud Muslim and native New Yorker. He is an academic, activist, and lecturer. Currently, he is a faculty member a Hofstra University and Associate Editor at Religion Dispatches. He is the convener of islamicate and a contributor to Talk Islam and AltMuslimah; his work has appeared at *City of Brass*, *Goat Milk*, and *CNN.com*. He has appeared on CBS Evening News, CNN, Russia Today, Channel 4 (UK), BBC, NPR, State of Belief—Air America Radio, and Iqra TV (Saudi Arabia).

He is also an instructor at Quest: A Center for Spiritual Inquiry at the Park Avenue Christian Church. He has been a visiting professor at Virginia Theological Seminary and Reconstructionist Rabbinical College.

As a Nizari Ismaili Muslim, he believes his faith guides him to do good in this world, and to leave the world in a better state than he found it for his, and others', children.

"If all the trees of the world were pens, and all the oceans were ink, with more oceans to replace, you could not write all that God could teach."
(18:27)

I grew up normal. Painfully normal. Our family had 2.5 kids, depending on how you counted my brother and the cats. We had a three-bedroom house and a small plot of land.

My parents were economic migrants from Tanzania. Much as they were a product of their parents, I am a product of mine. I also have 2.5 children, depending on how you count my brother and my kids. The kids will hopefully be the product of the best of my upbringing. I am the result of my ancestors' hopes and dreams, and I have hopes and dreams for my descendants.

While I feel I speak for all of them, ultimately, I can only speak for myself. "No one shall bear another's burden." (17:15)

The Past

I do not know what my parents wished for me, aside from happiness. It is something that I should ask them. I do know that they left Tanzania in difficult circumstances. I only knew one of my four grandparents. My nani, maternal grandmother, lived in three countries on three different continents. From her travels from India to Tanzania to the US, she said the only thing she was always able to take with her was her education. It was an ethic she instilled in the family. My mother was a teacher before coming to the US At her family reunions, many of her cousins remember her as their teacher. My grandmother would take care of my brother and I after school, when we were in our primary grades. We would sit and do our homework with her before we did anything else. Of all my US-based family, it has become something of a joke that we all have at least one degree from either NYU or Columbia.

The area I grew up in during this time was one of the most fascinating places I have ever known. We lived in Elmhurst, Queens in New York City. My grade school and my grandmother were located in Forest Hills, Queens. Forest Hills was one of the most diverse Jewish communities at the time. This spectrum of religious pluralism was to prove incredibly formative to me.

The Present

When I went to high school, it was a shocking transition. I went from a Montessori school in Queens to a public high school on Long Island. In many ways, my high school was as diverse, if not more so, than my grade school. At the same time, the idea of difference was more evident. My graduating class was the last in the school that was majority white. The racial tension was palpable.

My first identity consciousness was racial, not religious. I was a colored man before I was a religious man. The effect of a lack of a strong religious identification at this time was compounded by two things—adolescence and education. As an adolescent, one rebels against parents and everything they stand for. My parents were religious, both in terms of practice and in terms of service to the community. I could not be like them if I were to be a good teenager, especially a good second-generation American teenager. There was also the unintended consequence of a good education in the American context: an arc to world civilization that holds that religious belief must fall by the wayside. I bought into the idea that a well-developed individual did not need religion. It was the opiate of the masses. I had a teenager's understanding of Marx and Nietzche, a dangerous and heady brew.

The racial division in my school made me aware of a Black consciousness—a political awareness that impacts many communities of color. One of the markers of that consciousness was avoiding alcohol consumption. It was not what people of color did in my school, because alcohol was a poison to our communities. I stayed dry not out of faith in God, but out faith in myself. I carried this political awareness with me into college. I was excited because our summer reading before entering Columbia was *The Autobiography of Malcolm X*, a book I had not yet read, but was excited to get. It was the summer before Spike Lee's *X* was released. I knew it was important for me in developing my racial identity, but I did not realize what it would teach me about Islam. I started to think about Islam as something American. Ultimately, though, I was going to college to get an education and to get a job.

Like any good immigrant kid, even if I wanted to rebel, I was pre-med, which meant I was also a biology major. The other standard careers of lawyer or engineer did not appeal to me. The first clubs I joined were ethnic clubs, and I never went near a religious group. Then I realized I had to take a course in the humanities to graduate. I opted to take a course on Islam because I thought it would be easy.

It was not easy.

My parents may have taught me faith, but my professor taught me my religion. He was a former Jesuit of Syrian descent. He talked about Islam not just as a theological system, or a legal system, but as a system of life. It impacted the way people lived their lives, and because no two people were the same, no two "Islams" were the same. There was a diversity he showcased that resonated with the way I grew up. As a Shi'a Isma'ili Muslim, I was always aware of being a minority amongst a minority amongst a minority in America. What I learned in that class was that I was part of a larger spectrum of Muslims and their cultures.

The Jewish community I knew, from the Iranian Jew I bought my comics from, the Syrian Jews who played music in the area shows, the Bukharan Jews who ran the area restaurants, and the Ashkenazi Jew who was my best friend, made more sense to me. They had different religious understandings, food, dress and languages, but they could all respect each other as Jews. That had not been my experience as a Muslim, because there was never a place with that many different Muslims in my life. Unexpectedly, through this choice of Islam as a humanities course, I came to understand my place amongst Muslims. I understood Islam as the faith of my ancestors. I felt liberated. I could return to my fitra as a believer. The faith that my parents instilled in me, that had guided my life, no matter how hard I tried to deny it, animated me. I said I did not drink because it was poison to communities of color, which I still believe, but now I could also comfortably say it was because I loved God.

This growth changed my life's course. I finished my pre-med requirements, took my MCATs, and majored in biology. I also took on a major in Middle East/South Asia Studies. I studied Islam and Hinduism. I devoured books on Islam. I became enraptured by *qawwali* (a devotional musical form from South Asia), even though I barely understood what was being said. I could make out the things that were important to me: Allah, Muhammad, Ali, and *tawhid* (the unicity of God), *nubuwwah* (prophethood), and *imamah* (line of divinely ordained guides).

I went to Harvard for graduate school. I got a Master's in Theology, and then a Ph.D. in Indo-Muslim Culture. Even when I was majoring in biology, I wanted to be a teacher, perhaps a sub-conscious honor to my mother. I was working on my doctoral dissertation when 9/11 happened, and I had to be a "public intellectual." I was called to it. I felt obligated to serve God by serving my community. I was also one of the rising generation of American-born Muslim academics studying Islam. This fact made me appealing to many groups, as I seemed a natural interlocutor between things Muslim and American. I began to lecture outside of the academy and I launched a blog called *islamicate*. Both lead to further growth in my religious identity. I became an *al-waez*, or itinerant preacher. I worked the worlds of Religious Studies and Theology. I became committed to inter-faith *and* intra-faith conversations.

The Future

My experience, my education, make me think about the world I want for my children. I had become my mother—a teacher and committed servant to the community—without realizing it. I want my children to be educated. I want them to be committed to service. I want them to know the faith I now know—the one that makes my soul sing; the one that allows me see God in every bit of creation and to be thankful for it. To have faith that the most beautiful of books came through the most beautiful of role models. To know that we cannot deny any of God's favors, because those favors continue. To understand that every community, in all times, has been given a guide, and while prophethood has ceased, we have been graced with the imams. I want them to know that every privilege that has been extended to me has been given to them, and it is their responsibility to pay it forward. My faith teaches me that I have to leave the world a better place for them and their children. I want them to know that.

I speak for myself. I want my voice to be one that honors my ancestors and inspires my descendants. "All is by the blessing of God. Recall the blessings of your Lord." (93:11)

The Day I Left Islam
by Adisa Banjoko

Adisa Banjoko is an author and journalist born and raised in the San Francisco Bay Area. He is a pioneer journalist on the relationship between Islam and Hip-Hop. Adisa founded the Hip-Hop Chess Federation (HHCF) in 2007. The HHCF fuses music, chess, and martial arts to promote unity, strategy, and nonviolence. He has lectured on urban culture at Harvard, Brown, the University of California at Berkeley, Stanford, and many other universities. Adisa and the HHCF were honored in 2009 by the San Francisco School Board of Education for their contributions to the children of San Francisco. He was also named one of the "Hot 20 under 40" by San Francisco's 7x7 magazine.

"So why haven't we seen you around the masjid brother?" asked the voice on the phone. His tone was polite, but sharp. I answered, "I dunno man. You know, I don't live close to Oakland. I gotta catch like three buses to get out there. It's not easy. I mean, brothas never come out to swoop me to get to Jummah. Then they wanna be all at me about missin the *khutba*."

The response was a long silence. He spoke again "Do you still believe?"

"Do I believe?" I asked myself silently.

Before I could answer, my mind ran through the experiences that led to me taking *shahada* (the Islamic testament of faith) just a year and a half earlier:

I'm walking into Joe's Music Emporium record store with the money my mom told me to use to look for work and buying Public Enemy's *It Takes a Nation of Millions to Hold Us Back*. My spirit feels a shock during "Show 'Em Whatcha Got" as the saxophone plays and the sister speaks about, "The same God that gave wisdom to Rosa Parks, gave strength to Martin Luther King, to Malcolm X." I want to worship that same God—and I feel the fear of not knowing how. I see my lanky frame at SF State rapping on stage against the "justifiable homicide" of a young Black child. I meet two brothers who ask me if I'm Muslim. I'm at 82nd and McArthur taking shahada. I'm eating halal pizza from the shop of the nice Yemeni family. Now I'm rockin' thobes and kufis all day every day and my mom is asking me why I'm wearing a costume. I am in Eastmont Mall and an Arab man is yelling at me to take off my Hand of Fatima. I tell him no. He tells me if I don't take it off, I am no longer a Muslim. Because he is an Arab, and I am new to Islam and therefore still believe that Arabs have a sort of final authority on Islam, I unhappily take it off later that day. I am doing rap songs about praying to the East, opening for artists like Gangstarr and Organized Konfusion and no Muslims come out to support my shows at all (even though the jams are packed). Other Muslims are playing twenty questions with me about why I did not make it to Friday prayer. Telling me that like many brothers I have "post-shahada syndrome" and ain't keeping it real.

And now, one of the men who first brought me into Islam was asking me if I believed.

"No, I don't," I said, slightly above a whisper.

It was a lie.

But it was true. I believed in Allah and his Messenger. *But not in the way these brothers believed I should.* I didn't know *hadith* (the sayings of the Prophet Muhammad). I didn't know the Qur'an like they did. I loved Allah, just in a different way. Being Muslim and American did not have to conflict. Being Black and Muslim did not have to conflict. When I converted, I had a deep respect for my fellow Muslim brothers. But I saw them putting in overtime in their efforts to emulate Arab Islam, and it was causing tension and fighting between them. They were trying to be something they were not, instead of finding a way to be whole, nonconflicted, African American Muslims. I didn't sign up for this. I just wanted to know God. I didn't take off the chains of White Supremacist Christianity to replace them with the chains of Arab Supremacy.

"OK," was the response. Then the phone was hung up.

I sat in my room. My heart beat technically, but spiritually…I felt like my heart was in a vice.

These guys were the only dudes I knew that were Muslim. They *were* Islam to me. But once I told one of them I didn't believe, these men cut ties with me completely.

A month or so later, it was Ramadan, the holy month of fasting, something I had become used to participating in. But this year, I felt isolated from the Muslim community. I thought the Islam that my Muslim brothers were demonstrating to me was not what I wanted out of Islam at all. I did not fast because I wasn't sure about any of it anymore. I still read the Qur'an, but I also read Dr. John Henrik Clarke, Dr. Ben, Runoko Rashidi and Van Sertima. I talked with the elder sister, O. G. Panther Kiilu Nyasha about the African struggle abroad. I exchanged letters with Geronimo Ji Jaga Pratt, passed on some messages to Tupac and prayed to the East now and again. But I was on my own as a rogue Muslim.

Around this time, I had some powerful dreams. In one of these, I dreamt that I was standing, at night, in front of a marble masjid the color of rosé wine. My feet were bare and I stood on plush grass. Next to me was a wide pillar. The masjid was open and there was light inside. When I looked up, I saw a full moon. As I gazed at it, I started to lift off the ground. I looked down and realized I no longer had a body. I kept floating upward and when I looked down, I could see myself pulling away from the masjid, the city, the country, the earth itself. I could see the earth spinning on its axis, and the only sound I heard was my own breath. I began to think that I had died, and I felt completely at peace. After a minute of watching the earth spin, I began to drop back down. In that moment, I felt I was being forced to return to earth because I had somehow disappointed God. When I came back down to my bed, I felt my spirit come back into my body. I woke up and saw the same full moon from my dream glowing in the night sky.

It took me years to interpret this dream, and now I realize what it meant. Nothing was blocking me from Islam. I was standing next to the first pillar—the shahadah—and the door to the masjid was always open. The light was right inside.

Back then, though, I did not interpret the dream fully. But it did make me feel a closer connection to Allah, and between reading the Qur'an, contemplating my faith, and being touched by my dream, I was primed to reconnect with Islam.

About a month later, I went to The Gavin Convention in San Francisco. The Gavin, as it was called, was a musical conference by music heads in the rap world. Outside of the panels, every major rapper in the game at that time could be seen at the Westin St. Francis. Walking into the lobby you would see people like Jermaine Dupree, Da Brat, Eric B and Rakim, Ice T, Eazy E and others just posted—all trying to connect.

I was walking though the lobby wearing my sterling white trademark *kufi* (traditional Muslim skull cap for males) when a voice to my left said "Ramadan Mubarak." Not looking in the direction of the voice I said "Ramadan Kareem," as if on autopilot. "But I'm not fasting."

"Why?" asked the voice.

I turned to face the voice, ready to argue. And saw a man with an open mind and relaxed face. It was Stevie B, a freestyle singer from the mid-'80s. I'd seen him perform a million times at Studio 47 in San Jose. I was a serious fan of his music, and envious of his jerri curl mullet—and I had no idea he was Muslim.

Standing in the middle of the lobby at one of the biggest music events of the year (surely in my life), I just told him everything. I talked about everything I had endured. I told him how I felt misled.

I told him how I felt many people treated Black issues like they were nothing to be concerned about. I told him about the guy at the mall. I let it all go. And he just listened intently.

"So that's why I'm not Muslim anymore and I'm not fasting," I said almost defiantly.

He nodded, looked at me with patience on his face and said, "So why do you let these people define your relationship with Allah? Your relationship with God belongs to you. Don't let their actions push you away from God."

Wow. Such a simple answer. For a second I could not hear anyone but him. It was as if the lobby was empty. It made perfect sense. Now I felt deep shame. Deep fear.

"So what do I gotta do? I gotta take shahada again?"

"No man, just keep loving Allah, keep studying and do everything you do to stay connected to God."

Then he gave me his number, which I lost, and I never saw him again. Never got to thank him. He saved my *deen* (religion). Imagine: a chance meeting on a rainy day at a rap convention saved my deen.

I took his advice and studied. I read books on Islam with furious attention to detail. Since then, I have been lucky enough to speak at universities like Harvard, Brown, and Stanford on Islamic history and culture. I am a pioneer writer on the discussion of the relationship between Hip-Hop and Islam. I have taken to heart Islam's lessons about the oneness of humanity, and my hardline notions about race distinctions have melted away. I have learned to have authentic respect for my Christian, Jewish, Buddhist, Hindu, and atheist friends on the earth.

By keeping my deen intact I was able to marry a stunningly beautiful Black girl I met at Studio 47 back when I used to watch Stevie B. She'll tell you to this day that had I not become Muslim, she'd never have married me. She took shahada a few years later, the day our son was born. We now have three amazingly beautiful and talented children.

My life, despite having struggles now and again, is something I thank God for every day. I never really left Islam. I left the company of some people who were distorting my vision of Islam and warping my personal relationship with God. I used to be mad at them, but no more. I thank them for what they introduced me to and wish them the best, even if we don't talk. I now worship that same God the sister on the Public Enemy record told me about. I am a man at peace with my identity as an African American Muslim. Unafraid to be it all and thankful that it's what Allah made me.

Much respect to Stevie B, and all praise be to Allah.

Oh Good,
I Thought You Were Jew
by Jason van Boom

Jason van Boom is an historian, writer, and journalist. He is Director and co-founder of Nicholas of Cusa Institute (NOCI), an independent think tank, research and consulting organization specializing in issues of local, national and European identity. Jason's current research interests lie in comparative studies of Christian and Islamic thought. He did his doctoral studies at Graduate Theological Union, specializing in the history of Christianity. He got his M.A. in medieval philosophy from Dominican School of Philosophy and Theology, and his B.A. in liberal arts from Thomas Aquinas College, Santa Paula, California. He was the original host of *Islam and Authors*, the first program in America dedicated to new books on Islam and Muslims. Jason contributes to *Huffington Post*, *ILLUME Magazine*, and *Tikkun Daily*.

It's the beard.

The most basic reminder of my heritage and my religious beliefs hangs on my face. It's a full beard. None of these compromised facial coverings like muttonchops or a goatee. My Judeo–Islamic fur covers my cheeks, chin, and around my mouth. I usually keep it trimmed, but it's noticeable. I sport this beard mainly because I'm a Muslim, but it makes me look like a Jew.

So ironic. I'm only half-Jewish, but I've been able to grow a full beard since I was seventeen or eighteen. Because I was something of an atheist as a teenager, I did not use my "beard gift" for religious purposes. The main advantage it gave me was that I could buy liquor without bothering with any kind of ID, fake or real. As I've gotten older, I've accepted the Qur'an's view on this matter: alcohol has its benefits, but the disadvantages are weightier. So, my beard no longer has a beverage function. Instead, it's a way to blend masculinity and monotheism, a practice shared by both Judaism and Islam.

It's always seemed strange to me that the West has generally disapproved of beards, despite its Christian origins. Eastern monks always have beards, as do most priests and deacons. The patriarchs and prophets of the Old Testament had beards. Jesus and his apostles had beards, too. But the Christian West, for some reason, has usually gone clean-shaven. I know the practice of being clean-shaven was introduced by Alexander the Great and the Romans. But when clergy go without beards, they often look more like eunuchs than Julius Caesar. There's something softening about a ministerial vocation. Being devoted to things above this world and renouncing the more usual forms of aggression can make a man look less obviously masculine.

There's something very animal-like about the beard. Furry. Musky. Primal. Viking. Hun. savage. To wear a beard reminds a man of his earthly nature. And also is the most constant expression of his gender. And I've noticed that rabbis, imams, and Eastern Christian monks often have a masculine, non-eunuch vibe. Hence, my hypothesis is that the beard helps to keep a religious man grounded in this world. As much as his prayers and contemplations lift his spirit to heaven, he's still in his body, in the realm of matter, hormones, and beard lotion.

Those are general considerations. But because Western Christianity has usually rejected beards, facial hair has become a marker of a Jewish or Muslim identity. In the West, a Jew or Muslim man who wears a beard is making a statement that he follows a religious law the West has rejected. In that sense, having a beard can be a marker like hijab, although our Muslimah sisters certainly get more flack when they choose to observe that practice.

So, as a Muslim man, I wear a beard. I don't know that it's strictly obligatory. Religious scholars are divided. I just know that if it was good enough for Noah, Abraham, Moses, Jesus, and Muhammad— peace be upon them all—then it should be right for me, too. So, my beard is no longer the "I can buy vodka without a card" signature, but the "Yes, I believe in only one God and I practice Shariah," signature. It's the shahadah on my face. But again, here's the paradox. So often when I practice some part of Shariah to make myself more Muslim, I end up being reminded of my half-Jewishness. Sometimes I look in the mirror and what I see is—"Jew."

In fact, one of the things that made me realize my beard-wearing advertised my Jewishness was my first visit to a Muslim bookstore. Long before I converted to Islam, I once visited my Jewish grand- father, a professional sculptor, at his artist's studio in Brooklyn (this was before 9/11). Bob was a totally secular man—started off as a die-hard communist, and ended his last days as a kind of Episcopa- lian "soft agnostic." But when I visited him, he was very, very secular. In his studio that afternoon, we heard the far-off resonance of the call to prayer. I think it was the first time I had heard it. Grandpa was visibly annoyed. "I hear that damn thing every day," he said. But I was intrigued. Later that day, or on another day, I walked around the neighborhood to see if I could find the source of that Arabic call.

I found a Muslim bookstore and wandered in. The owner, or perhaps an employee, was behind the sales desk. We greeted each other and started an introductory chit-chat. It was normal at first, but then it changed. He surprised me when he asked me my reli- gion. I was a Christian, and had never practiced Judaism. My father was Jewish, but since he and my mom divorced when I was a baby, I had never been raised in my half-ancestral faith. But I was always conscious of it. And somehow, the beard on my questioner remind- ed me of my partly Semitic roots. I remember being very careful to say "Christian," because I had heard that Muslims were sometimes anti-Jewish. Just wanted to be safe.

"Oh, good!" he said. "I thought you were Jew."

I quickly left the store. I don't think I even looked at any books. I felt a mixture of embarrassment and anger. I had recently been hearing anti-Semitic remarks from a few Christian and secular acquaintances. They weren't aware that I was half-Jewish. But I hadn't heard blatant anti-Semitism from a stranger like this. And I didn't expect that in a bookshop. It didn't turn me off Islam. But it did make me a little more apprehensive.

For some reason, actual Jews almost never peg me as Jewish. Just the other day, a Jewish professor I've known for years was surprised when I told her I was half-Jewish. But non-Jews often see me as Jewish, especially when I wear the beard.

Years later, after I did convert to Islam, I was working for a friend who had a large Islamic library. He let me borrow a big, fat volume full of Islamic prayers and devotions, with Arabic lettering on the cover. I was wearing a beard. I had on a white shirt and black trousers. Twice that day, as I carried the book with me, people thought I was Jewish!

But the biggest shock of all was from myself, on the day I first wore a kufi. No one said anything, but I felt so Jewish. It looked too much like a yarmulke, the Jewish skullcap. I remembered the photograph of my great-great-great-great grandfather, Phineas Mendel Heilprin, my last ancestor to be an Orthodox Jew. That day, as I went about my business, my attempts to conform to Shariah reminded me of my Jewishness. Muslims and Jews both stand out from Christians and seculars because we both adhere to sacred law. Half of my ancestors practiced sacred law. When I struggle with practicing Shariah in America's white-Protestant-secular-consumerist society, I remember, "my ancestors also struggled with this." Sometimes, after washing my face in preparation for prayer, I look in the mirror, see the water on my face, and think—"Jew." On this day, when I first tried wearing a kufi, this consciousness became more intense.

It happened when I was reading a sandwich-shop menu, and being conscious of which items were forbidden. It happened when I went to pray. I couldn't keep that kufi on for long. It looked and felt too much like a Jewish skullcap.

The fact is, I don't want to appear Jewish. It always makes me feel unsafe when a non-Jew calls me that. I know the history. Muslims may think Jews now have it easy, but it's never easy being a minority. And who knows when people will restart religious bonfires or secular gas chambers? And being Muslim in America—there are so many headaches with that. I don't want to stand out, but so often I feel like a purple zebra.

But what can I do? I can't change my genes, and half of them are Jewish. And I can't change my affirmation of Islam. I know this sounds strange to secular people, but I really do find the philosophical arguments for my religion convincing. I can't change my conscience any more than I can change my body.

On the other hand, it's precisely because I'm partly Jewish that I dare act on my convictions and *be* a practicing Muslim. After so many years of being a Christian, I can feel overwhelmed at times with going so much against the anti-Judeo-Islamic current of the West. But my ancestors toughed it out. They survived pogroms and crusades and inquisitions. Up until the mid-nineteenth century, they were monotheists who stuck by peculiar commandments. That consciousness becomes a resource I draw upon.

Of course, this kind of struggling with multiple identities and crossed lines of heritage is very common today. Who can know how it all works out, really? I just submit and accept where I am in life. God has His reasons for making me the way I am. As Martin Luther, who was usually beardless but definitely a monotheist, supposedly said, "Here I stand. I can do no more."

On My Knees
by Fares Alhassen

Fares Alhassen received his B.S. in Electrical and Computer Engineering (ECE) at California State Polytechnic University, Pomona, in 1998 and his MS and PhD in ECE at the University of California, Irvine, in 2004 and 2008, respectively. He is currently an associate specialist in the Physics Research Laboratory in the Department of Radiology and Biomedical Imaging at UCSF. He was a fellow of the 2007 cohort of NewGround, a Muslim-Jewish interfaith dialogue group based in the Los Angeles area. He enjoys spending time with family, whether it is hiking with his dear wife or visiting parents, siblings, and in-laws.

I was on my knees. I raised my hands to the sky. I had to do something, any little bit that I could do.

That Tuesday morning, my mother had stirred me out of bed, bearing tragic news. Two planes had crashed into the twin towers of the World Trade Center. I almost didn't believe her, thinking that I was still dreaming. After all, hadn't I just watched *Executive Decision* the night before?

My mother was telling me that terrorists hijacked a plane, loaded it with chemical weapons, and planned to crash it into Washington DC.

This wasn't a movie. This wasn't a dream.

I went to the family room and helplessly watched the tragedy unfold. The South Tower had just collapsed. Undoubtedly hundreds, if not thousands, had perished. Many were missing. The Pentagon had been attacked too. And American Airlines Flight 93 had just crashed near Shanksville, Pennsylvania.

What could I do? I couldn't watch any more of the horrifying television footage. People were donating blood, but I didn't see how donating my blood in the Los Angeles area would help any of the wounded in New York or Washington. Besides, the local donor centers were probably packed.

So I went with my friend to work. We had been working for my father, full-time during our summer breaks from college and part-time during the school year, providing computer support services for his retail stores.

My mother had encouraged and nurtured my interest in computers since I was very young, in the days when computers were not so nurturing, with their green-and-black monitors, inexplicable beeps, and befuddling error messages. She taught me how to use a word processor, how to align paper for printing on those noisy dot-matrix printers, and she was my last resort whenever I had used up whatever limited knowledge I had. My interest in computers continued to develop, and I'd occasionally drop by father's office and help him with some minor computer issue. After entering college, my dad hired me along with one of my best friends to work part-time for him.

The summer of 2001 was wrapping up and my friend and I were trying to finish several projects before resuming our studies. However, there really wasn't much to do that day. We drove back and forth between the stores, the overcast sky only adding to the gloom. I remember one of the sales managers showing me a fax from one of our major suppliers: they were closed for business that day.

That evening, I picked up a call from a close friend of my father's. He wanted to make sure everything was alright with our family. I was stunned by his gesture. I was feeling so helpless, and here was my father's friend reaching out to our family. He was the president of the local state university, probably with a lot of other concerns on his mind. And yet he was making the time to check on us. He, like many others, was reaching out to his Muslim friends, making sure they were safe. I let him know that we were all okay and that we very much appreciated his call and his support—yes, I would let my father know—thank you.

My father emigrated from Syria to the US about thirty years ago, settling in with his oldest brother in an apartment near Los Angeles. He pursued a college education, earned his degree, and eventually started a real estate business with his brothers who joined him from overseas. About ten years after immigrating to the US, he married overseas and brought his new wife home. I was their first child— their first experiment in raising an Arab, Muslim, American child.

My parents regularly spoke to me in Arabic, and also taught me to memorize several of the short chapters of the Qur'an. I remember my little sister and me sitting next to my father on Sundays and listening to him recite, line-by-line, the seven verses of the first chapter, "The Opening"— the Muslim equivalent of the Lord's prayer:

> In the name of God, the Most Gracious, the Most Merciful
> All praise is due to God, Lord of the worlds
> The Most Gracious, the Most Merciful
> Master of the Day of Judgment
> It is you we worship and it is you to whom we turn for aid
> Guide us along the straight path
> The path of those whom you have blessed,
> not those who have incurred anger nor those who have gone astray.

My father would ask us to recite "The Opening" to family and friends and I would gladly oblige, reciting the 1500-year-old verses with gusto and pride. The same gusto and pride with which I would sing along to Disney-labeled recordings of "You're a Grand 'Ole Flag," "This is My Country," or "When Johnny Comes Marching Home," playing on my Fisher Price record player. The same gusto and pride as when I would bombastically recite the Star-Spangled Banner to my parents, showing off what I had memorized for my second-grade class.

Later that evening, I watched President George W. Bush's speech to the nation. After somberly recounting the attacks and the government's response, he made a plea:

> Tonight, I ask for your prayers for all those who grieve, for the children whose worlds have been shattered, for all whose sense of safety and security has been threatened. And I pray they will be comforted by a power greater than any of us, spoken through the ages in Psalm 23: "Even though I walk through the valley of the shadow of death, I fear no evil, for You are with me."

The guilt overwhelmed me. Why hadn't I prayed for the victims? As a Muslim, as a person of faith, shouldn't I have turned to God that very morning and prayed for their victims and their families? Why hadn't the thought occurred to me?

I couldn't put it off any longer. I went to my bedroom and rolled out my prayer rug. I stood up, raised my hands, called out "God is greater," and I began. The words of the prayer flashed in and out of my mind: "All praise is due to God, Lord of the worlds…it is you we worship and it is you to whom we turn for aid…."

I bent down, placing my hands on my knees. "Glory be to my Lord, the Almighty."

I stood up. "God hears those who praise Him. Our Lord, all praise is due to you."

I knelt down, placing my face and hands on the floor. "Glory be to my Lord, the Most High."

I then stood up and completed the remaining cycles of prayer.

On my knees, with my legs tucked under me, I held out my open palms. I called out to God, asking Him to comfort the families and friends of the victims of the tragedy on that day. I asked Him to bless the souls of those who had returned to Him. I asked for His forgiveness and mercy. And I asked him to accept my prayers and the prayers of all those who were grieving.

Then I got up and went to bed. Lying there, my thoughts shifted from concern for the victims to revulsion toward the terrorists. How did they justify such despicable acts? Did we really share the same faith? What about other terrorist acts committed in the name of my faith? Could I do anything, however minor, to help prevent such acts from occurring again? I wasn't going to go spelunking in the caves of Afghanistan, searching for armed militants, but at least I could be an advocate against terrorism, and, more broadly, against religious extremism. But how could I advocate without some real knowledge of my faith, more than what I learned at home and at Sunday school?

In the ensuing years I read more and more about my faith, educating myself about the fundamentals of Islam, the historical origins of the faith, and issues of power and authority. I began to question what I saw as erroneous interpretations of the religious texts. A friend recommended that I first learn classical Arabic and read the sources in their original language before going off and criticizing the status quo. So I took an Arabic intensive course that summer, learning how to read and write classical Arabic. I continued my studies for about two more years, taking weekend Arabic extension classes at the Univeristy of California Los Angeles.

During my studies, I began reading the Qur'an daily in the hopes that doing so would improve my Arabic reading skills. Gradually, the words became clearer and clearer and the meanings became more and more apparent. A new world opened up to me—the lyrical beauty of the text married with its meaning sings a beautiful, and at times haunting, chorus: songs of prophets and pharaohs, of paradise and hell, of parables of life, death, and renewal, of a loving, merciful God.

That night, years ago, I prayed for the victims of 9/11. What I've since discovered is that my heart had been broken on that day; my heart cried out to pray and connect with the All Merciful, the Almighty—for them and for myself.

Creating a New Normal
by Shahed Amanullah

Shahed Amanullah serves as Senior Advisor for Technology for the Office of the Special Representative to Muslim Communities at the US Department of State, working on digital diplomacy projects for the Special Representative, who reports directly to Secretary of State Hillary Clinton.

Before joining the US State Department, Shahed served as CEO of Halalfire, which produces compelling online content for, and market research on, global Muslim communities. He founded and served as editor-in-chief of altmuslim.com, a leading online newsmagazine focusing on Muslim issues. Together with zabihah. com, the world's largest guide to Halal restaurants and markets, Halalfire properties serve over 12 million unique users per year, in addition to over 100,000 iPhone app downloads.

Shahed was twice named (2009 and 2010) as one of the 500 most influential Muslims in the world by Georgetown University and the Royal Islamic Strategic Studies Centre in Jordan, as well as one of the top 10 most visionary young *Muslims by Islamica Magazine* (2007). He is the winner of the SXSW Dewey Winburne Award for Community Service (2007).

He has also worked in structural engineering, telecom construction project management, real estate development, project finance, and market analysis; he has served on the board of multiple community non-profits and startups, and founded a venture-backed software company in Silicon Valley that was sold in 2001.

In the end, all I want is to just be invisible.

That may seem unlikely given my role in articulating the voices of Muslim America, but in fact this goal has been at the heart of my twenty plus years of civic engagement, political organizing, and new media advocacy.

Allow me to explain, and give you a little background.

Unlike some young Muslims growing up today, I have fond memories of my childhood. That's because I had the fortune of growing up in a pre-9/11 world, in a leafy suburb in Orange County, California. It was a world where there were racial epithets for everyone, but few for South Asians and much less for Muslims.

I found my place among a small group of diverse friends— Chinese, Korean, Buddhist, Jewish, Hispanic, and white—some of whom remain among my dearest friends even now, thirty years later. It was a normal high school life, complete with beach bonfires, football games, and prom. It was normal because I *felt* normal.

My religious identity was simply another in the mosaic of the American cultural landscape—a bit odd, perhaps, but not very threatening. I remember the exact moment when my Muslim identity hit me. It was in the form of a rock, hurled my way while delivering papers as a twelve-year old, and being around 1980 it was accompanied by some blurred shouting that had the word "Iranian" in it. It was the only time in my first twenty years on this earth that I encountered any hostility for being a Muslim.

I was raised by my single Indian-immigrant father, who, like many of his generation, found himself so busy making ends meet that there was little time for passing down much of a religious tradition aside from the basics. After I turned sixteen and got a car, I asked my father about attending a mosque. The only one he knew of was the Islamic Center of Southern California (ICSC). It was there that I found the soul of my religion—a core that taught me to serve others and to strive to connect with my Creator.

I didn't know at the time that other communities considered the ICSC a pariah mosque because of its forward-thinking policies. Under the leadership of some visionary community leaders, this mosque was determined to be a place where a truly American version of Islam was taught. While most mosques at the time were mono-cultural, this one sought a diverse congregation and encouraged women to sit on the board and run mosque affairs. The youth ran their own youth group, and were encouraged to seek out creative ways to express their Muslim identity: feeding the homeless, sharing culture, exploring religious identity, and visiting neighbors of other faiths. We were encouraged to focus on affairs of our local communities rather than those of where our parents may be from. "Home is where your children will be buried," we were often told, "not where your parents were born."

When I left Southern California to go to college at the University of California, Berkeley, the harmonious Islam that I was steeped in contrasted sharply with what I found there. The Muslim student group at the time was male-dominated, governed by immigrant students to the exclusion of US-born ones, and highly politicized. They would, for example, place an Israeli flag in front of their table in Sproul Plaza so that people approaching them would have to step on it, and had bitter, or no relationship at all, with other student groups as a result of their confrontational attitude.

After having experienced something beautiful in my formative years, I decided I was going to fight this. Together with other Muslim students who felt ostracized by these actions, we formed the Progressive Muslim Alliance, which was arguably the first Muslim group in America to call itself "progressive." We elected a woman president, and immediately reached out to other student groups. We held a combined Ramadan iftar and seder with Jewish students, taught a class on Islam in America, and ran students for elected office—starting with me.

I found my Muslim identity going from personal to very public at this point. I spent four years in student government, and ended up serving as UC Berkeley's executive vice president. My newfound visibility as an elected official coincided with several issues in the news (most notably the first Gulf War and worldwide reaction to Salman Rushdie's *Satanic Verses*). This put me in the position of being an unofficial Muslim spokesperson, which included my appearing on *Nightline* with Ted Koppel.

I spent much of the next ten years trying to be a model Muslim man, driven mainly by the obligation of the spotlight. Muslim community work required working within frameworks set up by the older generations, so I did my best to fit in. I worked dutifully in community organizations, which were (and in many cases still are) driven by male agendas and constructed with rigid hierarchies that allowed little room for dissent from the often self-selected leaders.

After years of this, I finally gave up on working within Muslim community organizations, whose male leadership offered scant opportunity for new blood or creative thinking to take root. I found other outlets for my identity expression: working with the San Francisco group AMILA to plan Ramadan retreats and art fairs, and starting zabihah.com, the original Halal web restaurant guide.

As a Muslim man, I was already starting to realize that many of the problems Muslims had in both their image and reality were rooted in a misplaced masculinity. In the late '90s, I helped found a group called "Muslims Against Family Violence," which focused on the growing problem of domestic violence in our communities. Our message fell on deaf ears—mainly male ones in denial.

Then it happened—the day that would change America forever.

The attacks perpetrated on this country on 9/11 were the ultimate manifestation of Muslims' inability to properly contain and tame male energy. It was the logical, nihilistic result of feeding political anger, nurturing male impotence, stoking sexual frustration, and allowing testosterone-addled minds to turn men into vengeful gods. We Muslim Americans may not have been directly complicit, but too many of us allowed the worst of what a man can be—quick to anger, willing to use force to solve problems, etc.— to dominate our discourse.

Men were responsible for getting us into this mess, and so I decided that for the sake of my own soul, men—or at least this man—should work to get us out of it.

My first step would be to help change the emerging Muslim American narrative, which was extremely problematic. Muslim voices in the aftermath of 9/11 were either dismissive of the fears of ordinary Americans, tone-deaf (the "Islam is peace" mantra, for example, quickly became a mocking tag line), or defensive. I could find few honest discussions where Muslims and their neighbors were not speaking past each other.

In the wake of this PR mess, I created altmuslim.com to create a space where these issues could be discussed with intellectual honesty, without being apologetic or defensive. We identified emerging young voices and helped train them to craft professional op-eds that could be syndicated, cultivated a new class of pundits that could give honest assessments of the Muslim condition on TV and print (and help put the professional Islam pundits out of business at the same time), and introduced new stories about Muslim communities into mainstream journalism.

With altmuslim.com, I felt that I had a platform with which to address all the things about my Muslim identity that needed change—from encouraging critical thought and self-reflection within, to humanizing Muslim Americans in an increasingly hostile environment. I worked with religion journalists to help them showcase the diversity of Muslim communities, advised government officials on how to include Muslim Americans in the fight against violent extremism, and provided media analysis to everyone from CNN to the BBC to the New York Times. I found myself in the lucky position of having control over part of the Muslim narrative while building a profitable business focusing on the Muslim market at the same time.

But even as I managed to achieve a degree of success in the media space, I felt something missing. I had set out to help define the place of Muslims in America, to paint a picture of what it meant to be Muslim. But in the process, I ended up feeling less comfortable than I did while I was growing up with my faith being relatively anonymous. Identity is a strange thing—people seek strength in it, but it can also weigh you down with expectations and other pressures. I found myself envying normal people whose faith was a private matter. Couldn't I just be one of them?

In the end, all the PR in the world won't convince our fellow Americans of our worth any better than a typical Muslim can do by simply being a friend to their neighbor. In fact, if each American grew up with a Muslim friend, we wouldn't have the paranoia and tension we have today. I think back to my high school experience, where I was just one of the guys, albeit a Muslim one. Twenty years later, it appears that my high school peers were permanently inoculated from the anti-Muslim hysteria, and all it took was for me to be a genuine friend. It is facts like this that make me second-guess my quasi-career in Muslim identity cultivation.

Luckily for me, I see a whole new generation of young Muslims taking on the responsibility of expressing Muslim identity through film, culture, and the Web, and for the first time in twenty years I can contemplate stepping down from this mantle I built for myself and just enjoy the Muslim American experience. I've taken some steps in that direction by taking on a senior advisor position at the State Department, something that has forced me to take a step back from the constant media spotlight.

And now, for the first time in a very long time, I can see the life that has eluded me for so long—that invisibility that I remember so fondly from my childhood.

Memoirs of a Mighty Mite Muslim
by Shakeer Abdullah

Shakeer Abdullah is the Director of the Multicultural Center at Auburn University. He has worked at Auburn since July 2008. In his position, he is responsible for the programming, operations, and management of the Multicultural Center and he also advises its various student organizations. In addition to his work in the Center, Mr. Abdullah has also taught courses at Auburn and has served on a number of campus committees.

Prior to coming to Auburn, Shakeer was the Director of Multicultural Affairs at Capital University Law School. In that position, he was charged with facilitating the success of students of color at the Law School and supporting students with disabilities. Previously, he worked at The Ohio State University as the Coordinator of New Diversity Initiatives in the Multicultural Center. Abdullah earned his Master's in Higher Education from OSU. Before going to OSU, Shakeer was Director of Minority Recruitment at Wittenberg University in Springfield, Ohio, where he received his Bachelor's in Business Management. He is currently completing a Ph.D. in higher education administration at Auburn.

Originally from Canton, Ohio, Shakeer is one of seventeen children. His hobbies include attending live musical events, movies, reading, maintaining an active lifestyle, and traveling. He has traveled to more than ten countries and looks forward to visiting even more. Shakeer and his wife Alida are the proud parents of a son and two daughters.

I was born in Ohio in 1976. Canton, Ohio is the home of the Pro Football Hall of Fame and my story takes place against that backdrop. I remember my first day of Mighty Mite football practice with the Vikings. It all happened by accident. I was a small fourth grader who accompanied my older brother to a football tryout, and there just happened to be another team practicing at the same time that included my age group.

Another little boy had just quit the team that day, so they gave the extra set of pads to me. I remember putting the pads on over my t-shirt and jeans for the first time; that was a fateful day for me in my life as a football player. At that time, I knew very little about football and had just started watching it on television, but all of that quickly began to change.

My first contact as a football player was during a game called "Bull in the Ring." The team formed a circle with one player in the middle; other players were called by their numbers, and the player in the middle was required to hit as many of them as possible. I had no idea then that this drill would impact the rest of my life. It marked the beginning of my football career, a career that would ultimately take me to college and teach me life lessons that I would carry beyond the football field. In that moment, though, I was just concerned with doing this drill and hitting as many people as I could. I remember not having a mouthpiece that day and thinking these coaches must be crazy. Eventually, I got the hang of football. We won the B league championship that year and even had a reception to celebrate our win. Yet my biggest fear concerning the reception had nothing to do with football. I wondered, "Will there be pork on the menu?"

As a young Muslim boy, I learned my religion first at home and then during two years at Islamic school. I knew the alphabet and numbers in Arabic, some surahs from the Qur'an and a number of prayers to make before eating, bedtime, using the restroom, etc. And one of the things that I knew for sure was that Muslims did not eat pork. So as the football reception approached, I wished and hoped and prayed that they would not serve pork. Years later I don't remember what was actually served, but I know that this was not the last time I worried about how my lifestyle as a football player would fit into my life as a Muslim.

I continued playing football as a youngster and finding a balance between my identities. My teammates often asked me questions about my kufi and wondered why my mother wore a *hijab* (a traditional head covering for Muslim women). I remember being embarrassed by all of these questions and, as I got older, even taking off my kufi on the way to school. People would ask if I was from Africa and I would quickly answer, "No, my parents are from Pittsburgh." I turned down every invitation from a teammate to spend the night because I was worried that that there would be pork served and I would not be able to eat anything. I did not feel comfortable asking for alternative meals, so I always just said no. As I grew older, however, I came to realize that avoiding pork would be one of the simpler aspects of my Islam.

Football continued to open doors for me throughout middle school and high school. I went on to play football at Canton McKinley Senior High School, which had one of the most famous and successful high school football programs in the United States. Our games were played at Fawcett Stadium, home of the annual Pro Football Hall of Fame game. My high school football team was very competitive and young players rarely saw playing time. When I finally did play as a sophomore, the announcer mispronounced my name on my only carry of the season. I played more and more as the years progressed, but during my sophomore and junior years I was not large enough to be a starter. By the time I was a senior I finally figured out why it was hard for me to gain weight and get bigger. I had been fasting for the entire month of Ramadan since I was in fourth grade—right around the time I began playing football. This was great for wrestling season, but not so much for football.

I had a religious awakening in Ramadan during my junior year of high school. I had been Muslim all my life, but it was not until

I was almost seventeen that I really committed myself to Islam. I decided that I would be more conscientious about my *salat* (daily prayers) and my faith. As a result, my grades improved and my focus on football and exercise increased. The discipline it took to pray on time and observe the *sunnah* (the habits and example of the Prophet Muhammad), naturally carried over into other aspects of my life. My coaches noticed not only my academic improvement, but they noticed my increased self-discipline and focus.

At the onset of two-a-day practices before my senior year in high school, the head coach asked me to ride with him to practice one morning and told me that I would be competing for a starting position as middle linebacker, a position that I had never played before. I worked hard during camp and when camp ended, I was named the starting middle linebacker. This was the first two-a-day camp where the coaches made sure that there was always a non-pork alternative for lunch. And when our position coach invited us over to his house, there was no pork on the menu. These small gestures went a long way in making me feel included and acknowledged. Our team had a very good season my senior year, with a deep playoff run and the first regional championship for the school in almost fifteen years. Our rivalry game even got (then) unheard-of national coverage in *Sports Illustrated* and on ESPN!

My success on the field carried over into the classroom and gave me the opportunity to play football at the collegiate level. I received multiple academic scholarships and eventually decided to play football at a Division III liberal arts college, Wittenberg University. Football and academics were my ticket to college, and once I arrived on campus, I continued to grow as a person and as a Muslim. My parents were not around to remind me to pray. No one was there to wake me up for *suhoor* (the meal before sunrise) during Ramadan. It was all up to me to maintain my *deen* (spirituality). I found that the flexibility of a college class schedule and interaction with Muslims from around the world helped make this spiritual growth easier. I continued to evolve and grow while remaining true to my beliefs. People were curious about my faith and often asked questions, but unlike my experiences as a child, I felt supported and encouraged to talk more about Islam. I took Islamic history classes and was even invited to speak to the university president as the unofficial representative of Muslims on campus.

My experiences at Wittenberg encouraged me to work in higher education administration. I earned a Master's Degree in Higher Education and I am currently completing my Ph.D. in the same area. I know that I am successful in large part because of the discipline that comes from my Islamic faith and upbringing. I frame this story around football because the sport has been my ticket to many opportunities, from television appearances to a college education. In many ways football is like Islam. Football teams operate from a playbook that explains how to be successful on offense, and how to score a touchdown. Muslims follow their own playbook: the Qur'an, which tells us how to be successful in life and gives us the straight path to success. Football teaches you about defense and how to protect your own end zone. Islam shows Muslims how to be on the defense against our lower selves and the influence of *Shaytan* (the Devil). In football you must practice so that you can improve your skills. In Islam, Muslims practice following the Sunnah of the Prophet Muhammad in order to improve ourselves.

While football is not a perfect metaphor for Islam, the discipline needed to do well in both is undeniable. Do not get discouraged if your name is mispronounced; patiently correct people until they get it right. Do not go hungry if the menu is not halal (food that is permissible to eat); politely ask for an acceptable alternative. Allah is with those who patiently persevere.

The "Bull in the Ring" drill that I experienced on my very first day of football practice taught me a lot. It taught me that life sends lessons to you from unexpected angles and you have to deal with them whether you are ready or not. It helped me understand the *ayah* (Qur'anic verse) that says Allah places no burden on a soul greater than it can bear. The lessons I learned during that drill have helped me through many a rough practice session and they still carry me today.

Manhood
by Baraka Blue

Baraka Blue is an emcee and spoken word artist residing in Oakland California. Part of a Muslim musicians collective, Remarkable Current, Baraka Blue has performed all over the United States as well as the Middle East, Africa, and Europe. His first album, *Sound Heart* was released in 2010. He is acclaimed for his original synthesis of spoken word poetry with the tradition of Sufi poets such as Rumi and Hafiz. His book of poetry, Disembodied Kneelings, was recently published by Remarkable Current Collective Editions. In addition to his performances, he has taught classes and led creative writing workshops internationally. Baraka Blue is currently pursuing his Master's Degree with a focus on Sufism and Psychology. His sophmore album *Majunun's Lost Memoirs* will be released soon.

The crowd gathered around me, rushing to grab my hand and embrace me. I found myself wrapped up in the arms of strangers. A grey-bearded man with an ancient face, a towering man the color of night in cloud-white flowing robes, and a young boy who reached up on his tippy-toes to hug my waist. I looked up at the hundreds more waiting to hug me. Men with smiles of pure joy, some with tears in their eyes, all inching forward as fast as they could to shower me with love and words of encouragement and congratulations. Words in foreign tongues I could not understand tumbled about me, yet their meanings were crystal clear. It was all like a dream. Though everything about the experience was new to me, it all felt strangely familiar. When I replay the memory in my head it feels even more dreamlike than when I was present in the moment. For that was the pivotal moment that I entered the fold of Islam and embarked on that path.

That moment was surreal in its entirety. The significance of that experience in my life is completely immeasurable. Yet what kept running through my mind in that instant was, "I can hardly believe this! I've never been shown this much love from the friends I grew up with, or even the men in my family, yet these complete strangers are overflowing with love for me and are rushing past each other to show it!"

You see, I grew up in America around the turn of the twenty-first century. And among all the strengths of American boys and men, showing love and affection to other men is not one of them. We are quite literally emotionally inept. If, while playing video games, or watching a movie, or just chilling on the couch with your boys, one of them was to, by chance, move their leg over a little bit so that it accidently rubbed against yours ever so slightly, the instantaneous reaction would invariably be something like, "Hey fag, you gay or what?" And if you were ever to, say, broach the subject of your "feelings"—you would likely be met by your homies with a chorus of mock sobs and a definitive, "You sound like a little bitch right now, bro."

Our fathers and uncles didn't fare much better than us. In fact, they were often worse off because they grew up in an America that was even less welcoming to male expressions of love. Ninety percent of the conversations with my father never slipped passed the old triumvirate comfort zone of sports, weather, and news. If it did happen to somehow sneak past that protective threshold to any realm that resembled sincere feelings or affection, rest assured one of us would regain composure and steer the ship of conversation to calmer waters, wrapping it up with a pat on the head, a hug, or an occasional (and awkward), "I love you." That was the extent of it. But the fact that he was around at all and said the occasional "I love you" made him a proper Father of the Year compared to most of my friends' dads.

So from this world, which I consider pretty typical of your average American male's experience, I entered Islam. I was six months away from my twenty-first birthday and all of a sudden I was being welcomed into a community that would rock my preconceptions of appropriate male-to-male interaction and affection. And in the final estimation, my very conceptions of what it means to be a man at all.

Being that I have an all-or-nothing personality, within a year of shahadah, I found myself overseas wandering through the streets of multiple Muslim majority countries and immersing myself in the spiritual and cultural oceans of Islam and its adherents. I remember in Morocco how strange it was to see men kiss each other on the cheeks (both cheeks too . . . and sometimes the right one twice). I'm glad I saw that practice a few times before a man tried to do it to me because just when the old voice in my head said, "Sock that dude in the mouth and show him what time it is," a strange new voice said gently, "Just relax, it's his custom," be patient and show respect. Besides, aren't you comfortable enough in your sexuality?" And in Yemen, when men would walk down the street holding hands, the voice saying "That's really gay," was more quickly overpowered by the developing voice which responded, "It's amazing how men can show each other love here without their sexual orientation being in question." I still had my lingering doubts though, and when a Yemeni friend grabbed my hand and held it as we walked through the marketplace I couldn't quite get rid of the uneasy feeling, even when I realized that not a single person in the market cared to notice.

These Muslim men would feed one another with their own hands, ask each other about the state of their heart, and then lovingly argue over who was going to pay the bill, all while maintaining a level of dignity and honor I had rarely witnessed. What was interesting to me is that these men were all masculine. Many of them had survived wars, famine, occupation, and extreme poverty. These were no "punks." They had seen more hardship and struggle than most people claiming to live out popular American society's hyper-masculine ideal of a "Real G." They were often married (sometimes to multiple women), hard working, sincere, upright, strong, chivalrous and intelligent. Yet their conception of manhood seemed to include and even celebrate these strange elements of compassion, gentleness, sharing, concern, and loving kindness that I always associated with femininity.

One day I was in a Yemeni mosque, where the community was celebrating the birth of the Prophet Muhammad. The mosque was part of a school that is attended by students from all over the world. After the celebration, in which many poems and songs were sung and tea was passed and incense was burned, a few men were asked to stand up to address the crowd. This night happened to coincide with the second week of the 2006 Israel-Lebanon War. One of these men was a student from Lebanon and, after praising the Prophet, he spoke about the fragility of life. With tears in his eyes he mentioned that he had not been able to contact his family in Lebanon these last few days and had no way of knowing if they were alright. He asked that everyone pray for them and for all the people in this world who are suffering and caught up in the insanity of war. I noticed men around me start to sniffle and my close friend, a Lebanese American who was translating the speeches to me, went silent, his eyes glossed over with tears.

Next, one of the elders of the city arose. He was a saintly man with a beautiful white turban and red henna in his black and graying beard. A renowned Sufi master who was a direct descendant of the Prophet Muhammad, he spoke with an inward serenity that was piercing. After praising God, he raised his hands in prayer. Everyone's hands rose around me, a sea of hundreds of men, of every color representing every continent on earth, and all of a sudden every one began to cry. And even with my beginners' Arabic, the meaning and intention of his words were clear. He was praying for those suffering, those in fear, those in darkness, those in harm's way, and those who had harmed themselves. He was praying for the heedless, those turning away from God at that very moment, chasing after the fleeting world with each priceless breath. He was praying for the believers, the *umma*, the children, the elders, the women, and the men. He was praying for humanity. For those who had harmed us, or had evil intentions for us, or misconceptions of us. For every thirsting tongue and every starving belly, for every person dealt with unjustly and even those (perhaps especially those) who perpetrate injustice in the earth. And every man in the sea of men around me, black, and brown, white, and yellow, wept. They wept for their own souls, they wept for humanity, and they wept for God.

I didn't weep that night. Not a single tear. I have no doubt I was the only person in attendance who didn't cry. I tried—I really tried. I started to think there was something wrong with me. It's not that I didn't feel. I felt deeply the sincerity and the love in the room. I felt the compassion for those suffering in the world. And I felt my state of absolute need before my Creator. But I didn't cry. Even when I told myself, "Cry!" There was a voice inside, yet to die, that spoke what had been ingrained in me since youth: men don't cry. And men especially don't cry in front of other men.

That night, after the gathering was over, a group of us took the late night bus down to the coast for a weekend on the Arabian Sea. I sat in the back and shared my experience with an African American brother from Atlanta who had been studying sacred knowledge in the Muslim lands for many years. He laughed when I told him my inner dialogue from that night. "We all had to go through that, *Alhamdolillah*," he responded. "To be a real man is a high station. It means to be mature. Not just physically but mentally, spiritually, emotionally. We weren't taught that growing up. We have to learn that. It is the Prophetic way. A real man is in touch with himself. If you know yourself you will know God. Becoming a man, a *rijal*, is realizing that any good in you, any power or strength or wisdom or beauty comes from the Divine Source and life is just the return journey. Everyone else on earth is on that same journey, whether they realize it or not. This is the path of submission."

"I appreciate it bro. I really do," I told him. "It's nothing, *Alhamdolillah*," he replied, "That's what brotherhood is all about. The believer is the mirror of the believer. I love you for the sake of Allah."

As the bus plunged deeper into the night, and everyone on the bus had plunged deep into dreams, I looked out at the rolling sands illuminated by the brilliant stars above me. I reflected on those words, on my journey, and on my Creator—and I cried.

Stepping Across the Gender Divide
by Tynan Power

Tynan Power is a progressive Muslim leader and educator, as well as a professional writer and communications specialist. As the founder of Pioneer Valley Progressive Muslims, he is deeply committed to non-sectarian community building and encourages full participation and inclusion of those often traditionally excluded from congregational life and leadership, including women and LGBTQ individuals. His writing and expertise cover a range of topics including contemporary Muslim concerns, interfaith understanding, LGBTQ issues, transgender rights and realities, and disability rights. He is the parent of two young adult sons.

A few years ago I received an email from my friend, Sam, with a question that caught me completely off-guard.

"Would you come with me to Friday prayer at the mosque tomorrow?" he asked. That alone would have been remarkable, but he continued, "because tomorrow I'm having gender reassignment surgery."

I knew Sam, short for Samir, not through Muslim circles, but through the transgender community. At first, I hadn't known he was Muslim. Yet we soon found we had a lot in common—as Muslim transgender men, often the only Muslims in any trans group, often the only trans person in any Muslim group, and often invisible as both in the wider world.

I knew other transgender Muslims, of course. I'd been involved with Al Fatiha, an LGBT Muslim organization founded in 1999, and I participated in interfaith discussions and gave lectures about transgender and Islam. Non-Muslim friends and colleagues routinely sent trans Muslims my way for support.

Yet Sam's request surprised me. I'd never known a transgender Muslim for whom Islamic faith, at least in the traditional sense, played the kind of role that would lead him to seek out a Jummah prayer before undergoing surgery. For many transgender Muslims in America, the life-altering steps involved in changing genders— counseling, hormone therapy, surgery, legal document changes to reflect a new name and correct gender—are utterly separate from their faith.

That isn't true everywhere. In other parts of the world, transgender Muslims were seeking and winning *fatwas* (religious rulings) in support of transition. The first known case took place in Iran, where the Shi'a leader Ayatollah Khomeini issued a ruling in support of a transgender woman (someone born male who identified as female). Subsequently, Sunni jurists at Al-Azhar in Cairo issued similar rulings.

Yet in the US, the idea of approaching a Sunni imam to get permission to have a sex change seemed ludicrous. Since there is no religious hierarchy, nor are there religious ordinations in Sunni Islam, imams are not bound by decisions made by others—and may not even know about them. Though some imams are well-educated and informed, others are elevated to leadership by virtue of being "religious"—which can mean many things. If imams are uninformed about transgender, the average devout Muslim is often even more so. I can't count the times I've heard that cross-dressing is forbidden in Islam; mention sex changes and people start uttering prayers seeking protection from the devil. No amount of scholarly support translates automatically into tolerance—never mind acceptance or respect.

Years ago, as a young convert to Islam, I had been welcomed with open arms into a community of women whom I learned to call my "sisters." They asked about my conversion and my family's reaction. My spiritual journey was honored and my legitimacy as a Muslim was validated. If I had a question about practice—how to pray, how to cover, how to deal with family conflicts—my sisters offered their insight and support.

As I began to live as a man, I lost access to that community. Suddenly I was navigating alone, and this was new to me. Gender ambiguity is a real obstacle to the Muslim community. The division of sexes usually begins at the door of the mosque. The gender binary reflex—the notion that "man" and "woman" are clear, discrete categories with no blurring or overlap—is deeply embedded in the contemporary Islamic community, even though the Qur'an itself refers to biologically intersex people and to the blurred gender state of men it calls "like women."[1]

For "androgynous" or "genderqueer" people who don't identify within the binary, choosing between two gender-specific doors is alienating. Having the decision made for them by community members who police gendered spaces can feel intolerable.

Even for trans people like me who identify as men or women within the gender binary, the transition process creates a period of gender ambiguity. There was a time when my hair was short, but my face was hairless, and my body's curves were apparent even under clothes purchased in the men's department. I had no idea what that meant in Islam.

At what point, exactly, was I considered a man? When was I to guard my modesty from the navel to the knee instead of by drawing my veil down over my chest? When should I enter a mosque by the door for men? Was I a man at the moment when I first recognized myself as a man, before any step was taken to transition? At the moment when I began to look like a man? And how would I know, since the transition was gradual? Would I be a man only at the

---

[1]   According to some scholars, blurred gender states existed from the earliest days of Islam and, are mentioned in the Qur'an in the phrase "men who have no need of women." [Qur'an 24:31]

moment of waking up from anesthesia after surgery was complete? Which surgery, of the variety available? What if that was not financially or medically possible for me?

The choices I finally made were simple ones. I transitioned when I realized that my gender identity as a man was simply a truth—and there can be no deceit before Allah, one of whose attributes is *al-Haqq*, the Truth. I stopped covering to pray when I realized I was avoiding my daily prayers because I was dreading having to dress in "drag" as a woman. I knew, from the consistency of my prayers, that I'd made the right choice. My relationship with God is more important than what I wear.

I didn't go to a mosque until I knew the well-meaning believers who played gender police would not keep me from my prayer. After years of being an "insider," I had gone back to feeling like an "outsider" waiting for welcome.

Which is why, on a Friday in 2006, I nervously walked into a mosque for the first time in years, to be there for my friend, Sam. We chose a large mosque, hoping to be anonymous. We were. By then, we both looked like what we are: men. Together, we listened to the khutba, prayed shoulder to shoulder, and left with a mixture of emotions.

Sam felt relief that he had accomplished his main purpose: to pray Friday prayer among Muslims before taking an irreversible step toward living a more authentic and honest life as a Muslim man.

I felt relief that we hadn't been kicked out.

At the same time, the experience felt surreal. I was glad to have been there for my friend. I was grateful for the sense of being fully seen by Sam, in all the complexity of my experience as a Muslim man. I was deeply moved by joining the community of men in the mosque.

Yet as affirming as it was to be in the men's prayer space, Sam and I were both uncomfortable. We acutely felt the absence of women in the prayer hall. We both had spent many Friday prayers hidden away in back rooms. Now, as we had benefited not just from hearing the imam's words but also seeing his gestures and facial expressions—all those non-verbal cues that add so much to communication—the women, wherever they were, had not.

Part of me wanted—and still wants—to fiercely challenge that status quo. I want to use my privilege as a man to address what I perceive to be inequity in the treatment of women in the mosque. My history of living as a Muslim woman demands it. So does the example of the Prophet Muhammad (peace be upon him), who challenged the status quo of his time by empowering women.

At the same time, the privilege I carry as a man in the Muslim community also brings the danger of stepping on women's rights even as I try to champion them. Both Sam and I recall that just as we knew women who balked at being corralled in a back room for prayer, there were others who appreciated the sanctity of private space where they were shielded from male eyes, male voices, and male domination.

That is what Sam and I sat reconciling after our visit to the mosque, before he boarded a train for New York City and the awaiting surgery. In the months that followed, we had numerous exchanges about what it means to be a Muslim man. Ultimately, I realized that as Muslim men, we can challenge the status quo for Muslim women, but often our place is behind them: supporting them and giving them room to take the lead. In the last several years, I've been proud and honored to support Muslim women leaders— arguing for their rights, performing the call to prayer for a woman- led prayer in Washington, DC, and creating space in my community where women can choose where they want to pray.

When it comes down to it, there is not one "Muslim female" or "Muslim male" experience any more than there is one "Muslim" experience. Both sides of the gender divide are peopled with unique histories, perspectives, needs, and hopes. When I enter a Muslim space now, I strive to bring my whole self, as a convert, as an Ameri- can, as a man, as a parent, and yes, as someone who has experienced life as a Muslim woman—but only as one Muslim woman, just as I now experience life as one Muslim man.

Integration,
not Assimilation
by Aziz H. Poonawalla

Aziz H. Poonawalla, Ph.D. is a Medical Physicist specializing in diagnostic imaging. His scientific research is published in academic journals including Radiology, Multiple Sclerosis, and the Journal of Magnetic Resonance Imaging. He holds an honorary fellowship at the University of Wisconsin and is also an adjunct Assistant Professor at the University of Texas at Houston. A member of the Dawoodi Bohra Muslim community, he has authored the City of Brass blog (http://bit.ly/muslim) for over eight years. He also co-founded the annual Brass Crescent Awards for muslim blogs and bloggers, and administers TalkIslam.info, a global muslim debate forum. He lives near Madison, Wisconsin with his wife and children. Follow him on Twitter as @azizhp or visit about.me/aziz for more information.

Do I speak for myself? The idea that any of us speak for ourselves is in some ways naive. The truth is that I inevitably speak for my fellow Muslim Americans, regardless of my intentions. In that sense, my speech is not free, but rather bears the weight of that responsibility. Words have consequences.

A case in point: I've been blogging for over nine years, and I've seen firsthand how my opinions have been exploited to perpetuate stereotypes and anti-Muslim rhetoric. A few years ago for example, in writing about Israel and Palestine, I once took at face value a story in a British newspaper about genetic bio-weapons that had been definitively discredited. My motivation was to advocate for abolishment of nuclear weapons, but my lack of due diligence eclipsed the point I was trying to make and harmed not only my reputation for fairness and being a "moderate" Muslim, but also contributed to mistrust between Muslims and Jews. I have long since repudiated my mistake, but the lesson I learned was that credibility is hard-won and easily lost, and the ramifications of my laziness as a writer can extend well beyond just my own blog.

This and other experiences as a blogger have made me acutely aware that I speak for Muslims in general, to a non-Muslim audience. The same dynamic also applies within a Muslim-only audience. For example, as an Ismaili Shi'a, I am an unapologetic advocate of the "calendar" method for determining when Islamic dates such as Ramadan and Eid al Fitr begin. However, I always temper my arguments with respect for those who choose to adhere to the tradition of moonsighting instead, because otherwise I risk discrediting other Ismailis and Shi'a who observe Ramadan according to the calendar.

Like fractals, the pattern repeats—ultimately I speak not just for Muslims or Shi'a, but also for my own ethnic community, the Dawoodi Bohras. We are a small community, numbering only a million worldwide. We trace our religious heritage to the Haraz in Yemen and the Fatimids in Cairo. However, preserving that heritage is as much a challenge for us as for other minority groups, especially for those of us settled in the West. As we immigrate and establish roots into diverse societies, we strive to retain our language, our traditions, and our culture.

As a Bohra, I look to my community's leader, His Holiness Syedna Mohammed Burhanuddin (TUS), for guidance in navigating the challenge of integration without assimilation. In this context, "assimilation" is commonly understood as adopting the identity and culture of the mainstream, whereas "integration" is a harmony between my private traditions and my public interactions. The best example is prayer: I drag myself out of bed every morning for the sunrise prayer, and often find myself praying in parking lots, hallways, or wherever else I happen to be at sunset. While the thought of being a public spectacle is uncomfortable, the thought of missing my namaaz is even more so.

Another challenge is the repudiation of all interest-bearing transactions—I pay off my credit cards every month, wait for zero-percent financing on cars, and even insist to bemused bank tellers that no, I must decline the complimentary interest on the checking account. And of course there's food—no morning coffee during Ramadan, monitoring the kids' lunch schedules for "mystery meat," and doing the post-Halloween ritual of picking out the gelatin-containing gummi bears and candy corn. Note that I still use credit cards, buy cars, and go trick or treating with the kids, but I do it my way, without compromising on the fundamentals of my faith. I believe that even the smallest aspects of Shariah have meaning and purpose, and see no conflict between my religious orthodoxy and my cultural American identity.

However, there's more to integration than making Halloween halal. Integration also requires looking outwards as well as inwards. His Holiness has always stressed civic duty, to be "law-abiding citizens of your country." In this, he has invoked our Fatemid heritage of tolerance and diversity, a hallmark of that empire's governance. His wisdom encourages us to take pride in being citizens of our nations, even as we affirm our Bohra ethnicity and Islamic faith. From this premise, and the hadith "*hubbul wattane minal iman*" (patriotism is integral to faith), I have sought to be a model citizen, uphold my civic duties, and participate in the public sphere—and in so doing, exemplify to my non-Muslim fellow citizens the spirit of Islam.

In fact, as an eleven-year old child in 1985, I was one among dozens of children from across the US to welcome His Holiness to America, by singing the Star Spangled Banner in chorus. Fast-forward to this year, and my daughter chose as her third grade social studies project a biography of President Obama. Certainly at times my American exceptionalism grates on the ears of my British or Indian friends, but they know I'm a "typical American"—and proud of it.

And I'm proud of being a fundamentalist Muslim, too—literally, one who embraces the fundamentals of religion. Being a fundamentalist is hard, and to quote Tom Hanks from "A League of Their Own": "It's supposed to be hard. The hard is what makes it great." It's physically hard to overcome tiredness and laziness for morning prayer, it's emotionally hard to overcome the disappointment of fiscal constraints on my lifestyle by refusing interest, and it's mentally hard to function the first few weeks of Ramadan without my morning latte. And it's especially hard as a parent to refuse my children certain pleasures that their classmates enjoy. But despite all the inconveniences and hardships and disappointments that these choices often cause, I believe they are necessary material sacrifices for my and my family's spiritual well being. Having faith is hard, and the hard is what makes it great.

If I only spoke for myself, it would certainly be more tempting to assimilate, and take the path of least resistance. But I speak for all Bohras, when I wear my *topi* (cap) in public, or grow my beard, and especially when I blog or write public essays. And when I speak, my children listen—and more importantly watch—to see whether what I do matches what I say. So I am inspired to discipline, to integrate my duties to my faith with my equally incumbent civic duties. Like raising children, these are labors of love.

And I love my country precisely because it is here that I can perform these labors, freely. Unique to the modern world, unique to human history, the United States of America is as pure an example of freedom of speech and faith as is possible to achieve. Like all expressions of ideal principle, it is a simple one: *Congress shall make no law respecting an establishment of religion, or prohibiting the free exercise thereof.* Indeed, only the Holy Qur'an articulates the same sentiment more succinctly (109:6)—"*Lakum deenukum waleya deen*"—Unto you be your religion, and unto me, mine. The simple truth is that America is the greatest Islamic country on the face of the earth, and as an American and a Muslim therefore I am doubly blessed. Like all blessings, these carry a moral imperative, a welcome weight upon my shoulders, which keeps me upon the straight path, in faith and in citizenship.

But freedom is hard, too. A commitment to freedom of speech means responding to offense and insult not with censorship, but with more speech—to persuade is a harder task than to silence. I see this, the defense of offense, as part of my civic duty as an American, which also sustains my religious duty. If a cartoon of the Prophet offends me, it is my right to explain why I am offended, but if my limitations are such that I cannot persuade those who offend me to stop, then I must bear it with dignity. That is a price I pay willingly, even eagerly. Above all, I must not lose faith in my fellow Americans, Muslim or non-Muslim alike. This, too, is hard—but when we succeed, we are all great together. And God is greatest.

As the hadith says, "*al khalqo iyalullah wahabbul khalqe illullahe unfaohum le iyalehi*" (Creation is God's family, and the most beloved to God is the one who is most beneficial to his family). This is the teaching of my Prophet, and my *mawla* (an honorific for His Holiness, indicating my conviction in his spiritual leadership), today. As a good Muslim, a good citizen, and a good father, husband and son, may I be beneficial and beloved to my American family, and an example to my own children in that regard, *insha'llah.*

The War of Art in the Muslim Community
by Kamran Pasha

Kamran Pasha is a screenwriter and director, and is one of the first Muslims to succeed in Hollywood. Kamran recently served as Co-Executive Producer for Disney's new "Tron" animated television series. Previously he served as a writer and producer for NBC's television series "Kings." His other credits include serving as producer on NBC's remake of "Bionic Woman," and co-producer of Showtime Network's Golden Globe nominated series "Sleeper Cell," about a Muslim FBI agent who infiltrates a terrorist group.

Kamran is a published novelist as well. Simon and Schuster recently published his Mother of the Believers, a novel showing the rise of Islam from the eyes of Prophet Muhammad's wife Aisha. His second novel, Shadow of the Swords, follows the conflict between Richard the Lionheart and the Muslim leader Saladin for control of Jerusalem during the Crusades.

Kamran's Hollywood career launched when he sold his first movie script to Warner Brothers Pictures, an historical epic on the love story behind the building of the Taj Mahal. He is currently writing an epic film entitled The Voyage of Ibn Battuta, which follows the adventures of the famous Arab traveler who journeyed to China in the fourteenth century.

Growing up in New York in the 1970s, I was never really conscious of being "different" from my neighbors—until the fateful events that marked the beginning of the new Islamic century. In 1979, the Muslim world turned 1,400—and promptly turned the whole world upside down. The Soviets invaded Afghanistan. The Ayatollahs overthrew the Shah of Iran. And messianic fanatics led by a Saudi claiming to be the Mahdi, the awaited Muslim spiritual leader, took over the Grand Mosque in Mecca. I was only seven years old at the time, but had reached the age when kids in school were becoming aware of a world outside the sheltered life of the playground. While I was too young to understand global events, I sensed the world was changing from my parents, who stayed glued to the news. The world "Islam" began to enter the consciousness of the general populace as something that was foreign, unstable, and dangerous. And as a Muslim boy, I was part of that the threatening phenomenon that was sweeping through the world.

As political events in the Middle East seethed in turmoil through the 1980s, images of American hostages in Tehran and dead Marines in Beirut filtered through the media and became associated with Islam. And I started hearing the dreaded taunts in school—"towel head" and "camel jockey" were the most polite. Suddenly, being Muslim was a badge of dishonor that made me increasingly socially isolated in school. And as a result, I found myself becoming more immersed in my identity as a Muslim purely because it was the primary lens through which others viewed me. If the world wanted to attack me for being Muslim, then I responded by becoming the most fervent Muslim I could be. My teenage rebellion did not take the form of drinking and partying like other boys my age. Instead I became a mini-mullah, a zealous preacher who fought back against high school bullies through prayer and spiritual debate. Interestingly, this pressure to own my Muslim identity made me more religious than many Muslims living back in the Islamic world. During visits to relatives in Pakistan, I was surprised at how lackadaisical they were about their Islamic heritage—they rarely prayed or read the

Qur'an, and Ramadan was more of a social experience than a time of soul searching and transformation. In both America and the Islamic world, I stood out from the crowd as a pious Muslim teenager. Islam, for me, became a way to be different, to be unique, at a time when my own personal identity was still submerged in teenage confusion.

But time passed, and my innate personality did begin to take shape. And in the process, I found myself even more alone. I discovered that I was a writer at heart and had no interest in the sciences. Being raised in an American Muslim community where my generation was being funneled unquestioningly into careers as doctors and engineers, my love of literature and art was seen as bizarre by my friends and neighbors. When I suggested that I might become a professional writer one day, my Muslim associates looked at me as if I were mentally ill. The two most common responses were, "What can you possibly do with that?" and "You'll never make any money." It was painful enough to hear my dreams being quashed by the negative attitudes of my friends and classmates, a tragedy perhaps common to all budding artists, but in the American Muslim community there was another layer that I had to deal with—the use of religion as a shaming device to stamp out nonconformity.

"Art is *haraam*" was perhaps the most damaging message I received from the so-called pious lights of the community. Both young and old among the Muslims held the belief that creative work was worse than impractical—it was sinful. I remember an incident with a classmate in high school, a Tableeghi Jamaat evangelist who insisted on wearing only traditional Pakistani kurtas to class, because T-shirts and jeans were "un-Islamic." I had recently discovered the world of J.R.R. Tolkien and was excitingly sharing with him the wonders of Middle Earth, with its hobbits, orcs and magic rings. He looked at me with contempt and said something I would never forget: "Why are you reading books? The only book you need to read is the Qur'an." At that moment, I realized I was truly alone. Being a Muslim isolated me from the mainstream culture. And being an artist isolated me from fellow Muslims.

That was twenty years ago, and I have had a remarkable journey of self-discovery since then. My loneliness proved to be my greatest strength. Being different from everyone, even from members of my own community, allowed me to think for myself and to come to my own conclusions about what it means to be an American, and what it means to be a Muslim. Isolation gave me a path to authentic self-discovery. In looking for others like myself, I studied the world and history. I discovered that the vision of Islam that both Muslims and non-Muslims held up in the contemporary world, a dour Islam of rules and punishments, was an empty husk of the glories of Islamic civilization. In searching for other Muslim artists, I discovered the works of Islam's greatest thinkers, ranging from the philosophers like Ibn Rushd (Averroes) and Ibn Sina (Avicenna), to wondrous mystical poets like Rumi and Hafez. I found an Islam that, for over a thousand years, saw itself through the prism of art. I gloried in the memory of the Muslim architects who built the Taj Mahal as a symbol of eternal love, of the Muslim musicians in Spain that invented the guitar—who then inspired the European troubadours with their songs.

In my journey to find my own place in the world, I discovered it was my fellow Muslims who had lost their place. The fools who lectured me about art being "un-Islamic" were themselves outside the mainstream of Islamic history and culture. The Islam of great beauty that I found on my quest was something that had the power to change the world far more deeply than the political machinations and power trips that Muslims were using to advance themselves today. Art is a proactive tool of change. It can inspire, provide hope, and channel the creative spirit to solve problems far more effectively than the reactive and defensive approaches to politics that many Muslims are engaged in today. We had forgotten the Muslims of the past, who saw themselves as philosopher kings meant to guide human civilization forward. Our ancestors knew that art was Islam's grandest achievement and legacy.

And so, for my part, I have dedicated my life to re-igniting the artistic spirit of the Muslim community. I have worked as a professional writer for over a decade. I have become one of the first Muslim filmmakers to succeed in Hollywood, producing major TV shows such as *Sleeper Cell* and *Kings*. I have written screenplays that bring to life Muslim history, ranging from an epic movie on the love story of Taj Mahal to a film on the grand journey of Ibn Battuta, the Muslim traveler who ventured from Morocco to China in the fourteenth century. I have also become a novelist, bringing Muslim stories to life for a new generation through the prism of historical fiction. In *Mother of the Believers*, I tell the story of the birth of Islam from the perspective of the Prophet's wife Aisha, and in *Shadow of the Swords*, the tale of Saladin, the great Muslim king who liberated Jerusalem from the Crusaders.

My experience being raised as a Muslim artist in America was painful, but it was also Allah's greatest gift to me. It was a flame that forged the steel of my truly wonderful life today I am delighted to see that a new artistic consciousness is being born among Muslims in general, and in America in particular. Muslims are now rising as writers, filmmakers and musicians. And through the efforts of this new wave of Muslim artists, our community is beginning to realize that art is not an embarrassing outlier in Islam—it is its heart. A Sufi mystic once said this to me: "Allah reveals Himself to people with miracles that reflect their culture. The Egyptians valued magic, and Allah sent Moses with signs more wondrous than their magicians. The Jews valued medicine, and Allah sent Jesus to perform healings that surpassed their greatest doctors. And what miracle did Allah give the Arabs? They were proudest of their poetry, their art. And so Allah sent them the Holy Qur'an, which is the most beautiful poetry ever known on earth and cannot be reproduced by men."

His words guide me to this day. As a Muslim artist, I am waging a sacred struggle—a *jihad*—to remind Muslims that God's gift to Islam, His greatest miracle to the world, is art.

My Political Agnosticism
by Davi Barker

Davi was born in California, but spent much of his childhood traveling with his family. On this journey he was struck by the wonders of nature. A lightning storm over a primordial desert in Arabia, the cherry blossom petals sprinkling on the floating markets in Thailand, and snorkeling the coral reefs of the Maldives. The sun setting on the Bay Area always reminds him that God is a better painter than him.

Back home he felt alienated, and spent his adolescence as an outsider. He is realizing recently that his sense of separation is not the result of uniqueness, but of a universal similarity that crosses all cultures, and creeds. We can only be as alienated from each other as we are separated from our true self, and we can only be as alienated from our self as we are separated from nature.

In elementary school I was instructed to recite the pledge of allegiance. I refused, insisting that I could not make a pledge until I understood what it meant. I was sent to the principal's office and ordered to do as I was told. For a while I stood with the class, but didn't speak the words, until I was caught. Then I stood and spoke the words, but didn't place my hand over my heart. Again I was caught. It was not until I was sufficiently bullied and humiliated by the teacher that I finally complied. The meaning was never explained to me.

I was a precocious child. When asked what I hoped to be when I grew up I answered, "a benevolent dictator." The first time I was asked my political opinion was in the second grade. We were instructed to choose sides in a mock election. They told us conservatives wanted things to stay the same, and liberals wanted things to change. It was a wild over-simplification, but I chose liberal because as bad as things were, any change seemed preferable.

In 2003 I was a socialist, and like any good socialist I was begging for change along Pacific Avenue in Santa Cruz, California. My favorite strategy was to sit in a meditative position with one palm extended and the other holding a sign which read "take or give." Some people would drop coins. Others would take coins. One day a police officer approached me and told me that panhandling was illegal. I calmly informed him that I was not panhandling. That the coins in my hand and on the ground were not mine, but where left there by other people for someone else to take, and he was free to take them. He then informed me that sitting on the sidewalk was illegal and ordered me to move. I respectfully asked him if he would enforce such an ordinance on the statue of Buddha that was sitting nearby with coins in its hand. He said no. So, I graciously asked that I be given the same religious freedom as the statue, to emulate the prophetic practice of sitting still and keeping quiet. He said he had better things to do than argue the Constitution with me. I thanked him, and invited him to tend to those things. Befuddled, he left me alone, and I spent the day thinking about money.

In a flash it came to me that money was nothing at all—just an intermediate step between goods and services. It could not be eaten like grain. It could not be used in manufacturing like petroleum. It was not backed by gold or silver. There was no material difference between notes issued by the Federal Reserve and counterfeit money. It was some kind of magic, and it worked because of the public's pathological belief in that magic. In short, the dollar was backed by faith, and in reality it had little more in common with the value it represented than the statue had in common with Buddha—it was just an intermediary.

I began spending hours at the public library scouring through the congressional record trying to make sense of this strange machine. It was in those volumes that I discovered an unlikely political ally in a Texas Republican, Dr. Ron Paul. I joined the Tea Party for the same reason I chose liberal in second grade. As bad as things were, any change seemed preferable.

Contrary to common thought, the Tea Party began while President Bush was in office. It was not a distinctly conservative movement at first. It began as thousands of people brought together by their disgust with the two-man-con of party politics. It was a broad coalition of disenchanted rabble from the right and left under a common banner. End the war in Iraq and abolish the Federal Reserve. Now the angry mob rallies behind a former Chairman of the Federal Reserve Bank of Kansas City. The descent of the Tea Party reminds me in many ways of Malcolm X's description of the 1963 March on Washington. It is an authentic expression of public outrage co-opted by the same entrenched power structure it aimed to disrupt.

In 2007, on the anniversary of the Boston Tea Party, major demonstrations took place in every major city in the country. In San Francisco hundreds of us gathered at the Federal Reserve building and marched to the bay carrying tea crates labeled with all the government predation we abhorred. Then we chucked them off a pier. (All tethered of course. San Franciscans are nothing if not environmentally friendly.) A revolutionary spirit had seized us. It was as if we were confronting the most impenetrable of enemies armed with nothing but virtue. We had seen the face of the Leviathan and said, "Not one step further! You have trampled on mankind long enough." They would either take notice or perish. It really seemed that the tide of authoritarianism had reached its high mark and would finally begin to recede; that the momentum of our movement would soon shake the shackles of the world, replacing the old right-left dichotomy with a new paradigm: the people versus the political establishment. For a brief moment the future of this country seemed bright. I had found a political home among the libertarians.

I considered casting a vote for Barack Obama for the same reason I joined the Tea Party. As bad as things were, any change seemed preferable. But then I heard him say something in an interview with the *Military Times* that changed the way I looked at politics forever. Senator Obama said, "What essentially sets a nation-state apart is a monopoly on violence." This was no political gaffe. I discovered that the very definition of government in Western statecraft is, "a regional monopoly on violence against civilians." Learning this sent me on a political odyssey the end of which I have not yet reached.

Gandhi said, "Be the change you want to see in the world." As Muslims we might phrase it, "The means must contain the ends." Fundamentally, behind all the analysis, I only ever wanted two changes in government. I wanted them to stop impoverishing people by manipulating the economy, and I wanted them to stop committing atrocities on our behalf. But now I have realized that if my goal is to reduce economic exploitation and violence in society, a violent monopoly is precisely the wrong tool to use. If we know that a monopoly is economically undesirable, and we know that violence is morally undesirable, why is a violent monopoly desirable at all?

Many people call me an anarchist for even asking that question. Maybe I am. But I know that the American people demanded change, and elected a President for whom "change" was a one-word campaign slogan. The country swung hard from right to left, and nothing changed. Every conflict has escalated and more were started. Federal money flows toward corporations and banks faster than ever. America now surveils us without warrants and detains us without trials. It should be clear by now that begging the political establishment is not the way to change the political establishment.

As a Muslim, people often ask me if I'm proud to be an American. Basically they want to know, do I pledge allegiance? Well, I don't. I don't stand. I don't place my hand over my heart. And I don't speak the words. To me, being American is a coincidence of my birth. It's the plot of ground I landed on. There is an America in my imagination, the America they taught us about, built on liberty, equality and justice. But I am heartbroken by the oily nepotism of the real America, which has as little in common with its founding principles as the dollar has with gold, or the statue has with Buddha. The Declaration of Independence states that, "Governments are instituted among men, deriving their just power from the consent of the governed." I do not consent. As for anarchy, as bad as things are, any change seems preferable.

Wading Through the Seas of Contention
by Dawud Walid

Dawud Walid is a revert to Islam particularly due to the influence of conscious hip-hop music of the late 1980's, and is a student of the late Imam Warith Deen Mohammed, the son of the late Nation of Islam leader, Elijah Muhammad. He has traveled to sixteen different countries including making hajj to Mecca twice and speaking twice at the Malian Conference for Peace and Tolerance in Bamako, Mali. He lives in Detroit, Michigan where he serves as Executive Director of the Michigan chapter of the Councll on American-Islamic Relations.

As a Black American Muslim activist and preacher in America's most Arab-influenced metropolitan area in the nation, I find myself wading in and out of various cultural seas while trying to reconcile the misunderstandings and conflicts within them. That metro Detroit is one of America's most segregated regions with a long history of racial tension makes my interaction within the broader community challenging yet fulfilling. One of my more memorable moments in relation to this was the 2006 siege on Gaza and Lebanon by the Israeli military, and how these events played out in my professional and personal relationships.

As Executive Director of the Michigan chapter of the Council on American-Islamic Relations (CAIR-MI), I not only watched the devastation that took place from the military bombardment of Gaza and

Lebanon (primarily the southern region), but I quickly realized the direct consequences that that violence had on a significant number of CAIR-MI's constituents, who were a large percentage of the 25,000 Americans that were trapped in Lebanon due to hostilities, which lasted for approximately one month beginning on July 12, 2006.

On July 18, 2006, I was among the 10,000 people who attended a protest in Dearborn, Michigan, which was organized to criticize America's unconditional support of Israel and the assault by the Israeli military, whose causalities were approximately forty percent civilian. Many of the protestors were Lebanese Shi'a Muslims. To my chagrin, the protest's noble purpose of raising awareness about injustices was diminished by several occurences. First, it featured the fringe anti-Zionist group Neturei Karta, who pronounced Israel to be an abomination before the Creator. Secondly, a prominent ethnic newspaper publisher declared his support for the (US, designated) terrorist group Hezbollah. And thirdly, the presence of demonstrators who chanted slogans and held signs including a few abhorrent ones equating the Star of David with the swastika.

Consequently, in the days that followed, I found myself watching television news stories about the protest and fielding phone calls from concerned interfaith activists regarding counter-protests from the mainstream Jewish community, which declared complete felicity and acceptance of Israeli military actions and accused Muslims in Dearborn of having deep-rooted anti-Semitism. The neglect of Hurricane Katrina victims one year prior had affected me; I had been painfully reminded of the historical inequalities shown towards black Americans, the poor, and the working class in America, and I could not help but compare Katrina with the Bush administration's slow response in evacuating Lebanese-Americans during the hostilities in Lebanon. I stated this publicly during a press conference with a representative of Congressman John Dingell (D-MI), and re-stated it at another press conference in which a Lebanese-American boy from Dearborn was shot in the face by Israeli sniper fire. My experience in America has always informed me that despite significant progress our country has made regarding race relations, non-white

Americans simply are not treated as well as white Americans by the government or by the general population. The situation in Lebanon, sadly, reinforced my conviction, since America was slow to evacuate Lebanese-Americans despite having the world's largest military apparatus; in fact, it was the last Western nation to evacuate its citizens.

Seeing the actions and comments from some Arab community leaders and protestors made me equally upset. Whether it is true or not, Dearborn is seen by many as the "Muslim capital of America," and I am constantly in the position of defending the Muslim community. But this time I knew some of their actions were indefensible. Since I was the only black student in my seventh grade middle school reading class in Chesterfield, Virginia, and I was nurtured by Mrs. Davis, my Jewish teacher (who wore a Star of David in class), my visceral response to seeing the Star of David being compared to a Nazi sign was of complete disgust

And as I denounced the comparison of that sacred symbol with a sign of hate from an Islamic perspective, in the media and later in front of Muslim congregations, it was my old teacher's humanity that drove me. Moreover, my mind even swerved to how some Jewish Americans risked their lives, being imprisoned, beaten, and killed, to win Black Americans the vote. Others, such as Freedom Riders during the Jim Crow South, challenged segregation, while the parents and grandparents of those holding hateful signs were either not here in America or were missing in action during the Civil Rights Movement.

The rallies in favor of Israel in which killings of civilians were justified as necessary or "collateral damage," was another point of irritation, not to mention the defense by the local Jewish community of the long illegal occupation that continues to this day in the lands of Palestinians and Syrians. Having a mother who grew up going to segregated schools and knowing the history of America, led me to question how a community with members who were Holocaust survivors and were involved in the Civil Rights Movement could be able to justify anything similar to what they endured and fought against.

Everything about this scenario looked and felt wrong to me, and for saying so I was attacked on many levels. For instance, a young Lebanese-American activist cussed me out for interfering in "their business," and told me that this issue was "an Arab issue only, not a Muslim issue." Black Americans in Detroit told me that they were saddened that I was being used by Arabs, the same people who treated us poorly in their liquor stores and gas stations across the country. Some Jewish leaders told me that I sat with extremist Muslim leaders, though they themselves passively supported purveyors of Islamophobia. Yet, despite all of these challenges, which on rare occasions invoke disappointment, frustration, and anger within me, my spirituality and experiential knowledge pushed me and continues to keep me engaged in highly contentious matters such as this.

According to my understanding of Islam, it is incumbent upon me to be the initiator of the change that I want to see. The Lebanese-American activist who cussed me out is now my friend, because I engaged her on a human level and brought issues to her attention in the hopes of broadening her horizons. I am actively involved in discussions for the purpose of trying to clear up misconceptions between Arab Americans and Black Americans. I encourage young Arab Americans to get involved in broader societal issues and tell them that they are not responsible for what their parents' generation did or did not do as immigrants, and that they should be empowered to take ownership of today. And I meet and work on issues with some Jewish leaders in metro Detroit for the purpose of improving our locality, which is one of the most challenged areas in the entire country.

The conflict of 2006 is just one event in a series of events that highlights why I must stay engaged in the process of conflict management and building community. Though I wade through (and am at times submerged in), the treacherous waters of ethnic, racial, religious, and social-economic strife, I get back out and make some progress at my work in promoting justice and mutual understanding. This is my experience; this is my Islam.

All Eyes on Me
by Hasan Minhaj

Hasan Minhaj is a comedian, actor, and writer based in Los Angeles, California. He currently plays the role of "Seth" on ABC Family's *State of Georgia*, and is a series regular on MTV's improv comedy show, *Disaster Date*. Hasan has appeared on E!'s *Chelsea Lately*, Fox's, *The Wanda Sykes Show*, and Comedy Central's *Legend of Neil*. His debut album, *Hasan Minhaj: Leaning on Expensive Cars and Getting Paid to Do It*, is now available on iTunes and Amazon.com. Today, Hasan enjoys writing biographies about himself in the third person.

If you're a hip hop fan and the title of this essay is getting you excited, I need to give you fair warning—this is not an ode to the late, great Tupac Shakur. It is the story of a brown boy who felt like it was "him against the world." What I'm about to tell you is nothing new, and perhaps it has been told many times before. It is relatable to many nonetheless: being brown in America is tough. Being a brown, Muslim dude in America is tough-er. The problem? We're different. I got the pleasure of learning that valuable lesson through early heartbreak. When I was six years old I fell madly in love with the girl of my dreams—Nicole Bagood. One day on the playground I mustered up the courage to express my undying love for her. The following exchange happened verbatim, and I am not exaggerating this for comedic effect:

Me: Nicole, I love you.

Nicole: You're the color of poop!

Out of the gate, that's memory number one with a woman. Sadly enough, my memories with the female species since then have been more or less the same. But I digress. The point of the story was about the loss of innocence during childhood. In that moment I realized I was different in every sense of the word—my skin, my hair, and even my personal and religious beliefs did not match up with the Western norm. Why couldn't I eat pepperoni pizza? What do you mean I have to sit down when I pee? And where the hell is our Christmas tree? Defining your identity to yourself and others is a huge part of adolescence. Unfortunately, at my school I was the only one of my kind, so there was no one to grow up and share my pain with. I was like an X-Men character, but instead of having cool powers like adamantium claws or the ability to shoot lasers from my eyes, my superpowers were growing a mustache really fast and not being able to go to school dances.

Growing up as an outcast made me want to be like everyone else. My father didn't agree with this, though. Driving home from school one day, my father yelled at me for getting a "satisfactory" grade on my third grade report card. He roared, "You want to be like everyone else? What in your life is just satisfactory?" Apparently I didn't have pain receptors as a child because I replied, "this car." Just so you know, we had a 1992 maroon Toyota Camry. Base model. That night my dad rearranged my face so bad you could have called me Mr. Potato Head. Thanks to him, I'll never need Botox (I still have numb spots above my eyebrows). But I deserved it. I completely disregarded everything my parents stood for: hard work, taking nothing for granted, and being the best you possibly could be in America.

Eventually they started taking me to Sunday School—a weekly gathering where Muslim youth would learn about Islam for three hours, then eat donuts during break. I was there mainly because of the donuts. By the time I was midway through elementary school

I had a rudimentary understanding of Islam. And by rudimentary I mean that I knew how to pray, read the Qur'an, and fast during Ramadan without passing out in class.

I was far from being an expert, but unfortunately, being the only Muslim boy at my elementary school meant that I became the spokesperson for my people by default—not really the gig I signed up for as a nine year old. Imagine someone coming up to you and saying, "Congratulations! You are the Muslim representative of Davis, California. The public perception of 1.5 billion Muslims rests on your shoulders. By the way, you can't drive, shave, or vote. Good luck!" I don't care how you cut it, those are Shaquille O'Neal–sized shoes to fill.

In the fourth grade we studied world religion and were required to give a presentation on our religion or faith. Here was the breakdown of our class: twenty-six Christians, three Jews, and one Muslim. Yikes. My approach was both simple and lazy: cover the major bases of Islam without treading on topics I knew nothing about. I decided to bring in a Qur'an, prayer mat, and dates. Two minutes into my presentation, John Middlekauf raised his hand and asked, "If the Qur'an is your holy book, what happens if you burn it?"—Huh? I was literally baffled. Who's burning the Qur'an? Why are we burning the Qur'an? How do I even begin to dissect this verbal Rubik's cube?

What unfolded were arguably the most awkward eight seconds of my primary education. I turned to Ms. Ledington (who happened to be a lesbian atheist) for help, and she just shrugged as if to say, "How the hell do I know?" Luckily, our principal was in the back of the classroom, and he decided to be the one rational adult in the room by chiming in, "I suppose, John, that if the Qur'an were to burn accidentally, in, say, a house fire, Allah would understand the circumstances and know that it wasn't Hasan's fault. If you're talking about personally burning a holy scripture, that's just wrong regardless of your religious beliefs." Crisis averted—temporarily at least.

The past sixteen years of my life have been a continuation of my fourth-grade presentation. Whether it's at work or school, I've been asked all sorts of outlandish questions about my beliefs: "How many wives can you have?" "Can you hit women?" "What happens if you're gay?"

True, Muslims in America are a growing minority, but for the foreseeable future we're still going to be "that one Muslim kid in Ms. Ledington's class." I've heard the old saying, "Islam is perfect, Muslims are not." Unfortunately, people learn about Islam from Muslims. That means I have to be friendly, honest, and answer people's questions no matter how ridiculous they are. I just take a deep breath and let them know, "Right now I'm looking for just one," "My mother actually hits me," and "Didn't you hear my first answer?"

Ultimately, my Dad was right. The last thing I can do as a Muslim American man is just be "satisfactory." Being the token "Muslim guy" in the group means I have to be the best friend, co-worker, and comrade to both Muslims and non-Muslims alike. In fact, my first roommate in Los Angeles, a first generation Hindu engineer, admitted that after the attacks of 9/11 his parents and friends in the Midwest gathered in their living rooms and badmouthed Muslims for what "they did to our country" for weeks. We lived together amicably for nearly two years without him mentioning this once, and the day I moved out he admitted I was the first "real Muslim friend" he ever had. Because of our relationship, he now looks at most Muslims as moderate, amicable people. Funny, considering that all I did was pay my rent on time, give him a ride to the airport every now and then, and break off some of my Mom's finest Indian cuisine from time to time (apparently a lot of Muslims, and people in general, fail to have this common courtesy). Since then my room-mate track record has been like a "COEXIST" bumper sticker: I've lived, without any problems whatsoever, with a Catholic, a Bud-dhist, and an atheist gay guy.

Without compromising my personal beliefs, I've been able to learn about other religions and lifestyles by simply ingraining myself into the fabric of Western society. Sure, making friends at the masjid and Muslim camp is great, but perhaps growing up in Davis was a blessing in disguise. It taught me to embrace my differences, integrate myself into mainstream society, and ultimately not lose hope with the John Middlekaufs and Nicole Bagoods of the world. I've learned that maybe all the kids I grew up with didn't necessarily "hate" Muslims—they just didn't understand Muslims. (Actually I take that back—I've reached out to Nicole on Facebook several times and I think she actually does hate me.) Regardless, the work we're doing now as Muslim men and women is laying the foundation for ourselves and our children so that one day, when my son gives his fourth-grade presentation on Islam, kids will know that being pyro-happy with our holy scripture is a definite no-no. I just hope Nicole Bagood's future daughter doesn't turn him down for being the "color of poop." I know firsthand he's going to have a hard time dealing with it.

Faith and Politics
at Obama for America
by Mazen Asbahi

Mazen Asbahi is an attorney and community organizer based in Chicago and Washington D.C. As an attorney, he practices in the areas of business, healthcare and nonprofit law, counseling a wide variety of clients on transactional and regulatory matters. In addition to his legal practice, Mazen serves as a policy advisor to the Muslim Public Affairs Council and on the boards of the Council of Islamic Organization of Greater Chicago and the Institute for Social Policy and Understanding. In addition, Mazen remains active in the Democratic Party and is a co-founder of the National Muslim Democratic Council.

The following is a story about presidential politics, sacrifice and faith. It is also a story about becoming a story.

Tuesday, August 4, 2008. Obama for America Campaign Headquarters—Chicago. "Dear Mr. Asbahi, I'm a journalist with the *Wall Street Journal*. We want to write about you, your connections to fundamentalist Islamic organizations in the US and their connections to the Muslim Brotherhood. Call me, let's talk."

That was the gist of an email sent to me one morning.

I was at my usual seat at campaign headquarters, tightly squeezed next to other staffers working on outreach. Barack Obama had finally beaten Hillary Clinton after a prolonged primary battle. The vibe at headquarters, even at this early hour, was electric.

I stared at the email quietly while a flurry of thoughts and questions swirled in my mind. *What connections? The Wall Street Journal? Really?* Far Right-Wing blogs had written about me earlier with ridiculous guilt-by-association claims, which the campaign and I ignored. But this was different. I stared at the email a little longer, then closed my eyes. *This was big.*

I had joined the campaign on a full-time basis about a month earlier to serve as the national coordinator for Muslim American and Arab American outreach. To do so, I took an unpaid leave of absence from my job as an attorney at one of Chicago's large law firms. Thankfully, my wife and I had pulled together some savings and decided that the opportunity to be part of this historic race was too amazing to pass by.

Many community leaders and campaign veterans greeted the appointment with much enthusiasm. To have a campaign staffer solely dedicated to Muslim and Arab American outreach was a first, and reflected a significant step forward for both the Muslim American and Arab American communities.

Unlike political operatives and campaign professionals who move from campaign to campaign, I was a "true believer." I had first heard of Barack Obama twelve years earlier, during my first year of law school at Northwestern. My contracts professor asked me whether I ever thought of going into politics. I chuckled, responding, "Professor, if I ever wanted to go into politics, I would need to change my name." With a facial expression of genuine surprise and disbelief, he responded, "No, you wouldn't. You should meet a friend of mine out of Hyde Park, Barack Obama. He's got a name like yours—and he's going places."

From then on, I followed Obama's career path while I pursued my own, working my way up the law firm ladder. Then, one night, I heard Obama's now famous 2004 address at the Democratic

National Convention. While I've heard and been moved by many speeches before, particularly religious ones, I was riveted by the power of this speech. There must have been three or four different moments during the speech where I found myself crying. Obama's words that night struck something deep at my core.

Thinking back, it had a lot to do with Barack's personal story. I saw a lot of myself in him. Like him, I am the product of immigrants who came to America from the third world for higher education and opportunity. Like him, I love the study of law and the Constitution and stand in awe of the amazing transformation of America as a direct result of the Civil Rights movement. Like him, I am committed to community organizing.

But it was more than that. Obama's vision of what America is and *can be* resonated. He spoke of those fundamental aspects of American life we too often take for granted, such as the fact that in America, unlike my parents' Syria, we can think and write and speak out without worrying about governmental retribution. He spoke of an open and tolerant America—an America that made his own improbable personal story possible. And when Obama delivered that line: "The hope of a skinny kid with a funny name who believes that America has a place for him too," I nearly jumped out of my seat.

You see, in the aftermath of 9/11, many Muslim Americans, like myself, were at first shocked and then ashamed that other Muslims could carry out such a spectacularly evil act. They were murderers, plain and simple. But it was the ever growing hostility against Muslims following 9/11 that shook my sense of belonging.

"Damn right, Barack!" I thought, "America has a place for me too."

I forwarded the email up the chain of command. Almost immediately, senior campaign officials and I started thinking through the implications of the journalist's statement: "...your connection to fundamentalist Islamic groups in the US and their connections to the Muslim Brotherhood." All of sudden, my whole upbringing and work in the community became suspect. I gave them a quick personal background. I grew up in metro Detroit, in a fairly large community of Syrian physicians. During high school and college, I was active in the mainstream Muslim Youth of North America and Muslim Students Association. As a lawyer, I represented a number of Muslim nonprofit clients. I sat on the board of directors of the Institute for Social Policy and Understanding. I was a recent fellow of Leadership Greater Chicago. I had given talks, generally on non-profit governance, at the annual conventions of the Islamic Society of North America.

I believe that senior campaign officials knew that these affiliations were natural and expected of someone with deep roots in the American Muslim community. Nonetheless I sat down at my desk and pounded out a memo that could be shared with other senior officers of the campaign. In the memo, I explained that there was an organized effort to keep Arab Americans and American Muslims out of mainstream public life. Professional propagandists spread fear of Islam and Muslims and would later, in 2010, spearhead the contrived, so-called "Ground Zero" mosque controversy and anti-Shariah state legislation efforts. They found a home on the Far Right. In the note, I detailed their allegations against mainstream Muslim organizations.

A few hours later, the campaign was in communications with editors at the *Wall Street Journal* over the scope and content of the article being written about me. That's when I learned that the article would be published the next day and would connect me with an imam of one of the largest mosques in Chicagoland. At first, I drew a blank. I didn't have any direct connections with him. Then someone mentioned something about a mutual fund, and that's when I remembered.

About eight years before, during my first year as a corporate lawyer, I was asked to join the board of trustees of a new Islamic mutual fund that was being organized to offer Muslim Americans an ethical and socially conscious investment alternative. The board included the imam and a number of reputable scholars. The imam had been a source of some local controversy a few years earlier over alleged connections to certain Palestinian groups abroad. I was familiar with the imam, but I did not belong to his congregation, and I didn't agree with some of his more conservative and political perspectives. After an initial meeting of the board and only a few weeks after being asked to join, I resigned to avoid unnecessary controversy early in my legal career.

This was bad news to the campaign. The race was very close and the campaign was particularly focused on blue-collar voters in western Pennsylvania and Ohio. Each day was a competition to win the news cycle. The fear was that the imam would be yet another focus of the "Republican attack machine," and they would use me simply as a conduit to get to Obama.

Later that day, I met with top campaign officials. There was an air of seriousness in the room. We dove right into the issues and ramifications of what the *WSJ* might print. I started imagining the imam's picture next to Obama's picture all over the media. The discussion was frank and honest. The idea of stepping down from the campaign was floated around as the most effective means of mitigating the potential damage.

Recognizing what we were facing, the next move was clear: "Look, I'm here to get Barack elected. That's what this is all about. If stepping down is the best way to nip this thing in the bud, then I resign. It's that simple."

The *Wall Street Journal* ran the article the next day. As expected, it tried to paint a picture of me as some sort of radical. It also quoted from my resignation statement, which addressed the mutual fund board matter directly: "Since concerns have been raised about that brief time, I am stepping down...to avoid distracting from Barack Obama's message of change." Almost every major media outlet in the world picked up the story. Some observers were quick to attack the campaign as weak-kneed; others lamented the "politics of exclusion" and the "Kevin Bacon" game of six degrees of separation.

At the time, my emotions ran the spectrum. I was hugely disappointed to step away from this amazing role as a representative of the campaign. I was angry at the political environment—the ignorance and bigotry—that would even necessitate a resignation over such a stretched "guilt by association" attack. But I was also confident that I was doing the right thing—even if it hurt. It worked; my story became a minor news event in the course of the election.

A few months later, I attended the inauguration with my wife and son at the Mall in Washington. Standing in the twenty degree weather with my son sitting on my shoulders, I glanced around at the amazing diversity of people that day and felt the weight of this historic moment. The new president affirmed what I know is true of our country: "that our patchwork heritage is a strength, not a weakness"; and that "we are a nation of Christians and Muslims, Jews and Hindus, and nonbelievers. We are shaped by every language and culture, drawn from every end of the earth."

I am proud to have played a small role in the historic election of Barack Obama as our nation's forty-fourth president. My campaign experience has changed the direction of my professional and personal life. Soon after the inauguration, I opened a boutique law office and now split my time between community organizing and practicing law. Personally, I still retain a bit of that fire that I shared with many staffers at headquarters—that we can, in fact, change the world. Obama's election proves this simple but empowering notion beyond any doubt.

The last few years have seen a rise of anti-Muslim and anti-Arab bigotry. Our communities will continue to be a source of suspicion for some time. But the historical trajectory is positive. As Muslim Americans, we recognize that we must first pay our dues before we earn a seat at the table. My story only echoes the stories of earlier ethnic and religious communities who faced similar struggles and succeeded. There's no doubt that our challenges will require sacrifice, faith and may even involve a bit of presidential politics. It is up to us, working with all Americans of good conscience, to assure this positive trajectory. To shy away from the challenge would be a disservice to ourselves, our country, and our faith.

Undefined
by Aziz Hasan

Aziz Hasan has a personal goal to win the ultimate slashie award. While that may be a fictitious award, he strives to always learn new skills. He eventually wants to say, "I'm a designer-slash-marketer-slash-dancer-slash-etc, etc." But in the meantime, to keep some consistency and a day job, Aziz is the Marketing and Brand Director of the fashion line, *Eva Khurshid* and a Digital Media and Creative Strategist at *SAY Media*, an advertising and media company.

With *Eva Khurshid*, Aziz focuses on the vision behind the brand, ranging from its brand positioning to its visual expression. At *SAY Media*, Aziz is part of a niche creative department specializing in building custom programs aimed to help brands communicate their message in the digital space through engaging ad experiences. Beyond the desk, Aziz is a freelance graphic designer building brand identities for emerging companies. He builds their brand concept, visual identity and marketing collateral. Another passion point is dance. Aziz is an avid hip-hop dancer focusing on popping and waving. With a B.S. in Business Management from Case Western Reserve University, and a concentration in Entrepreneurship and Art Studio, Aziz hopes to translate his experiences and expertise into his passions.

I **often wonder what defines me.** It always starts the same way. Some scrap of paper, a pencil and some serious reflection. This time is no different. I pull out a page from my notebook and begin listing out what those things might be. About twenty minutes into this familiar exercise I have an interesting realization. Among one hundred plus traits and passions listed, not one of them is "Muslim" or "American."

I find that odd. So much of how we define ourselves begins with our roots, but for some reason the notion of roots didn't even cross my mind as I made my list.

I stare out of my living room window onto the street below, watching people pass by, marinating in this odd moment. Why didn)t I list those two defining qualities? Some people would start their list there.

Then I realize it stems from one simple principle: I hate labels. For as long as I can remember, I never wanted to define myself. But I always assumed that that unwillingness came from an inability to comprehend who I am. I now see it has always been deliberate. As I try to better understand how it was such a deliberate choice, I remember an experience that led me to this disposition. It was a blend of middle school, the Grateful Dead and a passion for art.

Like a typical middle-schooler, I spent most of my time trying on different sides of my personality and expressing them through my clothes. One morning I woke up and found myself scrambling through the drawers of my white IKEA dresser, late for the bus as usual. I spotted a handful of t-shirts crumpled in the dresser, and my eyes settled on a dark purple t-shirt. This was one of my favorite t-shirts. It was a Grateful Dead shirt that featured the iconic danc-ing bears riding into space. I liked this particular shirt, not because of the Grateful Dead, but because of my passion for drawing. The bears were jovial and lifelike; they had interesting details, jagged fur, small eyes that were so simple, but telling, and a silly open mouth expression. So I put it on and rushed out the door to catch the bus.

Well, on this particular day, the cards were not stacked in my favor. The latest middle school craze was identifying posers. In an effort to be cool, kids would don the latest fashion of indie band t-shirts and blockbuster movies to prove that they were part of the new fads. As I was walking down the halls of my middle school that morning, a classmate—a particularly loud and crass one who was always scanning for a chance to validate himself—cornered me. We were neither friends nor enemies, but knew each other existed. Once cornered, he pointed to my t-shirt and exclaimed, You're not a Grateful Dead fan! I bet you can't even name any of their songs! Name me three right NOW!

He was right. I wasn›t a Grateful Dead fan. I didn›t know who Jerry Garcia was. I›d never heard the music. For all I knew it was just some guy that Ben and Jerry named an ice cream flavor after.

Panic swept over me, and then a rush of guilt. Was I a poser? Did I have a right to wear this shirt if I didn›t know the band? Why did I pick *this* shirt of all the shirts in my dresser?

I concentrated hard to uncover any song titles lodged deep within my brain. I knew I had a few friends that were *actual* fans. What were they always talking about? Something to do with trains, trucks and magnolias…? Luckily my mind shot into action and I was able to rattle off two songs, but I struggled with the third. It was obvious—I really didn›t know what I was talking about.

The whole encounter spanned a total of five minutes, but to me it felt like hours. That moment, all five minutes of it, started to shape the way I thought about labels. I was upset that someone felt they could figure me out based on my t-shirt. I was appreciating a form of art! The masses assumed I was labeling myself as a Dead Head. Had we spent the five minutes of interrogation talking about why I was wearing that shirt, instead of what songs I knew, it would have been obvious that my alignment was with the art and not the music. And after five more minutes, he might have seen my sketchbook where I tried to expand on the bear designs with my own aesthetic. But, middle school will be middle school and it didn't go down like that.

I continue to peer out the window watching the people on the street, my list still lying on my desk. As I do, a woman walking down the street catches my eye. It then occurs to me, I don't care that this woman walking down the street is Latin American and a banker (or so I gather by the way she's dressed). I'm curious about her ambitions, the impact she wants to have on the world, her next move to turn dream into reality. I want to understand what makes her who she is. The fact that she is a banker is irrelevant. That label paints expectations of a stuffy, entitled, shallow person. I won't assume that.

I leave for work every day understanding that I might stumble into a situation where I will be labeled like I was in middle school. Not just because of my clothing, but more likely because of my religion, my skin color, and honestly, my beard. But this time instead of waiting to be cornered, I step forward and own who I am.

I use humor to my defense. I know people assume things about me when I enter the room, even if only for a split second. It's natural; we *all* do it—we label based on appearance. Yes, I'm the youngest guy at the table. Yes, I'm brown. And yes, I have a finely trimmed beard, and you *should* be jealous. But, I use that moment to disarm a room full of people by cracking a few jokes and letting them know, appearances aside—*I'm just like you.*

"Man, you guys have a low quota! Am I the only Muzzi (Muslim) guy at this table? "

"Am I the only one who went tanning this winter?"

I mention the label in my joke and then quickly dismiss that it has any relevance in the room. It's OK to think it, but not OK to cast judgment with it. Labels create a limited definition of who someone is. It's a first pass, a singular definition. It is far from the truth and only a fraction of the story. The story, a person, is dynamic and always changing, he or she cannot be summed up in a few simple words.

So I choose to remain undefined. It's not important to me to put parameters around who I am. And I don't intend on bending to the labels and expectations imposed upon me. Being Muslim,

American, brown or bearded…is no different than being in my own skin—living, breathing and evolving every day— *to me it's being human*. What *is* different is—understanding my intentions and aspirations. They are deep, complex and dynamic. They are as complicated as my destiny and as limitless as my creativity. Neither of which can be summarized or simplified into a few words.

Rather than define myself by a set of labels and the expectations that come with them, I will *only begin to define myself* by the things I do. I am forever on a quest for like-minded people who want to do something special and change the world.

Some people will tell you I'm a hip-hop dancer, an illustrator and a graphic designer; others will tell you I am a business man, a marketer and a storyteller… for me, those are just a few of the tools I put in my bag of tricks to help me on my journey.

It's the journey that matters.

So let's do something together. Something special. I don't care who they say you are, or how you are labeled, it just matters that *you* want to change the world.

The Exodus of Fear: Redefining Patriotism through Legacy
by Sami H. Elmansoury

Sami H. Elmansoury is a political activist, entrepreneur, orator, and community leader. While a student at Rutgers University, Sami co-founded the Human Development Project, an apolitical organization dedicated to Judeo-Muslim unity through the shared values of improving one's world and empowering communities through service. In 2005, he was the first recipient of the People of the Book Award, presented by Rutgers University for his persistent work in bridge-building, for promoting a stronger appreciation for the strength in America's diversity, and for positively altering the campus climate.

In 2008 and 2009, Sami actively served with national and state political campaigns, each time focusing in part on the strengthened involvement of traditionally disenfranchised groups. In 2010, he was one of just seventy young people nationwide to be invited into the Department of State's Generation Change initiative, which included an inaugural reception with Secretary of State Hillary Rodham Clinton. An avid writer and public speaker, Sami has spoken at events and conferences throughout the United States, and has been featured in various media outlets. He also serves on the boards of several local and national organizations. Elmansoury graduated from Rutgers University in 2006, and currently resides in Marlboro Township, New Jersey, with his family.

Iam a strong believer in our country and in the many profound things that the United States stands for. I am also a Muslim who appreciates his faith, and I recognize and will openly profess that I find no contradiction between my being an American with strong national pride, and my being Muslim. I also know that there exists a proud American Muslim legacy, which despite the calls of the naysayers, can never be expunged from our national history.

I realized some time ago that the sense of alienation admittedly plaguing many American Muslim youth today does not emerge from some pseudo-inherent evil within them or their faith—as fear-mongering pundits would have one believe—but often, rather, from a lack of connection to or rootedness in their country. While in college, I was told by other Muslims that a sense of Muslim community identity (*ummah*) could only be preserved if one puts aside one's national pride. But I never felt this to be an Islamic imperative. The frank truth is that the Muslims of China never gave up being Chinese—nor did the Muslims of India, Egypt, or Russia renounce their national identities. So why would American Muslims shy away from rooting themselves in the United States? My views differ, in part, because I recall a different story.

It is unlikely that many Americans have heard of Mohamed Youssef. Mohamed is a true American hero. An elegant, handsome man, with striking green eyes and a serene demeanor, he grew up in 1920s Egypt—a world of vibrant culture and diversity, and a place where Jews, Christians, Muslims, and others coexisted without question. Mohamed was a brilliant engineer in Sinai, but more than that, he became a devoted father to Sonia, Sammy, and Sameh. Mohamed was a man of profound wisdom, and a dear friend to many. Having lived and worked in Sinai, Mohamed's family was deeply affected by the Israeli-Palestinian conflict and the surrounding wars that violently shook the Middle East for three decades. Despite his pride in his native Egypt, Mohamed always held a spirited admiration for the United States—for its embracing of rare freedoms, and for the liberties that it espoused. Increasingly concerned for the safety of his wife and children in a war-torn region, and having reached a peak in his Egyptian career, he applied for emigration to the United States in the late 1960s, hoping that there he would find a more hopeful future for his family.

At the time, NASA and its research affiliates had been seeking engineers and scientists for an urgent mission that for many, would ultimately determine the United States' global position and lasting victory in a seemingly endless Cold War. The nation was racing to fulfill President Kennedy's declared promise that by the end of the decade, America would land a man on the moon. With a stellar record and the unmatched pride of an immigrant, Mohamed was selected as a Project Engineer for Apollo 11—to place America first—during an era of brutal international competition. With no dearth of uncertainties before them or behind them, Mohamed and his family emigrated from Egypt to Cocoa Beach, Florida in 1968, years before emigration from Egypt would become more commonplace, and he began his new post soon thereafter. The following year, he, his wife, and his three young children proudly watched in person as Apollo 11 took off from Cape Canaveral.

Mohamed and his wife of nearly sixty years, Madiha Elzeiny—both Muslims—are Americans, and continue to hold great pride in their American story and in the legacy that follows with it. I realize that it is quintessentially American stories like these—stories of national contribution and sacrifice—that far too often go untold to American Muslim youth. I remind my Muslim coreligionists that men like Mohamed, while being Muslim, are also deeply American at their core. Homeland pride is not limited by religion. Yet I often find myself having to stand up to Muslim youth and say: "Be proud, you have a legacy here."

I reflect on the paradigm that has been created for American Muslims: it is often assumed that to be a practicing Muslim today is quintessentially un-American. Yet my frustration with this absurd challenge drives me to be even more involved in my community, to present to both my neighbors and to my coreligionists the blatant fact that my faith values neither contradict my sincere American pride, nor my American culture. Because unlike many who have become radically absorbed into the misled notion that being both American and a patriot can only be derived from the fear of what is different, my patriotism does not come from politics or apologies—it comes from our Sputnik moments. It is derived from a proud legacy.

I recently met with Mohamed—now in his eighties, his hair swept back, his eyes still striking through mine, his belt matching his shoes, and his suit pressed as though it was his first day with NASA. He showed me a survey on the economy and other issues that the Obama Administration had sent, and read his thoughtful answers to me with pride. He was convinced, with a stunning smile, that "Dear Moh" meant that the letter had only gone to him. When I asked him for his wisdom on the challenging circumstances at work alienating the American Muslim community today, he said that every community faces a struggle; that to an extent, struggle is an inevitable part of becoming American, and that the post-9/11 era offered no exception. But he has been American for decades—since long before 9/11. I gazed into Mohamed's eyes, and I saw the pain behind his words. The same fear-mongering that had sought to strip away his American legacy, has also attacked many American Muslim youth. It has caused them to ask: "Am I American enough? And what does that mean?" And the fear and disconnect that ensues has caused many of them to reject an American identity. Yet 9/11 and similar political evils did not define Mohamed, so why should he be defined by it? His story spoke for itself. He was a patriot. He had served his country in one of the most profound ways. And the day that he arrived in the United States, he opened a new chapter in his family's legacy, a chapter that *is* American at its very core.

It is through stories like that of Mohamed that I have overcome any and all fear of the ignorant. I forbid myself from allowing them to stifle my patriotism, to prevent me from cheering my country on when it is right or speaking up when it is wrong, or to offer me a sense of alienation in the only nation that I call home. For fearing the disingenuous only permits them a sense of accomplishment. But it is time to raise our eyes once again, as a nation, and to understand that ignorant fear does not drive sincere patriotism. It forges expounded ignorance, and pushes the most vulnerable—those whom we are supposed to embrace—to alienation. The fear-mongering that would seek to debase Mohamed's name—*because* of his name—while simultaneously attempting to erase his legacy, is the same counterproductive force that lays challenge to the latest generation of young Americans. Young Americans who believe in our country, and who are yearning to find their calling and contribution, while maintaining the liberty to practice their faith in an era when "United We Stand" has outlandishly become the motto of *both* the uniters and the dividers.

And so I remain deeply rooted in the quest for the success of my country, and I am deeply proud to be an American who knows his own history. I stand as a patriot. For I am not a post-9/11 patriot, defined by fear and a desire for acceptance by those who feel that they control the dialogue, or by those who would seek to change my identity. My pride is not sourced from a self-coerced sense of patriotism due to a tumultuous political climate. It comes from Mohamed Youssef—my grandfather—an American and a gentleman, who, through his work on the ground, shot for the stars, and touched the moon. I am defined by my family's American legacy, and I am not waiting for anyone to tell me how American I am, or how American I can be.

It is upon every American Muslim young person to discover their own legacy, and to wear that narrative with pride. Ask questions. Document your story—whether it involves tragedy or hope. Draw upon your talents. Connect with your countrymen. And give back to your community. As for me, as just one American who happens to be Muslim, I will work with every breath to have a profound, significant, and remarkably positive impact on my country and on my world, and to keep my grandfather's proud legacy alive.

I will boldly defy those who seek to alienate me because of my faith, for neither fear-mongers nor coreligionists can erase a story that stays alive through example. And neither can take away the distinguished difference that any young American can make, as they build upon the courage that brought their families and their ancestors here, and as they discover the legacy that made them American.

I challenge the naysayers to recognize that we are still one nation, and that no troublesome force can separate us from each other's shared destiny. We will move forward together—we will have to.

Finding Myself in Tears
by Justin Mashouf

Justin Mashouf is a filmmaker and artist living in Los Angeles, California. Justin's most recent documentary film, "Warring Factions," follows him to Iran where he meets a group of young Iranian breakdancers for an impromptu boy battle. Justin's work deals with the blurring of borders and his unique interactions with the Muslim world.

It was at the age of twelve, alongside my best friend Mahdi amongst a small gathering of Muslims, where I would learn the meaning of being a Muslim man.

Mahdi and I met in our homeroom class in a middle school in Tucson, Arizona. It appeared to be no mistake that five of the six Iranians in the school were put in the same class. I was an awkward, shrimpy white kid who happened to be half Iranian, while Mahdi was a fluffy-haired brown kid who happened to be half white.

Our ethnic backgrounds were almost identical. Both of our fathers came to the US in the early '70s from Iran, and both of our mothers were white Americans from the East Coast. It didn't take very long until we were inseparable.

My exposure to Islam was worlds away from his. Mahdi's dad was the informal leader of the small Shiite community in Tucson, whereas my father was a retired physician who rarely identified himself to others as a Muslim, especially to those outside the faith. My father would never attend Islamic gatherings, so before I met Mahdi, Roman Catholicism was the only religion I was exposed to. My mother grew up in the Catholic Church with a strong faith in God but a shaky relationship with the Church. I attended church with my family for Christmas and Easter but never took communion. I always thought it was odd when they called communion wafers and wine the body and blood of Christ. If we should remember God by eating something, why couldn't it be chocolate?

Mahdi, meanwhile, had grown up attending weekly gatherings of the local Muslim community with his family, and he started bringing me along because we did everything together. Where he took me that first time was unlike any church I had been to. There were no pews, altars, candles, stained glass, or even chairs, for that matter. People would convert their homes into a space for worship, and there was no church or mosque that could re-create that humble but spiritually elevated environment.

At the gatherings Mahdi and I sat with the adults for no more than fifteen minutes before escaping to the kids' room, while the adults recited "Dua Kumayl," a supplicatory prayer traditionally recited weekly by Shiites. They were a group diverse in heritage and culture—from Iran, Iraq, Kuwait, India and Pakistan, who prayed together in Arabic and chatted together in English. We kids sat in a room alongside pots of simmering Persian stews and fragrant jasmine rice. Our usual entertainment with the handful of other boys always started with wrestling matches. One time it ended with detonating M-80's and small bottle rockets inside discarded soda liters. Our attempt at silencing the bangs by covering them with pillows was one accident away from the wrath of Mahdi's father. Thankfully, our juvenile explosive adventures were never discovered by the adults, or the FBI.

Every year during the Islamic month of Moharram, the adults would drape the rooms in black curtains, sheets, and green embroidered calligraphy. Dressed in nothing but black, flocks of our dormant community would rise out of their daily routines and enter this uncomfortably small space. Knees awkwardly rubbing up against one another, these believers sat on the floor to read Dua Kumayl and commemorate the martyrdom of Imam Husayn, the grandson of the Prophet Muhammad.

Who I was about to learn of, and what I was about to see, changed me. I had known of this man, Imam Husayn, but for the first time, amongst these strangers I felt his spirit. From the day of his birth the Prophet was aware that his grandson would die a violent death in a land called Karbala. Sure enough, it turned out to be the most gruesome, heart wrenching death in the history of Shiite Islam.[1]

In the early years that Mahdi had been bringing me here, we were rarely deeply engaged with the gathering directly. Things were different when Moharram came around. The rooms of the house became so packed that there was no such thing as a kids' room. We had no choice but to exist as quiet observers, unable to resort to our childish mischief. The combination of body heat and kitchen steam prompted the women to periodically splash rosewater over the crowd to calm the odor of men. Individuals of each ethnicity would recite poetry in their native tongue, recounting the events of the battle of Karbala, which climaxed with the dramatic murder of Imam Husayn. The variety of languages, dialects, and styles joined our cultures into a symphonic hum. As I sat leaning against the wall,

---

[1] The story of Imam Husayn is a complicated historical narrative of the rise of the Umayyad's from the time of the assassination of Ali ibn abi Talib, the cousin and son-in-law of the Prophet Muhammad. Shiites see Ali ibn abi Talib as the legitimate successor to the Prophet. Ali's son, Husayn, was threatened by the Umayyad ruler Yazid, that if he did not pledge allegiance and therefore legitimize Yazid's leadership of the Muslims, he would be killed. Husayn set out to Iraq, where his followers wrote him letters proclaiming their allegiance to him and their willingness to rise against Yazid's rule. Yazid's army intercepted Imam Husayn and his small band of under one hundred followers in the deserts of Iraq, killing all of the combatants, including Husayn's six-month old son, and cruelly capturing the women, children and those too weak to fight, marching them to the court of Yazid in Syria. This killing of the Prophet's grandson and dishonoring of the Prophet's closest family members was lamented by most Muslims. The martyrdom of Husayn became a central Shi'i religious observation commemorated with lamentations in the retelling of this tragedy.

my senses overwhelmed, the lights were turned off, and all attention shifted to the sincere voice of the reciter as attending believers cried and wept in solidarity over their fallen leader. The tears of men and women alike sounded in one continuous harmony. Even though I could barely understand the words that were being said, I knew the pulse of the gathering was something I wanted to feel forever.

Everything I knew about being a man was challenged.

The first time I saw my father cry was when I was six. He had received the news that my grandmother had passed. Until that point, I had the illusion that my father was this indestructible character from a movie. At 5'3" inches, he was a champion power lifter amongst an Iranian tradition of men built like heroes. From my comparably shrimpy stature, I wanted to be just like him. And like him, my tears were reserved for my mother only. She was the one who could handle my childhood waterworks.

All of my television heroes, Thundercats, G.I. Joes, and Teenage Mutant Ninja Turtles, were warrior men. Playing rough with the boys at school was expected and any boy seen crying was violating the archetypal rites of passage of becoming a man.

As a twelve-year-old, sitting in a room full of crying men, I felt my worldview oddly, yet naturally, shifting. My first year of being in this gathering would be as a novice observer. In the years that followed, I became an appreciative participant in this ritual, letting my inhibitions dissolve to engage in the story as if I were there to witness the tragedy and come to the sobering reality that my tears were acts of repentance for my personal inaction against injustice. I felt liberated by the vulnerability of the men around me, and even the boys at school could not shame away this experience.

Whether the believers gathered in that dark space were acting out of traditional habit or by honest expression, their collective energy was contagious and had the power to affect even a stranger to the tradition. This lamentation went beyond an act of solidarity and remembrance. It was a religious experience aimed at softening the hearts of believers. So etched into their hearts was this love for

Imam Husayn, that the mere recitation of the events of Karbala was a wound in the Shiite soul that bled each year. So they sang:

Een Husayn keest ke alam hameh divaneye oost
Een chesham eest ke jaanha hame parvaneye oost

Who is this Husayn, who the world has gone mad over?
Who is this candlelight, who all of the moths fly around?

The tradition of *azadari* (mourning congregations, lamentations, chest beating and all such actions which express the emotions of grief and solidarity with Imam Husayn) slowly became part of my life. The oral histories, performed in ways that trigger emotion, continue to inspire me on multiple levels. Seeing azadari's effect throughout the Muslim world, playing a role from tradition to revolution, has taught me the power of storytelling. This phenomenon has strengthened my drive to become a storyteller. Today, I continue to draw inspiration from these traditions as a filmmaker.

My first feature film, *Warring Factions*, was inspired by this desire to invoke human emotions and remind viewers of our common humanity. As an Iranian American, I set out to find breakdancing in Iran and in turn I learned a learned an ancient Iranian martial art. Living with the tense culture of war and politics between the US and Iran, my film was an attempt to shift the dialog to the universality of movements, music and emotion. Just as telling the story of Imam Husayn is a tradition that invokes powerful emotions and inspires Husayn's mourners to live righteous lives, I have seen my film as an extension of this tradition.

To think, it all started in a room of crying men—an annual renewal of Shiite identity, dignified, proud, and reverent. I felt even then that azadari was a reminder for believers, particularly men, that humankind is not made of steel. Our modern heroes are foolishly, not bravely, stoic. True heroes, and my identity as a Muslim man, must maintain a soft heart for the oppressed that drives fearlessness in the battle for justice. Being a Muslim man retains my humanity.

Coming Home
by Mohamed Geraldez

Mohamed Geraldez converted to Islam during his junior year in college. Upon graduating, he went overseas to study the Islamic sciences for nearly four years in Syria, Morocco, Mauritania and the Saharan Desert, with some of the most renowned scholars of the Muslim world. After studying abroad, he returned to the US to obtain his Master's in Business—MBA. Mohamed is an entrepreneur and co-founder of a few companies in different industries, including the first and largest vegan necktie company in the world www.JaanJ.com. He enjoys surfing, fashion, academia, basketball, skateboarding, business, and drinking coffee. Mohamed currently resides in Southern California and travels throughout the world for business and speaking engagements. Find him on Facebook at www.facebook.com/mgeraldez.

"Get out! Get out of our room…NOW!" As I stared at the Las Vegas strip from our eighth floor hotel room, tears of sadness and strength fell from my face as I realized that a past life was coming to an end, but a new one had just been ushered in. After all the arguments, I was broken and knew that I overstepped all boundaries of respect, and I had nothing else to blame except my newfound self-righteousness. But like any other religious zealot, I was oddly happy. My new state of mind ultimately took its toll on my innocent family and with that, my dad wanted me out...now.

Born into welfare and raised in a poor Latino neighborhood with its fair share of gunshots and drug abuse, my parents were committed to raising their children right. In the tenth grade, we moved to a beautiful tract home development, but unbeknownst to my parents, I still found myself gravitating towards the people and neighborhoods that resembled my childhood years. Although this new phase of my life should have made life easier in general, it actually left me confused, troubled and searching; but that is what drugs, drive-by shootings, lawless partying, alcohol and losing friends to gang violence can do to you.

Despite the mental turmoil during my late teenage years, I was still able to maintain a 4.2 GPA. At the time, I viewed excelling in school as my ticket to staying out late and for long periods of time rather than as a stepping stone to establishing a successful life. But in spite of all the late night and all-weekend partying, I felt empty.

My double lifestyle inevitably led to spiritual chaos, and I started looking into God.

The religion I was born and raised into, Christianity, was simply confusing to me. I teetered on the verge of becoming an atheist, but before I took that final step, I wanted to look at the world's religions closely. I researched, read and talked to many people about Taoism, Buddhism, Rastafarianism, Christianity, Judaism, Islam, Hinduism, atheism and even animistic faiths. I was now twenty-years old, and during this period serious conversations about philosophy, current events and religion became more and more a part of my life. After many discussions on so many topics, and engaging the leaders and adherents of numerous faiths, especially a Muslim classmate from Geology 303 named Eugene, Islam appealed to my intellect due to its radical view of one God with absolutely no divine associates. Soon after this realization, I converted.

When I became Muslim, I felt a sense of physical relief and renewal that I have never felt before. Spiritually, I felt an unexpected euphoria.

It is said that when one converts, all of his sins are washed away. I felt this. It is hard to explain but I can tell you one thing: before I went to bed on the night I converted (February 14, Valentine's Day), I sincerely thought that I was going to die in my sleep. I did not expect to wake up, because my once-heavy heart felt a beautiful but strange lightness that I had never felt before, as though it was not tied to this world any longer. My soul felt fresh and new.

Within months of accepting my new faith, I thought I was becoming religious, but in reality I was becoming intolerant. My family and I argued all the time about religion, because all I did was attack their belief system. This created a tense atmosphere in our household and was the main reason why my father kicked me out during that family vacation in Las Vegas. "No wonder they call this place Sin City"—and other self-righteous comments, pushed my happy family over the edge during that weekend.

Several months later, in the fall semester of my senior year, I decided I was going to study Islam with the scholars of the Middle East and Africa. Months of studying my new religion on the weekends and in my spare time were inadequate. Additionally, studying Islam in English instead of Arabic was frustrating because I felt that I had limited access to religious knowledge; not knowing the language of the Holy Qur'an was, in my opinion, an impediment. I wanted my knowledge straight from the source; therefore, I decided to set off for the Middle East right after graduating from college.

For nearly four years, I studied in Syria, Morocco, and Mauritania. While in Syria, I studied Arabic at the University of Damascus Language Institute. After becoming competent in Arabic after one year, I moved to Morocco to live with one of my teachers and would travel back and forth to my other teachers who lived in the Saharan Desert of Mauritania.

Gone were the days of orderly lines, waiting for your turn to speak, and "common" courtesy. My new life consisted of ignored driving laws, overcharged goods, and gawking. In fact, while in Syria the gawking bothered me so much that I contemplated leaving, but

I eventually realized that the local population had just never seen a Filipino before. In Morocco, I would force a smile when greeted with "Kon-nichiwa;" they thought I was a Japanese tourist. In Mauritania, they called me "Al Filistini" (The Palestinian) instead of "Al Filibini" (The Filipino), because the words sounded similar and they didn't know much about the Philippines.

The true test of patience, however, would occur during my Arabic conversations in the marketplace. Once I opened my mouth, I became the local sideshow inducing smiles, whispers, and stares from onlookers. Thankfully I overcame any annoyance at this by examining the countless reasons for their conspicuous reactions every time I spoke. The rarity of a Muslim convert in their country, the impossible thought of Americans converting to Islam, and the anomaly of hearing a non-Arab speaking Arabic, would compel anyone to stare. It must have been a sight to see a strange creature effortlessly destroy centuries of eloquence with just a few sentences. But as I became more fluent, people and their opinions drifted to the periphery for what lay ahead of me was the greater challenge: myself.

My first lesson in the Sahara Desert was how to become accustomed to solitude. Once labeled the life of the party, I was now cloistered for countless hours in order to read and memorize. During the first several weeks, my social personality had difficulty adjusting to solitary life. I could not have Mozart as background music while reading a passage, or take study breaks to justify meeting my friends. For the first time in my life I had to concentrate as never before, and I had to do it all alone.

Loneliness and daydreaming had no place in the Mauritanian method of education. To combat them, ironically, I would study more to occupy myself. With this approach, came a rebirth. The sound of my breath was no longer deafening as I became enamored with the pursuit of knowledge. I would stay up late, reading and memorizing by candlelight, or by flashlight, depending on the weather. I would sometimes catch myself thinking, "I never knew my life would end up this way. I'm quite glad it did." It was truly a victory for my soul over the destructive path I had been on earlier in life.

Self-discovery and intellectual pursuit, however, were not the sole means of learning. Life with the Massumi tribe, well-known for their Islamic scholarship, also taught me many valuable lessons. I found myself at times sitting in the middle of my dark tent for hours as sandstorms halted daily life, preparing for flash floods at the first sight of lightning, and eating tortoise and lizard meat because of the lack of available food. If I never displayed any patience in my life up to this point, the desert forced a semblance of it to appear. Strangely, I loved every second. Not every city boy can say he learned how to calculate time and direction from the position of celestial bodies, or can say he transcribed fragile manuscripts by hand into a notebook. Yet the real reward was witnessing myself mature into a man that I never imagined—adaptive, forbearing and thoughtful. These were traits I never thought could exist within me because I was always impatient, wanting it my way, right away, forcing things to go according to my plans. Life in the Sahara Desert taught me otherwise. If it were not for my neighbors, my tent would have been destroyed countless times in desert storms. When I would run out of my daily ration of water, I was thankful that I had generous people around me. Events like these made me realize that life was not about "I, me and my"—it was about "us." If I wanted to succeed, let alone survive, I had to care for others. This train of thought became so regulated as to become routine, and I truly hope it still exists within me to this day. If not, may God forgive my soul.

My life abroad, especially in Mauritania, was the most transformative phase of my life. It was a period of determination, growth and reflection due to the sheer absence of distractions and everyday Western amenities. My time overseas can best be summed up by what my father told my mother on their flight to visit me: "Your son is not a little boy anymore. Traveling makes people grow...exposes you to other opinions and cultures. You'll see that he's matured."

After four years of studies abroad, I returned home.

Since 2005 my once anti-Islamic family has entirely converted, I have co-founded a few companies, returned to university and obtained an MBA, and decided to go back to volunteering at the local state prison. To my parents, their ambitious and goal-driven son was back and I was no longer "far-off" into religion to the detriment of my worldly life. I had finally returned and they could not be more happy and proud of their boy.

Muslim After Midnight
by Obaid H. Siddiqui

Obaid H. Siddiqui is a writer based in Philadelphia. He was trained as a journalist, but upon realizing he was the only one interested in reading his byline, he changed fields and is now a marketing professional for a global firm. Born the youngest of four children to Indo-Pakistani immigrants, multiple relocations in his youth led him from the deep South to the Mid-Atlantic region, where a lone year spent in a south Jersey Italian neighborhood eviscerated his strong southern accent. With the soul of a Bedouin and the appetite of a Viking, he is a voracious consumer of conversations with friends and family, quality journalism, self-reflection, Alabama football, and cheese steaks. When not with loved ones, Obaid can be found slowly stroking his beard and staring off into the distance, while thinking of cheese steaks and world peace. He plans to retire at the age of thirty-five and move to Greece. He's also a poor planner.

Nothing good happens at 3:00 a.m.

Of course, that is what you hear only after something bad has happened at 3:00 a.m. I'm a night owl; I relish the calm of the pre-dawn hours when the weather is cool, the streets are quiet, and my mind is most apt to channel creative inspiration. So that popular refrain never meant much to me. Until that one night, at 3:00 a.m.

The warmth of the Wawa convenience store was a welcome relief from the crisp, bitter cold of that February night. I was dressed for the weather: a burly, brown wool carcoat accented with a maroon *keffiyeh* (traditional Arab male headdress) that served as my scarf. Now, I'm not a fool. I understand that in Western countries the keffiyeh serves as more than an article of clothing. It's a political statement. At least it was until Urban Outfitters usurped and rebranded it as a must-have for the young, liberal-chic hipster crowd. Let it be known, though, that I was wearing it prior to the commercialization of the fabric design. But I digress. It was 3:00 a.m and buying a drink at the local Wawa would be my last stop prior to turning in for the night. Given the time, other customers were not likely, so I figured my scarf would go unnoticed. Plus, I'd been a patron of this particular Wawa for over a decade. By now, I was well aware of all the store employees and their corresponding shift schedules.

Lost in this aura of familiarity, I didn't even notice the couple standing at the sandwich counter as I walked straight back to the refrigerators to grab a half-lemonade, half-iced tea beverage (Arnold Palmer is a genius). I opened the clunky glass door and was accosted by a cold fog that I fought to ignore. I braved the artificial elements, reached in and secured a tight, kung-fu grip on my prized possession. Before I could retract my hand and close the refrigerator door, my ears clued in to the incoherent ravings of a man behind me.

"Hey Habib! Go back to Iraq!"

I turned around, and about four feet in front of me stood a drunken white man in his 30's. Despite the intoxicant coursing through his body—the smell of which permeated the air directly around him—he had a steely resolve in his eyes. With lips pursed and fists clenched, he stood as though he had an army behind him ready to set his command into action.

It's amazing how in the tensest of situations, in the briefest spans of time, everything can slow down. A lifetime passed in those few seconds. Psychologists say when in a threatening situation, one immediately has to choose to either fight or flee. I, however, chose to criticize. Instantly, I tried to make sense of the man's rantings.

First off, habib means friend in Arabic. *If you hate me, it's a bit misleading to address me as "friend."* I was expecting to see an affable face when I turned around, and instead I saw *American History X.* Not cool. Secondly, I'm not from Iraq—nor is the keffiyeh a particularly Iraqi garment. I was born in Birmingham, Alabama—though I grant you it's a part of the US still considered a foreign country to those in the Northeast, and I bought the keffiyeh at the shops on 52nd and Market Streets in Philadelphia—again, a land considered foreign territory to white suburbia. But, even so, my father is from India and my mother is from Pakistan, so I really have no business going to Iraq. Apparently, this wasn't a man concerned with details.

O.k. So he's clearly speaking out of a drunken ignorance. What now? A rush of emotion and thoughts began to cloud my decision process. Fear for my safety quickly evolved into anger, which then quickly progressed into an assessment of my fighting skills. *When was the last time you were in a fight? No answer. That's not good.* Nonetheless, dramatic fight scenes from American movies jockeyed for position against proverbial stories of Islamic peace and tolerance in my head.

I wanted to hit him. *Is that the American or Muslim in me?* I had it all planned out. I'd get very close to him and disarm him with a pleasant smile. The moment he opened his mouth again, I'd use his torso to guide my upwardly mobile fist into the underbelly of his stupid little chin. *Violence will just embolden his bigoted beliefs.* And I've never been much of a fighter. Although my stocky build and beard can intimidate some, I'm more teddy bear than thug. In fact, when I was four years old my father and I walked by a karate studio. He stopped and lifted me up to watch the action through the glass storefront window. I began to cry and begged to leave, much to the chagrin of my uber-alpha-male father. Alas, I would only look like Ralph Macchio in my childhood; I would not have his karate chops.

I wanted to dispel the bigot's hatred through open, careful dialogue. *Is that the American or Muslim in me?* Surely, a calm, diplomatic discussion would allow us both to exit this situation without partaking in a horribly choreographed fight sequence. *He's too drunk to allow logic to convince him.*

I just wanted to leave the store. *Is that the American or Muslim in me?* But I could not avoid acknowledging the situation and drop my much-craved lemonade/iced tea, and walk out. This jerk has challenged my manhood! *Something needs to be done and it needs to be done quickly.*

I looked around the store. The two black employees buried their heads downward indicating they wanted no part in the ensuing drama. (The interplay of racial, social, ethnic, and religious elements in this little dance of bigotry would make David Mamet blush.) My antagonizer's female companion—who resembled a cross between Courtney Love and a corpse, but was seemingly less intoxicated than her man-friend—stayed quiet as she anxiously anticipated my move.

It's go time. I looked directly into his eyes, gave him a head nod, and walked around him. *That is the American Muslim in me.* I made my way to the counter, paid for my drink, and slowly exited the store. The employee behind the counter never made eye contact with me.

There have been many instances of similar prejudicial bigotry hurled toward me prior to and since that occurrence. However, I reenact that event in my head the most often. To this day, I still want to punch him. Yet, to this day, I still think I made the right decision. The decision-making skill that has emerged from my shared identity is now one of my greatest strengths. As an American Muslim, I see both sides. I've learned when to stand for the rights of my faith and when to acknowledge the separation of mosque and state. Unfortunately, events like the one I described force many American Muslim men to doggedly tether themselves to one side at the expense of the other.

On one end, are those who identify solely as American and shed their Islamic beliefs to chase after the elusive, and often illusory, promise of hedonistic delights and consumerist gluttony that is the

American dream. On the other end, are those who identify solely as Muslim and remove themselves from society at large by escaping to an isolated life, surrounded only by those who share their strict adherence to a particular belief set and cultural legacy.

Then there's the third group—those for whom the two identities cannot be separated. We *American Muslim* males are our own breed. I understand and enjoy the most vulgar references of American pop culture, and can substantively discuss, from an Islamic perspective, why such references are wrong. I can hang out at bars with friends who drink without having the slightest urge to partake in the same activities. I can befriend women without the goal of treating them as a notch in the belt of sexual conquest. My faith is Islam and my nationality is American. I am as much American as I am Muslim. There is no inherent contradiction between the two. Membership to one does not exclude me from the other. I've learned— through trial and error, both painful and comical—to walk comfortably in the skin of each. It's easy now.

Just as long as I'm in bed before 3:00 a.m.

My Detroit *Surah*
Khaled A. Beydoun

Khaled A. Beydoun is a lawyer, author and consultant. He is Arab American, with roots in Egypt, Lebanon, and Detroit. He graduated from the University of Michigan, earned his J.D. from the University of California, Los Angeles School of Law, and an LLM from the University of Toronto Faculty of Law. Mr. Beydoun is an experienced attorney, education consultant, and avid writer. He has published scholarship and a book addressing affirmative action and education, human trafficking and human rights, multiculturalism, and Islam. He is most proud of being the son of Fikrieh Beydoun, his mother and hero. Khaled can be reached at kabeydoun@gmail.com.

M y mother and I drove northbound on Evergreen Drive, deep into the northwest side of Detroit. I sat quietly in the front seat of our blue Dodge Caravan, gazing out the rolled-down window at boarded-up homes, un-mowed lawns, Joy Road's feared housing projects, and ultimately, our destination: *Frank Cody High School*. My mother handed me two dollars for lunch and drove back to Warrendale, leaving me alone in a neighborhood I had never set foot in before.

The metropolitan Detroit area ranks as the most segregated region in the United States. The city's school system vividly represented the racial stratification on the ground, and Cody High's largely black student body was nothing like *Fordson High*, my home school. Fordson boasted a student community that was more than ninety percent Arab American, while I walked into Cody's summer school classes as the lone member of my ethnic group. I felt a barrage of stereotypes thrown my way, and within hours of my first day of summer was called "camel jockey," "terrorist," and "sand nigger." I responded to these slurs the only way I knew how, by stepping up and fighting back.

After school, I ran up to the blue minivan parked on Cathedral Street with my books in hand, certain that my first day at Cody would be my last. The scratches and bruises on my face, surely, would persuade my mother to relocate me to another school. However, her words emphatically declared the opposite, as did her rigid Arabic tenor: *"You chose to fail freshman year, now you must deal with the consequences. You are staying at Cody."* I returned the next day, the following week, and the full three months of the summer of 1993. I fought more, earned the respect of my classmates, and, eventually, earned an education that no textbook or course could extend.

The students at Cody were largely poor and black, and the surrounding community rife with violence and drugs. Cody was only a few miles away from our home on Mettetal Street, which was situated in a largely Black and Arab neighborhood. Yet, I traveled to Dearborn for school, and Arab families in the enclave mingled little with their Black neighbors. Therefore, even though Cody was only a ten-minute drive, the school felt worlds away. That was Detroit, where roads separated one community from another and ethnic intermingling oftentimes resulted in violence. My friends were largely Arab American, and while they spent their summers visiting family in Lebanon, Yemen or Palestine, I migrated across Detroit's racially segregated landscape every morning to Cody High, with my Egyptian mother behind the wheel and WJLB's "strong songs" playing from the car speakers.

"Asalaamu alaykum," greeted Terry, a classmate from the north-west side of Detroit who sat next to me in biology. I was surprised at first to hear refined Arabic coming from the mouth of Terry, a Black fourteen-year-old who emerged as my first friend at Cody. Like-wise, Terry was floored when he looked into my Walkman to find "Rock Dis Funky Joint," the single from Poor Righteous Teachers. We were both perplexed, but this served as the catalyst for discover-ing the many commonalities Terry and I shared. Apart from failing our freshman years at Fordson and Cooley High, Terry and I were poor, listened to Boogie Down Productions and Public Enemy, and seldom traveled beyond the neatly demarcated boundaries of our neighborhoods. We were also both Muslim, raised by single mothers.

Since coming to Detroit in 1981, my family and I had lived in a total of twelve homes. My father, living abroad in Lebanon, left my mother to care for my older sister, Khalida, youngest brother, Mohamed, and me, all by herself. She was uneducated, spoke little English, and struggled to make a decent life for us in an unfamil-iar, economically depressed, and gritty city. We lived on welfare for many years. I remember coming home from school and making cheese sandwiches wrapped in pita bread from government issued cheese and staples. This was the life I knew as a child, and I never sensed that we were poor until my teenage years. My mother taught herself how to sew and make clothing; she worked as a tailor and later at a laundromat, while my sister eventually assumed the role of my second parent.

Terry lived right off Seven Mile, around the corner from the landmark Hip Hop Shop. His father was locked away in prison, while his mother worked as a janitor at a downtown hotel. Like me, Terry's attention deviated from his studies, and he also failed the majority of his ninth grade courses. His eldest sister Raheema, a freshman at Wayne State University, looked after him while his mother worked twelve-hour days. Both of our mothers were strict disciplinarians, whose belief in faith navigated them beyond poverty, broken marriages, feeding four mouths with a limited budget of food stamps, and the trials associated with raising derelict sons. Our narratives paralleled one another across Detroit's racially polarized blocks and sections, but intersected that hot summer at Cody High.

It was weeks into July, and I grew accustomed to being the only Arab in the classroom. Instead of responding to jeers like, *"Yo Khaled, is you gonna hook me up when I come to your daddy's liquor store?"* with a punch, I jabbed back with a slick comeback. The same individuals I fought with earlier evolved into friends, or at worst, tolerated acquaintances. Besides, we shared the same tattered classrooms, read from the same worn textbooks, and learned from teachers who wanted to be anywhere but at Cody High. While Fordson ranked at the bottom of the State of Michigan's public schools, Cody was *the* bottom. My classmates were intelligent, but victims of an educational system that perpetuated their poverty and did anything but prepare them for success at college. While nearly one-third of freshmen eventually drop out at Fordson High, the number was more than half at Cody. The lessons I learned outside of the classroom at Cody had a revolutionary impact on my understanding of justice, equality, structural racism, and the debilitating impact of an inferior education.

Terry and I shared a love for music that galvanized our friendship. The words of Chuck D, KRS-One, Wise Intelligent, and Rakim made sense of our situation, and the economic and social trials both Terry and I faced. Boogie Down Productions exposed the failures of the public education system, while Public Enemy called for the structural reform needed to enfranchise people of color in the United States. While the subjects of the songs were largely African American, I felt a great affinity for their message, being both Arab and Muslim. Indeed, many of the artists infused Muslim phraseology and imagery into their lyrics, which resonated deeply with Terry and I.

Terry, hip hop, and especially my experience at Cody High inspired me to be a better student, a better son for my mother, and an advocate for social justice. I returned to Fordson with a broadened worldview, empowered by my summer education across town at

Cody High. My GPA jumped from a 0.9 to a 3.9; I buried my head in the works of Rumi and Naguib Mahfouz, Franz Fanon and Alex Haley, and maintained the friendships I made that summer throughout my life. Islam was colorblind. I read and mandated Muslims to fight for justice, equality and individual rights. I coupled this mission with the lessons I learned at Cody and on the streets of my home, Detroit, which led me to the University of Michigan, the UCLA School of Law to study Critical Race Theory, and shaped me into an advocate for social and racial justice.

I returned to Cody for the first time in thirteen years in 2006, poised to educate a crowd of largely black parents about an anti-affirmative ballot proposal. Many of the audience members were perplexed that an individual, perhaps of my complexion or ethnicity, would helm the American Civil Liberties Union campaign to safeguard affirmative action in Michigan. Yet, Terry—who sat in the front row, now an attorney for a large Detroit law firm—knew that my commitment to educational equality and racial justice was birthed in that very same building, and was an extension of the brand of "God's work" our mothers taught us in between long work days and cross-city drives.

So, How's it Going?
by Sameer Sarmast

Sameer S. Sarmast is a very active member of his local communities throughout Bergen and Passaic County. Sameer's educational background includes a B.S. in Finance and Management Information Systems from Rutgers University in New Jersey, and a M.S. in Management from Northeastern University in Massachusetts. While maintaining his career as a V.P. in financial services, Sameer also maintains a Halal food web show, *Sameer's Eats*, with his Creative Director, Saad Malik. Sameer strives to deliver quality episodes as a guide to the best Halal restaurants throughout North America, and hopes to make it to the Food Network as the face of the Halal Food industry. He is also the Treasurer and Public Relations head for the Rutgers University Muslim Alumni Association. Sameer currently resides in Bergen County, NJ, and enjoys volunteering, increasing his Islamic knowledge, socializing with his friends, eating at Halal restaurants, travelling, BBQing and spending quality time with his family.

"Alhamduli'llah, things are good." That is the truest answer I can give if someone asks me, "How's everything?" or "kayf haalak?" But there was a time when I could not say that honestly.

A couple years ago, I experienced two life-changing events. One broke me, and the other is healing me. The first seemed too sudden, and the latter is still underway. In the same year that I went through the darkest period of my life, I began to see the purpose of it. My days since then—the brighter days full of what I hope is constant maturity and spiritual growth—are a blessing, but they wouldn't have happened if I didn't first feel the agony.

It started with my divorce. For many Muslims, divorce is an alien concept. Muslim couples, for better or worse, stick it out for the long run. Divorce is allowed, but only as the ultimate last resort. And even then, it is frowned upon. I know full well why Islam frowns upon divorce: the emotional price is just too high. The anguish, frustration and fear that I experienced during my divorce were trying. It took a toll on everyone I came into contact with. Prior to it, I felt like I was the life of the party. But during this period, I sucked the life out of the room. I know my public persona might be a happy, joyful person, but if you saw me a few years ago, you might not have recognized me.

I thought I got married for the right reasons. You would think that I had found a perfect match: someone I knew for a while, who went to the same university, and the clincher—she was a Sunni Muslim, so I knew that our families shared similar religious values. In nine out of ten cases, this is a good recipe. But maybe I was too young and naive. I know now that Allah has a plan for everything. But back then, I didn't know much about my faith, and I mostly just followed what the community around me did. It wasn't until the first Ramadan after we got married that I realized the values we each had were not exactly the same. Values is probably the wrong word—maybe rituals is a better one, or even *fiqh* (Islamic jurisprudence). I always thought the deeper things were what brought people together. I had no idea that it would be fiqh that drove us apart.

During Ramadan, my family opted to follow our imam's example and prayed eight *raka 'ah* (an element of prayer) for the *tarawih* prayers (extra prayers during Ramadan) at the mosque closest to my house. This was the beginning of the end. Her family prayed more than eight raka 'ahs and she was confused that I did it differently, so she consulted with her relatives. One of them said that my fasts wouldn't count if we only prayed the shorter tarawih. Things escalated from there.

I was a person who barely knew about my faith, but somehow I earned the label of a "Wahhabi" from her family because I attended a mosque where the beards were long and the *thobes* (traditional Arab dress for men) were wide. Did I accept this notion? Let's just say that I would've denied it outright, if I even knew what it meant! I didn't know exactly what *Wahhabi* meant, but I realized that it was a misused label for someone who is extreme in their religious views. But the mosque I attended was conservative and featured on Jon Stewart's *The Daily Show,* highlighting their interfaith services! I also thought, "me? extreme?" I didn't even have a beard! I barely fit the profile of a Muslim. You would probably identify me more as a Bollywood star than as a Wahhabi extremist Muslim, but there it was.

I guess a bad guy or villain of sorts was needed and a convenient label had just become prevalent, thanks to Fox News. So, to her family, I became the scapegoat—the extremist, Wahhabi, jihadist/Islamo-terrorist. All because I prayed eight raka 'ahs during an optional prayer done once a year. There were other reasons that led up to the divorce, but when it got to the point of name-calling, it was obviously too late. Especially when it was the kind of name calling that put me in the same company as men who were vehemently hated or sent to Guantanamo.

If it sounds like I am being bitter, well that might be true. Divorce brought out the worst feelings in me. I was no longer the happy and energetic person I had always been. I felt that my divorce would permanently scar me, would make me permanently angry. No wonder divorce is considered one of the worst permissible things allowed in Islam. But during the worst of it, just as there was a cloud cast over my head, the light seized me. This light is difficult to describe in words, but I guess you can call it that feeling just after your morning grogginess goes away. When you're suddenly alert and you can see all the colors around you. This light was like the moments right after you've made yourself dizzy by spinning in a swivel chair. That might seem corny to people who have not experienced it, but during the grayest days, one can feel this light—if God wills it. And he willed it for me.

Allah took the accusation of the divorce—my supposed extremism—and made me really examine it. It was for this very reason that I began to seek Islamic knowledge through various institutions, coursework, books, and lectures. In the meantime, I got a better job offer with a different company and developed strong relationships with my bosses and co-workers. You know how people say, "When it rains, it pours"? Well, what's the good version of that? Because as a result of my divorce, that's what started happening—I was seized by the light, and I let it lead me to a better life.

That good ole Wahhabi mosque in Paterson that I was attending turned out to have the nicest, coolest people I've ever met. They definitely weren't extremists and they weren't hiding. They were, for lack of a better word, just chilling. Luckily, I had the type of schedule where I could extend my lunches. In going to Paterson every week, I also got the chance to share meals with some other people I met at the mosque. We grabbed lunch at a new place on Main Street on the way back to our jobs. Soon, everyone started asking me where the best place to go for a meal was.

Finding halal food can be a challenge in some areas and finding *amazing* halal food is an even bigger challenge. My search was made easier by the website Zabihah.com, but when asked for a recommendation, I did not want to disappoint anyone. So I turned my zeal for finding the best halal food into a mission. I started my online halal food show, *Sameer's Eats*. I might have aspirations for the Food Network, but honestly it's primarily about finding a good, halal bite to eat. Through this project I found a way to mitigate my past and move on and up.

There were still times when I felt like I hit rock bottom and I could not bring my colorful self out on camera, and when that happened, my partner, Saad Malik, was there for me. As *Sameer's Eats* grew, so did my popularity: I began getting phone calls from different organizations and companies to partner up for various cross-promotions domestically and internationally. This was exciting and I truly felt my life was turning around.

Now, what can I say? I felt blessed working for His sake and at the same time, humbled to be in the presence of major *shayoukh* (learned men of various Islamic sciences). My personal relationship with these men grew because their kindness and compassion brought me closer to Islam and alleviated the pain I had experienced in my past. I have made a lot of friends and hope to continue to meet new people through *Sameer's Eats*. It is safe to say that I was not as connected with Allah before my marriage. Now I can go back to saying, "Alhamduli'llah, things are well," and still be honest about it.

Touchdowns and Taqwa
by Ibrahim Abdul-Matin

Ibrahim Abdul-Matin is a New York native who has had ample adventures in the woods of upstate New York, Oakland, California, the Joshua Tree desert in California, Boston Harbor, and Rhode Island. He would most likely beat you in a (short) foot race. He sings Marvin Gaye to his infant son, and blogs about social justice, sports, the environment, music, and other pedestrianism related topics. He has been described as artistic and socially conscious. Ibrahim rides a fixed-gear bicycle, reads comic books, loves cold weather, Black people, and his native New York state. He also very seriously formerly worked as a policy advisor to Mayor Bloomberg, and is the author of *Green Deen: What Islam Teaches About Protecting the Planet* (buy it). Ibrahim is a regular contributor to WNYC's *The Takeaway*, (listen to the show) and one day you will read some of his fiction (inshaAllah!). If you see him on the subway, don't act like a stranger. Ibrahim lives in Brooklyn with his wife, Fatima Ashraf, and their son Ismael.

Taqwa involves fulfilling obligations inwardly and outwardly and avoiding what is prohibited inwardly and outwardly. It requires struggle and sacrifice, focus and commitment, cooperation, physical health, eating healthy wholesome foods, prayer, and the right attitude. A lot of what it takes to attain that state is also what it takes to be a good athlete.

In fact, being a Muslim is like being an athlete. In Islam no one can excommunicate you and say you are no longer part of the faith. Your status in the "deen" is between you and God alone. Sports are the same way. I have not played organized sports in thirteen years but I will always be an athlete. If I call myself an athlete, nobody can take that status away from me.

Islam and sports go beyond that similarity for me, though. Sports played host to some of the most dramatic moments in my life and events that, to this day, helped define who I am as a Muslim. Most importantly, some of my most significant ideas about Islam came about through the lens of sports. We know how memorable a championship moment is when it involves our favorite teams. For me the most memorable moments in sports were when I got a better understanding of my own soul and a deeper connection to God.

Let me first offer a little context. I am a city and a country kid. I was born in New York City. However, six years after my parents ended their marriage, my father moved out of the city and I began spending the school year in upstate New York (first in a small town called Sidney, and later in another small city called Troy), and summers in Brooklyn. Upstate is where I became an athlete. In Sidney, like most small towns in America, sports rule the world. By the time I was in middle school I was excelling in football, basketball, and track, and I was committed to getting a full scholarship in whatever sport I could, to help my father, who had six children to get through college.

We moved to Troy when I was fifteen, and here I found myself on a winning football program. It was my success in Troy that led to me being offered football scholarships from a number of universities. I ultimately accepted an offer from the University of Rhode Island. I played there for four years, lettered, and played against some people that ended up in the NFL, and even one who won a Super Bowl. Today I am no longer a competitive football player: the extent of my current athleticism is an occasional run here and there, pick-up basketball, bike riding, and my role as a radio sports contributor for WNYC's *The Takeaway*.

Now that my playing career is over, I am able to look back and see how, in my life, sports intertwined with Islam. One example of this is how football helped me keep my family bonds tight, in keeping with the teachings of Islam. The Prophet said, "The best of you are those who are best to their families." During most of my daring athletic achievements, I was away from my mother. She never saw me score four touchdowns in one football game, or score twenty-two points in a basketball game. She never witnessed me in the state semifinals, coming within a yard of making it to state in football, or being just a hair away from making the finals in the fifty-five meter dash at the Indoor State Championships. But in my senior year in college, my mother finally came to see me play. It was my last home game at URI, a tough game that featured a bone-crushing hit leveled by one of our cornerbacks on an opposing player. I wondered what my mother would have thought if that had been me on the receiving end. We lost the game, but I ended up a winner because the true blessing of that day was that it brought my siblings, mother, and father—all of us, to one event. During the game, a good friend of mine had snapped the only pictures I would ever have of my parents together. By that time football was simply a means to an end; it was a job. But later, when my friend developed the film and brought the photos to me, it was clear what its purpose was: football was there to show me that God works in mysterious ways, that everything happens for a reason, and that we are never tested beyond what we can bear. In that picture I see my family united with beaming smiles on a sunny autumn day.

Track and field was the setting for one of my greatest Islamic lessons on personal responsibility. I was a junior in high school and it was during Ramadan. I had missed dinner one Thursday night after breaking my fast because I was so tired from participating in indoor track and being on the basketball team at the same time—each day I was doing full practices for each sport while fasting. The next morning, Friday, I missed suhoor (the meal before sunrise that gives one some sustenance for the day of fasting ahead), and that night I also missed eating a proper dinner after breaking my fast. The next morning, Saturday, I also missed suhoor and woke up in time for fajr (morning prayer)—only this time I also had to prepare for a track meet. I had not eaten a proper meal in two days, and I did not know what to do. I was exhausted, hungry, and parched from thirst. I went to the kitchen and paced around looking into the cabinets and fridge. I even poured myself some water and stared at the glass. Eventually I went to my dad, who was preparing to take me to the track meet, and asked him what to do.

"Daddy," I said, "I have not eaten in two days and I have a HUGE track meet today. Should I eat? Or should I fast?"

My dad shook his head and paused. If you know him, you know that he never rushes to judgment. His response was simple and profound.

"That," he said, "is between you and Allah."

Needless to say, I fasted. The best part of the story is that in all my events that day, I not only won, but had personal bests. I discovered the benefits of thikr (engaging in constant remembrance of Allah) that day. Dhikr (chanting or silently repeating divine names), was what sustained me throughout the grueling track meet. I also understood through this experience that my status before God has everything to do with my own intentions, choices, and actions.

At times I did not always fit into the culture of sports in the USA. If I could go back, I would have insisted on taking breaks to pray and I would have pulled my coaches aside when they were being insensitive to my race and my religion. However, in employing struggle and sacrifice, focus and commitment, cooperation, physical health, eating healthy wholesome food, prayer, and the right attitude—I overcame those obstacles.

People measure their athletic careers by how much they won or lost, or how many points they scored. These are fair measurements, but I think it is easy to overlook some of the most important lessons that come embedded in the games and in our approach to them. We should measure our success also by what we learn about our own selves and our own souls. As an athlete and a member of the Muslim American community, I hope I can be an example of the fact that sports are a healthy outlet for our youth, and that sports can be an enriching part of the Muslim experience. I feel that each one of us has untapped potential in our community to be ambassadors of our faiths, cultures, and families, as well as athletes who can power our local teams to championships.

For God and Country
by Suhail A. Khan

Suhail A. Khan is a Washington D.C.-based attorney and conservative activist who serves as Chairman of the Conservative Inclusion Coalition (CIC), an organization dedicated to promoting the conservative message to Americans of all ethnic, racial and faith backgrounds. He has experience serving on Capitol Hill, the Executive Branch—including the White House, political campaigns, and on the boards of various advocacy organizations including the American Conservative Union and the Buxton Interfaith Initiative. In 2010, Suhail led a delegation of major Muslim American faith and community leaders to Auschwitz and Dachau concentration camps. Upon returning to the US, the delegation issued a statement and testified before Congress condemning Holocaust-denial and anti-Semitism.

Suhail earned a B.A. in political science from the University of California, Berkeley, and his J.D. from the University of Iowa.

"We can meet our destiny—to build a land here that will be for all mankind a shining city on a hill."—Ronald Reagan

My earliest memories include playing in Colorado's snow, tentatively touching wild deer, and later, riding in the front seat of our landlord's big green Ford enjoying a popsicle as he performed his daily duties. When I entered kindergarten, I began to experience the things that boys enjoy: bicycles, skateboards, camping, horseback riding, guns and lusting after all things fast, especially cars and motorcycles. Indeed, my upbringing was one of adventure, opportunity, hope, and infinite promise.

My heroes were likewise Americans associated with a Western spirit of adventure, bravery, rugged individualism, and of doing what's right—even when that was unpopular or even dangerous. As I grew up, John Wayne, Evel Knievel, Richard Petty, Steve McQueen, Audie Murphy, Clint Eastwood, Waylon Jennings, Johnny Cash, Merle Haggard, Dr. Martin Luther King, and Malcolm X were the figures I looked up to, for what they represented—individual courage and strength of character.

And some heroes were more personal. I'm proud that my late grandfather, Major Shaikh Adam, served with distinction in the English Cavalry, fighting the Fascists and Nazis in the North African theater of World War II. My late father, Mahboob Khan, was the first in his family to finish high school, to graduate from college, to turn down a coveted scholarship from the Soviets in Moscow, and to instead leave his family and everything familiar for the opportunity of the US.

From my heroes, I learned about hope and promise at a young age. I recall the excitement of the bicentennial celebrations of 1976, the election of Georgia Governor Jimmy Carter to the presidency, and then the nation's economic "malaise," including long gas lines. In 1980, as a ten-year-old, I could feel the renewed sense of optimism when Americans elected former California Governor Ronald Reagan as president. In addition to restoring our national economy, Reagan was especially bold in challenging the "evil empire" of the communists. As I got older, I began to take more interest in politics. As a Muslim whose parents escaped the poverty of the then-socialist India of the 1960s, I was especially drawn to Reagan's conservative message of a strong defense, family, economic liberty and the unparalleled creative energy of free markets. Reagan stood strong against the communist invasion of Afghanistan and the threat of communism elsewhere in the world, bravely calling on the Soviet leader (in the context of a divided Germany), with the invocation, "Mr. Gorbachev, tear down this wall!"

My Muslim faith was central in my upbringing. I was taught to cherish God, to strive for peace and justice, and to respect all others, including friends of other faiths, and so I enjoyed holidays surrounding Ramadan and the hajj, but other holidays as well. Whether it was the gift-giving of Christmas, the solemnity of Easter, or the celebration (and potato latkes) of Hanukkah, I enjoyed the holidays. When I later attended a Christian school, I was honored to be included in regular church services (as an observer), and cherished the freedom I likewise enjoyed to attend regular Jummah prayers. I knew well that ours was a nation where religious freedom and liberty was foundational and that this important freedom—along with other cherished freedoms—was endowed by our Creator (and not by government), and enshrined in our Constitution.

And so it was natural that, as a seventeen-year old college freshman on the campus of the University of California, Berkeley, that I would walk up to a table of the fledging chapter of the Berkeley College Conservatives and sign-up as a member. I would soon join Young Americans for Freedom and eventually, upon turning eighteen and proudly registering for Selective Service, register as an active member of the Republican Party. As someone who was taught from the earliest age the power of liberty and individual responsibility, I was drawn to the conservative message of individual freedom, faith, family and a strong national defense. I believed our nation should rely on the entrepreneurship and virtue of its citizens to be a great society, not on the power, as well-intentioned as it may be, of bureaucratic government. And this isn't just a political notion, but one based on faith as well. Islam emphasizes humanity's generosity, compassion and virtue. I believe we should strive to free individuals, faith groups, and civic organizations to engage in what we do best by our own virtue.

Upon joining groups such as Young Americans for Freedom and the Berkeley College Republicans, I was immediately embraced by my fellow conservatives in our effort to share the message of liberty. I was soon given a leadership position in which I helped to organize issue forums, wrote letters to the editor and op-eds, attended political conventions, and worked on campaigns including the presidential campaign of 1988. By the time I graduated, we had grown the Berkeley College Republicans into the largest college chapter in the state.

Dr. King stated that "we know not what the future holds, only who holds it." Little could I imagine that those experiences of campus activism would lead to my choosing a career in public service and, ultimately, serving on Capitol Hill—in the White House and other Executive Branch agencies, as a presidential appointee. Just months after graduating from the Iowa College of Law, my college campaign experience helped me secure a campaign job with a congressional candidate from my hometown in California. That candidate, Tom Campbell, won his election and hired me to serve in his Capitol Hill office.

My experience serving on Capitol Hill served to only reinforce my belief in American exceptionalism, and indeed in my Muslim faith. When I arrived in Washington, D.C., I was the only Muslim congressional staffer on the Hill. Congressman Campbell is himself a devout Catholic, and he assured me that he would not hold staff meetings on Fridays at mid-day so that I could go to prayers. He even offered his office to me to use for prayer.

Soon a second Muslim arrived on Capitol Hill and eventually our prayers grew into a regular Friday prayer of congressional staff, interns, and federal employees from nearby agencies. And while we would pray in empty meeting and committee rooms on Capitol Hill, our growing numbers warranted a regular space. I suggested identifying an appropriate place in the US Capitol building itself. The Capitol Dome, I explained to my friends and colleagues, is a symbol of democracy and freedom including religious liberty. What better way for the Capitol to come alive than to have a religious minority praying under the majestic dome? After approaching then Speaker of the House, Newt Gingrich, for a space to pray, Speaker Gingrich assured me, "As long as I'm Speaker, you'll have space to pray every Friday afternoon."

Today, almost fifteen years later, well over a hundred staff, Members of Congress, US Capitol Police, federal employees, friends, and guests continue to gather together to freely exercise their right to worship as guaranteed under the US Constitution. I'm a proud Reagan conservative, a Muslim, and an American. I believe that every American has the right to live their life as they see fit, free from government interference or dictate. I believe that government should not discriminate against anyone because of the color of their skin, their ethnic heritage, or their faith and religious belief. This confidence in American exceptionalism extends to the difficult time we, as Americans of the Muslim faith, are currently experiencing in the era following the tragedy of the 9/11 attacks. The ugly face of religious bigotry and hatred has, as it has at darker periods of our history, once again emerged in a most insidious manner. Some have raised questions about Islam and Muslims and whether our faith encourages violence, some have questioned our patriotism, and others have even claimed that Muslims should not serve in the armed service or in government.

And some have attacked me personally in blogs, newspapers, and popular media.

But I'm confident fairness will prevail. Why? Because America is a great nation, a beacon of hope, and time and time again, we've overcome hate and ignorance to welcome new Americans to become a part of our great national fabric. President Bush appointed Americans like me, and despite all the lies and the shameful attacks, the President stood with me and not with the hateful bigots who attacked me.

As people of faith—Jews, Christians and Muslims, as Americans—we should join together to promote life and liberty—political, religious, and economic liberty—for all people. Those who wish us harm must be defeated. And in doing so, we should work with all freedom-loving people in this important cause. Likewise, we should resist the call to respond to the hate of our enemies with a bigoted hatred of our own making. We are Americans, and we can take great pride in the fact that, regardless of ethnic and religious heritage, we stand united as one American people.

At the turn of the last century, a rabbi remarked at the variety of ethnic names of those entering Ellis Island, that all were American names. As we begin the new twenty-first century, I'd add that all faiths are American faiths. And as Americans, we are united in defending our cherished liberty in the many long days ahead.

Stranger
in a Strange Land
by Aamer H. Jamali

Aamer Jamali, M.D., is an interventional cardiologist in private practice in the Los Angeles area, and an Assistant Clinical Professor at the University of California, Los Angeles School of Medicine. Born in Detroit, Michigan to Indian parents, he moved to California when he was ten years old and has never left. Aamer received his undergraduate degree from Berkeley, and his medical training from UCLA and Stanford University, where he received awards for his medical research and for his contributions to medical literature. He currently lives in Los Angeles with his wife Sakina, and their two daughters. He is a member of the Dawoodi Bohra sect of Ismaili Shi'a Muslims, and is active in the Los Angeles chapter of the community. Aamer has also received the honorific status of "Mullah." He is indebted to the spiritual guidance of his Da'i, His Holiness Dr. Syedna Mohammed Burhanuddin (TUS), who served as a beacon during the tumultuous times in his life. When he is not working, Aamer enjoys golf and training in the martial arts.

"*D*octor, the blood pressure is dropping quickly, and the patient is becoming bradycardic!*"

There I was, in my final year of medical training—obviously Muslim by name and appearance, working in a predominantly Jewish hospital. I was scrubbed into a cardiac case in the operating room and needless to say, things weren't going well. My attending physician was well liked and highly regarded. He was a virtual celebrity in Los Angeles' large Jewish community. He wore a yarmulke to work, spoke excellent Yiddish and some Hebrew, and even participated in the hospital chapel services during the High Holy Days. So it surprised me to no end when I heard him mutter under his breath at that point of crisis a short Islamic prayer, "Allahumma Sale Ala Mohammed."

After the surgery was over and the patient was stabilized, I asked him about this. Taking me into a corner, he confided in me that he was actually Muslim born and raised, but living in this area and working in this hospital, "being Muslim is bad for business, so I let people believe what they want."

His confession shocked me, and I found myself re-evaluating all I knew about him as well as what I knew about the local community. I realized that walking around in a yarmulke and participating in temple services is a long way from "letting people believe what they want." But what surprised me most was the fact that he felt the need to put on this charade at all. After all, I had worked at that hospital for the last four years and for the most part the other physicians, and even the patients, had made no issue of my religion. Of course, I was always there as a trainee and my livelihood had never depended on their acceptance or referrals. When all was said and done, I could not say for certain what I would do differently if I were in his place.

As I left training and transitioned into private practice at another Jewish hospital, the world was forever changed as three jetliners were used as weapons to kill thousands of Americans. Suddenly, being Muslim was not just an interesting novelty, but to some, a grievous sin. I found myself tempted to take the easy road, and to try to hide my Muslim identity behind the guise of religious freedom. After all, I reasoned, I was not obliged to confirm my identity to anyone, no matter how Muslim I looked. If someone could not confirm my identity, I could potentially avoid uncomfortable follow-up questions and lengthy explanations. Thus, those who dared to question were treated to evasive answers and quick changes of topic. Rather than placate their curiosity, however, this seemed to only make matters worse. After all, nothing was more suspicious in those days than a Muslim trying to hide something.

With time, the true depth of the challenge Muslims faced became clearer. I watched with horror as my faith was time and again represented by the worst among us. The thieves, murderers, drug dealers, and illiterates all had their requisite television time. I knew in my heart that they had hijacked my faith just as they had hijacked those planes. That I shared no more in common with them than those passengers shared with their tormentors—was small comfort; I was seemingly helpless at the mercy of a falsely powerful minority. The cacophony of violent and extremist voices grew so loud that the peaceful Muslim majority was totally drowned out. As an American, albeit a Muslim one, I was so overwhelmed by violent messaging that even I began to wonder—where were the sane voices in Islam and, if they truly existed, why didn't they speak out as loudly? How long could I walk around saying, "No, really…most Muslims are not like that," before I began to doubt that fact myself?

Over time, this seed of doubt began to slowly grow. Rather than risk being relegated to a mere island of tolerance flooded by a churning sea of violence, I found myself wanting to abandon my religion completely—to just "be" something else—or nothing else. After all, why should I continue to affiliate myself, however loosely, with such unsavory characters? I was overcome with curiosity about how it would feel to no longer be Muslim—to "fit in," and no longer have to explain myself to my peers. To not be constrained by the rituals and restrictions of Islam. That sort of freedom was enticing; yet somehow it remained out of reach. I realized how naïve I was to think that this was possible—that I could simply choose not to believe the history, subscribe to the theology, or practice the rites. I found I could not be outside at sunset without feeling pangs of guilt for missing my prayers (though admittedly I did not always act on them); I knew, at a restaurant, I would not be able to order anything made with alcohol or pork; and if someone asked me what my religion was, my lips would always form the word "Muslim."

It was during this period that I realized that though Islam may have begun as a choice made for me by my parents, it did not remain so. Nor is it my choice. It is quite simply an indelible part of my being, my worldview, and my sense of self. It is a hue on my soul that even the harshest bleach of willful rejection would not be able to remove. Everything I say, everything I do, and everything I think occurs in the context of Islam, or simply does not occur. Other outlooks and belief systems are foreign; they seem to be immediately rejected by my internal psychological immune system.

My mentor in the operating room that day was there to teach me cardiology, but he ended up opening my eyes to a far more significant issue—the implications and perceptions of one's identity. I still feel that his method of dealing with the challenges posed with being Muslim were disingenuous at best, and deceitful at worst. However, the underlying message about the need for some degree of integration in order to breed comfort was well received.

Now that I truly am in his position, I have taken his lessons and made them my own. No, I do not wear a yarmulke. I am, however, a member of the local Jewish Community Center, which is the social center of our community. I joined as an avowed Muslim, however, and not under cover of deception. My family and I are also quite active in the local Muslim Community Center, and as such I have assumed the informal role of cross-cultural liaison. When our Community Center was under construction, this role came in handy, as the local conservative temple allowed us to host our weekly religious classes in their buildings.

I am active in our local masjid community and try to attend regularly. I also occasionally attend functions at one of the local temples (such as when invited to a bris or a bar mitzvah). When I do, I don a yarmulke and I, too, will speak Yiddish or even a little Hebrew there. I do not pretend to be Jewish, but rather attempt to emphasize my respect for Jewish culture, religion, and beliefs.

I have tried, through my actions, to demonstrate that Muslims are respectful people, tolerant people, and normal people: a lesson that is lost through much of the current media coverage of Islam. In return, I have been greeted with an acceptance and tolerance that I never expected. Despite occasional instances of intolerance, I have come to realize that the urges my mentor and I felt to suppress or deny our identities were likely rooted more in our own insecurities than any real threat.

Through this journey, I have come to embrace my identity as a proud Muslim. My Islam may not be about in-your-face observances and demands for equal rights (laudable though they may be), but it is surely not hidden under a guise of deception and whispered in hushed tones out of fear. Rather, it is imbued with the quiet confidence of the inevitable.

The Good Fight
by Umair Khan

Umair Khan is Counsel to New York State Senator Kevin Parker. He previously served as the Assistant Counsel in the office of the Majority Whip. He started in the New York Senate as a Graduate Fellow with State Senator Bill Perkins. Umair graduated from Albany Law School, where he was the founder/director of the Appellate Advocacy Project. Umair and his classmates filed *amicus curiae* briefs with the US Supreme Court in Safford v. Redding and Ashcroft v. Iqbal. He published a law review article titled, "Tortured Pleadings: The Historical Development and Recent Fall of the Liberal Pleadings Standard." The House Judiciary Committee, in its hearings on the Iqbal decision, cited his works. He has also worked for US District Judge Lawrence Kahn, US Magistrate Judge Randolph Treece, and the Albany County District Attorney›s Office.

Before going to Albany, Umair served as a Legislative Assistant on foreign policy to Congressman Bob Filner. He coordinated ethnic outreach for the Kerry Presidential campaign and served as the APAICS-Frank Horton Fellow with Congressman Mike Honda. Umair was also a founder of the Congressional Muslims Staffers Association. Umair received his B.A. in Government and Near Eastern Studies from Cornell University in 2003.

I recall sitting in the subway reading the *New York Times*, the first week of June 2003. I had graduated from college a couple of weeks earlier, and I was still attempting to figure out what I would do now that I was grown up. Like most *desis* (persons with roots in the Indian subcontinent), the career path my parents sought for me was medicine. But after a year, I decided to pursue a liberal arts degree in Government and Near Eastern Studies.

That afternoon, as I flipped through the paper, I came across an article discussing a recent report by the Inspector General of the Department of Justice. The report highlighted abuses by the Justice Department toward nearly a thousand Muslim men who were arrested and detained in the months following the September 11th attacks. None of these individuals were convicted of terrorism or related charges; most were held for immigration violations. Yet many languished for months without access to counsel, and their families were deliberately misinformed as to the detainees' whereabouts. Furthermore, many of the men were subjected to extensive physical and psychological abuse.

Sitting on the A train that afternoon, I was upset—partly for these abuses, but also because I was disappointed in my own limited knowledge of our laws and the Constitution. What did it mean to be denied access to legal representation? What recourse does one have when abused in this way? The following Friday after the prayer service at my mosque, the imam paused to introduce a few men in suits. They were agents from the FBI. The agents introduced themselves and explained the purpose of their visit—to educate the congregation on the role of the agency and enhance community relations. Following their presentation, the head agent opened the floor to questions and answers. I raised my hand and asked how they sought to accomplish building relations when that requires trust. I mentioned the serious abuses identified by the article I had read. My father sat near me, shocked that his son would ask such a question to an FBI agent. The agent acknowledged that some missteps were made, but would not discuss the matter further.

In the following weeks and days, I did not give the issue much thought, but six weeks later, after being selected for a fellowship with congressman Mike Honda, one of my first assignments was to write a letter to the Attorney General. Earlier in the summer, the congressman, along with thirty-one other members, requested a meeting with the Attorney General to discuss the Inspector General's report. In our follow-up letter we confirmed subsequent reports of repeated pattern of abuses by the Bureau of Prisons and potentially unlawful activity by the FBI. The Attorney General did not respond to either letter. I would learn five years later why. To this day I keep a copy of that letter.

As an aide, I had the incredible opportunity to learn about a multitude of policy areas and relevant laws. It was a very steep learning curve, but it sparked a curiosity to search for answers and oftentimes that meant learning history. This started on day one. I recall walking out of a meeting my first week. As I left his office, the congressman handed me a copy of *Personal Justice Denied*, the Report of the Commission on Wartime Relocation and Internment of Civilians. I read a lot of history during my fellowship that helped put in perspective the challenges of the Muslim community in the post-9/11 era. In watching, listening, and speaking with Congressman Honda, I gained a tremendous appreciation for the struggle involved in protecting constitutional rights—especially as it relates to conflict and security. Over the next couple of years as I worked with attorneys both on and off Capitol Hill, I realized that in order to continue growing as an individual, but also to better affect change, I needed to go to law school.

Near the end of the summer of 2008, I approached one of my law professors, who, while in law school, took on the Justice Department in the detention of Haitian refugees at Guantanamo under President George H. W. Bush. We met to discuss the possibility of getting involved in a civil rights case at the appellate level. As kismet would have it, some of his former colleagues were representing a Pakistani man detained following 9/11 named Javaid Iqbal, so together we assembled a team to file an amicus brief.

Iqbal had commenced a civil action against a series of government defendants. A cable repair guy, Iqbal was arrested on immigration charges on November 2, 2001 as a part of Operation PENTTBOM (Pentagon/Twin Towers Bombing), a massive investigation under the aegis of the FBI. The government sought to dismiss his case on procedural grounds, but lost at the district court and the Second Circuit Court of Appeals. The case was headed to the Supreme Court.

As I mentioned earlier, federal law enforcement officials established various policies and procedures that included the arrest of nearly a thousand Arab and Muslim men, primarily on immigration related charges. The government identified these individuals as "September 11 detainees." After a thorough investigation, the Inspector General of the Department of Justice concluded that many detainees were repeatedly beaten, denied medical treatment, deprived of religious freedoms, and denied due process rights while in custody. These September 11 detainees were held in solitary confinement, under conditions reserved for the most dangerous criminals, that included repeated body cavity searches, sensory deprivation, and physical abuse. Iqbal lost over forty pounds while in custody, and to this day suffers from medical issues related to his detention.

I remember sitting alone in my law journal office at two in the morning in shock as I read Iqbal's complaint against the Attorney General. I felt as if someone had punched me in the stomach as I read each line of the complaint. These individuals were held in Brooklyn, not rendition facilities. I was deeply saddened that my government—my country—deliberately denied the most basic legal and human rights to detained individuals. We were supposed to be better than this. As disheartened and frustrated as I felt that night, I realized the need to channel the feelings into a constructive struggle. I recalled the perseverance and determination exhibited by some of the people I had the honor of learning from who endured greater obstacles. I was reminded of the sacrifices and patience of those who lived in the internment camps, and the Freedom Riders who were beaten and killed by racist mobs in the south.

After spending a couple of months and many long nights preparing our brief, our team and I were able to attend the oral argument at the Supreme Court. On a mild December morning by New York standards, we walked into the entrance of the Court. As I entered the chamber, I was surprised to see the marble walls lined with sculptures of the law givers of human history, including Hammurabi, Confucius, Prophet Moses, and Prophet Muhammad. This seemed ironic in light of not only the policies of our government, but also the growing anti-Muslim fervor following President Obama's election. We sat in the front of the chamber in an area reserved for guests of the justices, a minor coup courtesy of a former colleague who had just finished a clerkship there. I had the opportunity to witness firsthand the judicial philosophies of the justices as they peppered the attorneys with questions and brought forward arguments that the parties themselves had not. I was excited to see and hear the oral arguments. As a law student, I had only read the decisions. In their writings I could sense one justice's wit, another's humor. Now I had an opportunity to see them in action.

Five months later, the Supreme Court ruled Iqbal's pleading was insufficient, but the Court did not dismiss the case. Frustrated with the outcome and the Court's adoption of a new pleading standard, I approached a former colleague who was counsel on the House Judiciary Committee. He graciously listened to my argument, that the Court rebuked seventy years of precedent and the will of Congress. Four months later, I learned the chair of the Constitution subcommittee would hold hearings entitled "Access to Justice Denied," and introduce a bill called the "Open Access to Courts Act of 2009." The title of the hearing itself was a play on the congressional report on the internment of Japanese Americans. The bill would effectively reverse the Supreme Court's decision in *Ashcroft v. Iqbal*. Similar legislation was also introduced in the Senate.

Although neither bill passed, it was heartening to see a public discourse emerge as numerous papers, including the *New York Times* and the *Wall Street Journal*, wrote editorials on the litigation and subsequent legislation. There was, and continues to be, discourse in legal and academic circles on the issue. The government would go on to settle with Mr. Iqbal.

There is a hadith, or a saying, of the Prophet Muhammad that many will recall from Sunday School that I paraphrase: if you see an injustice, stop it with your hand. If you cannot, then speak against it. If you cannot, then know in your heart that it is wrong. As an attorney today, I have the opportunity to work on policies that impact the lives of New Yorkers and address injustices every day, from developing economic policies to creating sustainable well-paying jobs to protecting the environment to continuing to stand up for civil rights. On occasion, I even get to participate in litigation. Working at the state level, I have gained a greater appreciation that policies aren't established in a vacuum. Thus, although legal challenges are important, it is equally important to educate the general public in support of your view.

The decision to get a law degree and the opportunity to collaborate, work, and learn from those who seek to address the injustices we see today has been greatly rewarding. You don't always win, but there is a satisfaction in the journey and the effort that I find comforting.

The Walk
by Wahid Momand

Wahid Momand is an IT professional. He is a graduate of San Jose State University and has worked in Silicon Valley as an IT professional since 2000. Ever since Wahid arrived in the United States at a very young age, he wanted to tell a story: the story of an Afghan family's struggles in post-Soviet invasion Afghanistan; a story of escape through the mountains, deserts, and across the minefields of Afghanistan under the watchful eyes of Soviet gunships across the border, and finally settling in California. Wahid finished writing his story in 1996. After the events of 9/11, he decided to share his story with the world, and is currently working to polish the manuscript for publication. He currently resides in Newport Beach, California.

My earliest memories are that of life in Rishkhor, a town just south of Kabul, Afghanistan. I stood on the patio of our military home on a lonely forked road that slithered toward the base. Scattered on this road were modest two story houses, exposed and lacking any sort of wall or barrier. This was the norm in Kabul and its surroundings. They were strategically nestled in the foothills, sitting beneath crisp blue skies while the giant snowcapped mountains looked on in silence, keeping in their rocky bosoms memories of the days gone by.

Next to the hills were the army barracks and military compounds of the Republic of Afghanistan, and on the other side were homes of military families. It was a place I knew well. On a weekly basis my father and I would walk out of our home into the garden, past the rose bushes, and onto the dusty paved road towards the local market, while children played soccer on the fields near the foothills. My father was a tall, wiry man with broad shoulders and huge hands. I held tightly onto his finger as I hurried to keep up with his long paced steps towards the kindergarten and elementary school and beyond. Every time we passed this area, he reminded me that I would soon be attending that school. On our walks he would purchase hot *naan* (Afghan bread), fresh meat, and locally produced vegetables for supper and we would walk back past the local mosque to home.

My father's vision of my future never came to be in Afghanistan. He was killed during the gruesome Russian invasion of Afghanistan and the subsequent cold war between the Red Army of the Soviet Union and the US-backed Mujahidin. A war that killed 2 million innocent Afghans, left over 3 million Afghans wounded, over 2 million more internally displaced, and 5 million refugees outside of Afghanistan who would be repatriated in faraway lands.

Ten years later I found myself in Fremont, California, better known as "Little Kabul," along with thousands of other Afghans. I felt at home in Fremont, a multicultural city east of San Francisco. I walked down Fremont Boulevard towards the local market and while in line, I observed a diverse crowd of Americans and multigenerational immigrants from far corners of the world, as they waited inside the small store to buy hot naan and had animated conversations with each other about anything and everything. I purchased my naan, fresh halal meat, and local vegetables from the Afghan Market and walked back past the local mosque situated inside a small office building next to my home.

On the way I stopped by the basketball courts and stood on the sidelines watching the pick-up game. I offered a piece of naan as a bribe to anyone who would let me play for them a few minutes.

Chris would always volunteer because of his love for naan, and then Fred, Waleed, William, big Bilal and I would play a full court game against the other assembled team. The camaraderie and teamwork between a dozen teens from diverse backgrounds culminated in a beautiful, yet competitive, game of basketball. With sweat dripping and half the naan devoured, I would deliver the groceries late to my waiting mother.

As a young man living in California, I considered myself an Afghan American by nationality and a Muslim by faith. I was mistaken as Caucasian or Hispanic until I introduced myself, and that was when I would receive confused looks.

"Wade?"

"No, Wahid."

"Joaquin?"

"No no, Waa, eeed", I would enunciate.

"Where are you from?"

"Afghanistan."

"Where is that?"

"Central Asia," I would reply.

"Hmm, never heard of it."

"It's surrounded by Iran, the USSR, China and Pakistan," I would say, busting out some geography, "near the Indian Ocean, the Indian sub-continent."

But that confused them more.

"America is fighting a cold war against the USSR in Afghanistan."

That was where the inquisitions ended.

At school when a dispute occurred, sometimes I would hear ethnic slurs.

"Yo Gandhi!" to which I replied, "That's India, buddy."

"Freakin' camel jockey!"—to which I smiled and said, "That's Arabia."

"Damn Khomeini!" would come the reply. I would answer, "Nope, that's Iran, dude."

"Saddam!" Wrong again, but nice try.

I would smile as the situation became so comical that it diffused the hostility, culminating in a smile on my adversary's face and a handshake between us.

September 11, 2001 changed all that. In the blink of an eye the whole world not only knew where Afghanistan was, but the ethnic compositions, the languages, and the religion of the country. I heard factoids on cable news networks describing Islam and it was something completely alien to me. A consolidation of religion, cultural, and ethnic practices were presented on a daily basis to the American people as the ways of Islam. The treatment of women, the destruction of the Buddha statues at Bamiyan, the suicide bombers, the terror plots—these were presented as Islam, yet these values were so far removed from the ones I was raised with I could not recognize what was being presented as Islam. I was taught to wish peace upon people I greeted. Hospitality was encouraged. Elders were to be respected for their experience and knowledge, women and girls were upheld as our treasured mothers and sisters. I was taught that heaven is under the feet of mothers and that individuals of different religions were valued as people of the Book.

Days later I started receiving weekly fliers on the steps of my house that sent chills down my spine. The fliers called the Prophet of Islam the anti-Christ, described Islam as the religion of hate, Shariah law as a threat to the US Constitution, and they called on business owners not to hire Muslims as their staff. For the first time in my life I felt out of place, an outcast and outsider. My neighbors, co-workers and friends who knew Islam through my actions, and me—were now receiving a distorted image of Islam and of myself.

I tried to explain, to anyone who would listen, that women were in the Afghan parliament long before their counterparts could even vote in America, and about the first Afghan astronaut in space. I pointed out that Muslim countries (Pakistan, Turkey, Bangladesh, and Indonesia) have had women as their leaders long before a woman was seen as a serious presidential contender in the US. I explained that the Bamiyan Buddhas were protected in Afghanistan for thousands of years under Islamic rulers. I presented the passages from the Holy Qur'an that specify life as sacred, and that killing one person is seen equal to killing all humanity. But my efforts were to no avail. My voice was silenced by the constant thrashing of Islam and Muslims in the media, especially on Fox News. I found comfort in a poem I had memorized as a child, which roughly translates as:

> Rise of evil is due to our destruction—union of the immoral is due to our disbandment

> Islam in its foundation has no flaw—any fault that arises is that of a Muslim

My decision was not to let the faults of a few radical, extremist Muslims ruin the peaceful image of Islam. Though Islamophobia was in its infancy, I decided to reach out to a mass audience by creating a comprehensive website about Afghanistan and Islam that I named afghanland.com. Any information I had collected from family and friends, I placed on the site. Overnight I received thousands of emails, congratulating and thanking me for successfully portraying the undisputed facts about Islam and Afghanistan. Hundreds of people shared articles, essays and commentary on the site.

I saw it as my duty as an Afghan American and Muslim man to fight back against the bigotry, discrimination and fear that were brewing in America post 9/11. I wanted to preserve the America I grew up in, the multicultural America where nationalities, ethnicities, religions and races are part of its tightly knitted fabric. A place where one day I could grab my own child's hand and walk past children of all races and cultures and religious backgrounds playing basketball. A place where we walk past the synagogues, mosques, churches and temples towards our local Afghan Market to purchase delicious Afghan naan, halal meat and walk back home without any fear of reprisal for things unrelated to us.. That is the American Dream, the place Ronald Reagan described as that shining city upon a hill whose beacon light guides freedom-loving people everywhere.

Searching for Ummah
by Ehab Zahriyeh

Ehab Zahriyeh is an independent multimedia journalist based in New York. Born and raised in Brooklyn to Palestinian parents, Ehab studied political science, journalism, and history at Baruch College, the City University of New York, where he graduated in 2008. Since then, he has work for NY1 News as a video journalist, and has had his work published with various other outlets. He has traveled to Palestine/Israel, Jordan, Morocco, and recently to Egypt, to freelance report for Press TV about the nation after the fall of Hosni Mubarak's presidency.

The most breathtaking experience of my life was taking my first steps onto Jerusalem's Al-Aqsa compound, home to Islam's third holiest site in the world. At that site, I witnessed evidence of an ummah that had planted its foot in history hundreds of years ago and remains in place today. But finding the ummah in my own life would be an ongoing personal journey.

Growing up, I've always known I was different. It was almost as if we were brought up with two sets of personalities: the all-American one and the one reflecting our family's blurred traditions of Islam and culture from the old country. We played basketball and Super Nintendo games and ate cheeseburgers. We also fasted during Ramadan, spoke broken Arabic, and filled our neighborhoods with strong aromas of Middle Eastern spices. Learning to balance the two identities, and eventually merging them into one, meant I had to search for what Islam would come to mean to me.

I didn't go to Islamic school or take Sunday Qur'an classes like many other Muslim Americans. My father was born in Jerusalem, but moved to the United States as a toddler. And my mother, also of Palestinian background, was born in Venezuela and moved to the US at a very young age as well. Both were raised Muslim, but also without a structured education in the faith. They didn't read or write Arabic like many other Muslim parents. They were conservative, but only became "religious" later on. When I was growing up, they were against dating and my mother always dressed somewhat modestly. However, they did not pray, recite the Qur'an, or search for deeper spirituality. Most of the Islamic knowledge I gained had been from Friday prayer service, which at times was in Arabic, so I did not understand much.

Despite my primitive knowledge of the faith, I knew I was Muslim. Islam for me, growing up, was not much more than a list of do's and don'ts.

"You should fast, it's Ramadan."

"No pork, it's haraam in Islam."

With a strong extended family, it wasn't always so bad being different because there was enough support at home. But eventually my ignorance of myself would hit a wall and I would no longer be able to complacently accept knowing too little about my faith and identity.

News about Palestine seemed to always exist. And living rooms were often used as a place where relatives would vent over Israeli occupation of Palestinian lands, debate US foreign policy, and share personal experiences in the Holy Land. The discussions only existed in the background for me. I was much more interested in playing *Manhunt* with my cousins and siblings, or *Street Fighter* on Super Nintendo. But all that changed for me in the fall of the year 2000.

Intifada

I was beginning my first year in high school, and like always, the Palestinian-Israeli conflict had been making the news. What was the difference about the sensational, decades-long fight and peace-process this time? Initially, to me—nothing. But then images of hundreds of Palestinian deaths, thousands of people uprising, and suicide attacks on Israeli centers began making daily news coverage. A Palestinian American at school was passing out flyers for a protest in Times Square against Israeli aggression. I really did not know much about what was going on, and my ignorance was frustrating me. Aren't I Palestinian, Muslim, and Arab? Aren't those my people being killed?

I had heard the term ummah plenty of times at Friday prayer. *The Islamic Nation:* we are supposed to defend one another against injustice. We are supposed to be *one.* But there had been no ummah. Where was the unified support for the people of Palestine?

Family discussions in living rooms became almost completely dominated by the topic of Palestine. I became confused. What my uncles and cousins were saying about what was happening was different from what newscasts were saying.

I wanted to do something. Stand for justice. Stand with the ummah. But I still knew too little. I didn't know the significance of Jerusalem to Muslims. I didn't know why Palestinians seemed to be fighting alone without support from the ummah. More importantly, I didn't know myself. But I wasn't exactly ready to learn. I was struggling with my identities of being Muslim-Palestinian-Arab and being American. High school was a playground for me where I made friends, hung out, and played basketball, all of which was more exciting than researching my roots. I wasn't much of a reader, and I wasn't ready to pick up books.

But finally, I did. The book I picked up wasn't about the conflict, Jerusalem, or Israel. After watching a six-hour film about a Black-Muslim-American rebel, I became fascinated and wanted to learn more about his life. I got a copy of *The Autobiography of Malcolm*

189 American Men on Being Muslim   189

X, and it was the first book I ever read un-assigned. His book, I hoped, would give me insight into my identity. I became frustrated with injustice; I was American and Muslim, just like him. Towards the end of the book, Malcolm X writes about his journey to *hajj* (pilgrimage to Mecca) and how impressed he was with the ummah. He writes about praying, eating, and sleeping with people of all colors and backgrounds.

Reading about his experience wasn't enough to convince me that this abstract "ummah" actually existed. I still hadn't seen Muslims unified globally, and still hadn't experienced it in my own life. At this point, I became hungry to find it.

In my freshmen year in college, I had the opportunity to visit Palestine/Israel; something my parents hadn't been able to do. With two weeks in the Holy Land, I got to see up-close the conflict, occupation, refugee camps, destruction and disparity between the Israeli and Palestinian neighborhoods. All that was extremely overwhelming for a Brooklyn boy who had never stepped outside the US before that trip.

It was rainy and cold and I was quite exhausted from a full day of traveling throughout the country. I passed through the Damascus Gate in Jerusalem and walked on the slippery paths where Jesus had walked. Chaos. Noise. Filth. Merchants competed for every tourist, selling them grape leaves, desserts, and anything else made in China. In one, single moment, all of that froze for me. I reached Al-Aqsa, and the golden Dome of the Rock shined so brightly it silenced the old bustling city for me. I stood there in complete awe. The rain and cold became non-existent. It was a moment of truth; a moment where a long journey had reached its destination. Here was evidence of an ummah that had built a house of God that transcended through centuries—and I had finally witnessed it with my own eyes.

I came home from that trip with a sense of urgency to find my place as a Muslim-Palestinian-Arab in America. I began inserting myself into the family discussions and debates regarding Palestine. I began reading more and paying closer attention to events taking place in the Palestinian territories as well as other places like Iraq and Afghanistan. I became passionate, but alone in my sentiments. *Where is the ummah?* I wondered. Where was the Muslim community of humanity that stood unified against injustice? I still didn't know. I struggled to see it globally and I struggled to find it in my own life.

I searched for my place at my college's MSA (Muslim Students Association) and only became more frustrated. My experiences there were negative. The fellow Muslims I encountered, I felt, were sometimes rude and distant. Some were immigrants from South Asia or Africa, and I just couldn't relate. I had almost given up on finding the ummah. The atmosphere felt unfriendly to me. I didn't fit in.

October 2005

A tragic Earthquake had pounded South Asia, killing over 75,000 people. The devastation was something I, and so many others, were truly saddened to hear of. Together with members of the MSA and a few others, the decision was made to do something to help—anything we could. We began raising money on campus between classes and started a clothing and food drive. We knew the little that we collected wouldn't be enough to relieve the millions of people struck by the vicious earthquake, but it was all we could do, and it helped us cope. It also helped us appreciate our blessed lives.

I still had my reservations about the MSA, but I put them aside. During our efforts, I became closer with some of the MSA brothers and sisters. There were Malaysian twins, an Albanian American, a couple of Afghan Americans, and others with backgrounds from all over the globe.

For Ramadan, we continued to raise funds for the earthquake relief while fasting, praying, and breaking our fasts together. We spent all day and night together. Classes and sleep were the only times we were separated. We volunteered our time to feed other Muslims. We stayed late to pray evening prayers together. We learned about

Islam, different traditions, and each other. They would ask me about Palestine; I would ask them about Afghanistan. We all shared our family and personal experiences with each other. We were learning more together than we were in the classroom. Many of us grew more religious as we grew together. The MSA was not always a friendly place, but the earthquake and Ramadan surely humbled us and taught us how to appreciate each other's differences.

Baruch College MSA was a micro-example of the ummah. We represented all parts of the world with many languages and experiences, but we were one. We all cared about the tragic earthquake in Pakistan, wars in Iraq and Afghanistan, and the occupation of Palestine and Kashmir. I never thought I truly knew Islam, but in finding my ummah in college, I also found my Islam and I am now closer to God than before.

I always knew I was different growing up. That different-ness that defined me, and that different-ness that defined the other brothers and sisters I came to know and love, is what made our mini-ummah and us so special. Unbreakable bonds had been built between those brothers and sisters and myself, and between my faith and me. Finally, I've found my ummah. It lives with me beyond college and surely for the rest of my life.

The Trouble Maker
by Irfan Rydhan

Irfan Rydhan is a "Multi-Media" Muslim activist who lives in the San Francisco Bay Area. He is an architectural designer by profession (B.A. Architecture, 1997 University of California, Berkeley), and a passionate enthusiast in media arts and activism. His background includes non-profit management, film/video production, and graphic arts and design. In 1998, Irfan co-founded, with Javaid Malik of Jam-Productions, an international video/film company which was the first Muslim-owned independent video and film production company in the Bay Area. Irfan, along with his partner, created several Muslim themed projects, most notably the forty-five- minute documentary: *The Aftermath: American-Muslims After Sept. 11th*, which aired locally on San Jose and Oakland television channels, and was featured in the ISNA Film Festival in Chicago in 2003.

Irfan is one of the founding members of the SBIA Media Committee (www.MediaAndIslam.com), which conducts training programs and classes on how to effectively interact with the media in its coverage of issues relating to Islam and Muslims in the Bay Area. Irfan is currently serving as the Public Relations Director for *ILLUME Magazine* (www.IllumeMagazine.com), and has his own featured blog about Architecture, Islamic Art, Media and Halal Food called: "Al Mihrab: The Place of War" (www.almihrab. wordpress.com).

My late father, Abdul Sattar Rydhan, was a founding member of one of the first Islamic organizations in the San Francisco Bay Area in 1978, the South Bay Islamic Association (SBIA). While growing up, my siblings and I went to Sunday school at the SBIA and attended most of the Muslim community events there. It gave us a good, basic understanding of Islam, as well as the opportunity to meet fellow American Muslim children. Since I was a quiet, shy kid, I did not have very many friends in public school. I mostly kept to myself and preferred the company of my Muslim friends.

It was not until I went to college at the University of California, Berkeley in 1995 that I started to open up more and formed strong friendships with several non-Muslims. I was studying architecture, which not too many Muslims studied at that time, so I was forced to make new friends. I went for Jummah organized by the CAL Muslim Student Association (MSA), and also attended a few community events during Ramadan, but most of my time was spent in the architecture studios of Wurster Hall on the Berkeley campus. I became good friends with a diverse group of people of different ethnicities and religions, including an Indian Hindu, a Mexican Catholic, a Greek Orthodox, a Chinese Buddhist, and a Persian, who was a non-practicing Muslim. Although we did not discuss religion very much, people did ask me about Islam once in a while and I took the opportunity to explain the basic beliefs of Muslims. For example, my Greek friend was surprised to learn that Muslims believe that there is a devil!

During college, I also had several close Muslim friends. One of them, Javaid, was studying TV Production and Film. This was another field I was very interested in, because when I was younger my father had given me a book called *Reel Bad Arabs* written by Professor Jack Shaheen (a Christian Arab-American), who had researched the television and film Industry of the US and its portrayal of Arabs and Muslims. After reading the book I was shocked at all the negative images and stereotypes of Arabs and Muslims on many of the TV shows I grew up watching. After reading the book, I felt the need for Muslims to be more involved with the media, specifically television and film.

In 1996, Javaid began working on a video for one of the leaders of the MSA at UC Berkeley. I took the opportunity to help out with the filming and became Javaid's camera assistant. We recorded a large conference on campus that had the theme of *wahdah,* or unity for Muslims. As part of this conference, some Muslim students organized a "Rally against Oppression" on the famous Sproul Plaza of U.C. Berkeley in 1996. Javaid was assigned to record the rally and get some behind-the-scenes footage. The rally was theatrical in nature, consisting of a handful of Muslim students dressed in military fatigues marching through campus in support of Palestine. Many students, including myself, did not realize that there were local news outlets there that captured the scene on TV and radio. On the news the rally was portrayed as a bunch "militant" and "anti-Semitic" Muslims on the Berkeley campus. After hearing reports from family and friends on how bad the Muslim students looked on TV, I began to realize how powerful a tool TV is in shaping people's opinions and views on an event.

Javaid and I formed a production company called JAM- Productions in 1998 and we began to promote ourselves in the Muslim community. We even conducted a presentation at the neighborhood masjid on the television industry, to encourage young Muslims to study this field.

Fast forward to 2001, Javaid and I were working on a documentary about the Wahdah Conference called "Wahdah: 5 Years Later," where we interviewed the organizers of the infamous rally held in 1996. As we were finishing up the documentary, the tragic events of September 11th happened, and everything changed. There was a media explosion on Islam, Muslims and anything related to terrorism and violence. There was very little, if any, input from American Muslims in the media's coverage of the attacks and its aftermath. We decided to hold off on releasing our "Wahdah" documentary because of its controversial subject matter and instead, started a new documentary in October, 2001 called *The Aftermath: American Muslims after September 11th,* in which we would allow American Muslims to give their views and opinions about being Muslim in post 9/11 America. We ended up interviewing seven different American Muslims from various backgrounds, ages, and religious levels. Since it was only Javaid and I, with our trusty Canon XL-1 camera and an Apple G4 desktop with iMovie as our editing suite, it took us fourteen months to shoot, edit, and complete the forty-five-minute documentary. It was broadcast on San Jose and Oakland Community TV channels. We were able to create a DVD with additional footage a few years later, and in 2003 it was shown at the ISNA Film Festival in Chicago. Students and professors at Stanford University, Santa Clara University and the University of Michigan also saw the documentary.

In November of 2001, I was recruited by some of the leadership at SBIA to help them form a Media Outreach Committee to better prepare both the masjid and also our community members on how to effectively interact with the media. This was the beginning of my increased involvement with SBIA. In 2002, one year after helping to form the Media Outreach Committee, I became a board member of the masjid. I was encouraged by my father, who told me that new blood and new ideas were needed on the board. I agreed, not only because I wanted to make my father happy by following in his footsteps, but also because I knew that I could accomplish bigger things if I was on the board. At twenty-seven-years of age I was the youngest board member of one of the major Islamic organizations in the South Bay. With the help of the Media Committee, as well as a few other younger and more "progressive" board members, we were able to accomplish a lot of great things, not only at SBIA, but also for the larger Muslim community in the Bay Area.

As one of the most active committees at the masjid, the Media Committee was sometimes mistakenly seen as a separate organization; one that sometimes went too far and pushed the limits of the charter. I earned the nickname "The Trouble Maker" by some members of the board, because I always had an opinion about how things should be done differently. Some people got upset that I was always asking for money for new programs. Yet despite the occasional negativity, our Media Committee came up with some very unique events which had never before occurred at our masjid, let alone any other mosque in the Bay Area. Some of the events our committee helped to organize included a Halal Organic Cooking Show (which we recorded with a live audience inside the basement of the masjid), Free Media Training Seminars for the local community, and one of the first Ramadan Open Houses, where our Non-Muslim friends and neighbors were invited to the masjid to learn about Ramadan (the month of fasting for Muslims).

But one of our most ambitious endeavors, which still continues to this day, was the implementation of SBIA Eid Program enhancement which included inviting non-Muslim political, interfaith, and community leaders as guests to observe and participate in our community's most joyful time—the Eid celebrations (which happen after the month of Ramadan and at the end of the hajj). Our Eid program had been a very large and successful *mela* (festival) for over fifteen years, but our community did not know how to effectively use this happy occasion to show a more positive image of Muslims to the general public. So as part of the new initiative, we invited interfaith and non-Muslim community leaders, as well as provided a venue for our local government officials to come and meet with our community. Our committee also created a Press Release and invited the local media to cover the event. After watching the local news and seeing happy Muslims being interviewed on the day of Eid, I was elated that we were able to show a positive image of Muslims in America, rather than the usual tense or upset Muslim American reacting to negative events happening on the other side of the world.

One of the most positive and surprising outcomes of the new Eid program was the announcement by the Police Chief of San Jose at the time, Rob Davis, that he would like to fast the whole month of Ramadan, so that he could get the full experience of Ramadan. This became international news. In 2004, Chief Davis, with the help of our Imam Tahir Anwar of SBIA, fasted every day in Ramadan and also came to several *iftaar* (breaking of the fast) dinners at our masjid and at some community members' homes. During our Media Awards and Eid Banquet later that year, we presented Chief Davis with an award for his outreach efforts to the Muslim Community of the South Bay.

My experiences going to an Islamic Sunday school as a child, producing documentary films and even a TV show, and serving on the Board of Directors at SBIA for eight years, all helped shape the person I am today. I gained valuable experience working with different kinds of people and I learned to express my point of view. As that shy kid growing up, I was not really used to speaking out very often; I had to teach myself to make my voice heard through my films and my community service.

I strongly believe that American Muslims should be involved in some form of media work, either professionally or as a part-time hobby, in order to better train and prepare ourselves when we want to get our voices and opinions heard in the public. We can no longer rely on others to tell our stories; we must do it ourselves.

My Moment of Clarity
by Kofi Rashid

Kofi Rashid describes his conversion to Islam as very anti-climatic. For him it just felt like the most logical thing to do, given how he was raised and what he was learning about this amazing way of life. Born to a Jewish mother and an atheist father, he nonetheless converted to Islam at nineteen and says that it forever clarified his outlook on life. At the age of twenty-six, Kofi was given the opportunity to work and live in Malaysia, and jumped at the chance to fulfill a new longing to stretch his horizons beyond the shores of North America. While overseas, Kofi was very fortunate to have worked on projects which directly served the prime ministers of three different countries: Malaysia, Vietnam and UAE. As an American Muslim who lived for eleven years in a Muslim majority country (UAE), and worked for the private office of a Muslim leader (His Highness Sheikh Mohammed bin Rashid Al Maktoum), Kofi's perspective about the world, Islam, his community, and his life went through many evolutions. Now back in America, Kofi is taking the opportunity to use his experience, knowledge, and values to have a more direct impact on the Muslim American community and still stay connected to the global network of friends and colleagues he built over the years. This essay is a brief introduction to Kofi's experience of becoming a Muslim and the impact and influence it has had on his life.

I believe my story is uniquely American. I am a product of this country and her complex history; a history that is rich, diverse, dynamic, exhilarating, and traumatic. My conversion to Islam at nineteen years of age was made possible by these complexities.

I was born to a Jewish American mother from New York City and a black nationalist African American father from San Diego, California, which is not unusual for someone raised in Berkeley, California. My family's story is one of immigration, assimilation, and ascension in America, as well as one of slavery and subjugation.

I grew up in neither the church nor the synagogue, but was well exposed to both. My family infused me with a sense of spirituality that prepared me for Islam. I always knew there was a God or a higher spiritual power, but I could not make sense out of the idea of the Trinity. It just never felt right to me.

My father's brother is a pastor and my brother is a Baptist minister, so I have had every opportunity to become Christian. However, when I would attend church as a youth, the emotion was always too over the top for me. All of the singing, dancing, crying, and screaming was just not the way I wanted to praise God, and it often seemed contrived.

On the Jewish side, I participated in Passover and Hanukkah with my mother's family, and attended a few synagogues for the occasional Bar Mitzvah and weddings. Yet I never considered myself Jewish, and this never seemed like a realistic option for me spiritually. I did not feel comfortable in the synagogue. My discomfort was because I rarely saw any other brown faces in the audience and I didn't seem to feel a spiritual connection to Judaism.

Based on my experiences growing up with both Christianity and Judaism, I determined after high school that I would just be a good person and be led by my own moral compass. I felt like I did not need any organized religion in my life. I was never a part of a religious community and never felt the need to find one.

My first exposure to the word "Islam" was through *The Autobiography of Malcolm X*, when I was a sophomore in high school. My mother had this book in her library and it connected all the dots for me in regards to my family's black nationalist experience and my own realization that there is more to life than my own selfish wants and needs. Yet it wasn't until I matriculated into Howard University that I started to actively pursue this philosophy called Islam.

As a university freshman, with a fresh sense of independence, I was led by my curiosity and the excitement of being in the nation's capital, where intellectual and political events were constantly in play at my university. It was a new and stimulating atmosphere for me, and I think that this fresh start, combined with the fact that I was so far away from my family, gave me the freedom to explore new ideas and thoughts on my own.

The moment that I accepted Islam was when I read the Qur'an for the first time. I purchased a Yousef Ali's English translation from a bookstore about 200 feet from my freshman dormitory. I remember the moment like it was yesterday. I grew up reading the Christian Bible, and on occasion the Torah, and I was used to finding a lot of allegory and metaphor. But when I opened this green, thick book, with silky pages and foreign letters on one side and English words on the other, I was transfixed. I read Al Fatiha—the opening chapter. It made sense. It was clear. It was straightforward. Then I started to read the second chapter, Al-Bakarah. I read the third ayah: "for those who believe in the unseen..." Those five words spoke to my heart like nothing I had ever experienced. I had many instances growing up where I would pray to "God" and I really felt my prayers were answered. So this belief in the unseen was always real to me and I had it even though I could not articulate it the way this Qur'an articulated it. To have a religious book that was the word of God say this to me in such a clear manner made everything fall into place. This was my moment of clarity. I felt a complete sense of peace and fulfillment. I wasn't exactly sure what I had gotten myself into, but I knew this book was from God and if it was from God, I had to follow it. My heart believed in Islam before my brain knew what it really was all about.

I understood what I was reading and there were explanations to certain words or phrases at the bottom of the page, which helped to explain things further. As a math-oriented person, I could not deny the pure logic of the Qur'an and the simple truths that were articulated in it.

I read the entire Qur'an and began attending classes on Islamic law (fiqh) at my university. I was amazed by the depth of this way of life. One of my Islamic Studies teachers would spend hours talking about one Ayat of Qur'an. This class was critical to my confidence in this new religion and in reinforcing what I knew in my heart. The imams who taught me at this early stage were patient and always answered my questions in the most straightforward and clear manner.

I was raised in Berkeley, California, that beacon of anti-establishment activism in America, and my parents were both skeptics. So my natural inclination is to question everything: authority, information, motives—and especially religion. But the more questions that I asked about Islam, the more light began to shine on my quest for truth. The imams presented the religion in a logical framework that made perfect sense to me. At the time, I wasn't looking for a religion, but I was looking for answers about why we exist and who is God. I found my truth in Islam.

The Islamic way of life appealed to my nature and I appreciated its simple approach to worship. Although I was new to Islam, I found its tenets simple and familiar. Islam teaches us that you are to respect others, and that if you do not have something good to say, you should stay quiet. I have always lived by this sage advice. I found no pretenses in Islam and understood that everyone is equal in God's eyes. This is explicitly demonstrated in the hajj (and in the umrah, a smaller, less involved hajj) and its rituals, where a king has to wear the same clothes as the most impoverished person. This corresponded precisely with my own worldview. Only God determines someone's fate and there is no one that can tell you that you are going to hell because you don't believe what they believe. Only

God determines that, and this is echoed by my own sense of justice as well.

I learned that there were over 1 billion people that believed like I was beginning to believe and prayed like I was being taught to pray. I wanted to meet these people. I wanted to work with them and understand them and be a part of them. Feeling a connection through Islam with people all over the world made me feel like there were endless possibilities for my future; I could broaden my horizons in terms of finding meaning and purpose to my life. I was not limited to finding my identity in only an African American context; rather, I was becoming a citizen of the world. I had never really known my purpose in life, but now I had a much wider canvas on which to draw my potential—professionally, spiritually and educationally. Having this understanding made the world smaller and more within my reach. It also gave me confidence that God had a greater plan for me than I realized.

Shortly after I accepted Islam as my way of life, I was fortunate to meet and marry the love of my life. We met at my university, both twenty-year old students. She was born Muslim and shared my life aspirations and balanced me perfectly. Islam has made me whole in so many ways. It opened up my worldview literally, and after graduation I began to focus on how I could live and work to support the development of Muslim countries. My journeys throughout the world and my experiences as a Muslim have reinforced my belief that Islam has perfected the way of life for mankind. Islam teaches me the purpose of life. It teaches me to do something positive to improve this world, to treat others with respect, to live with humility and give thanks to the One that has given me everything. When I read the Qur'an, it is all clear: the meaning of our existence, how we should live, and how we should worship.

Although I grew up with a Christian family and Jewish family, when I converted to Islam, I received nothing but love from both. My Baptist minister older brother is still my hero, even though we don't share the same faith. One of my childhood mentors, who also became a pastor, is still one of my closest confidants. My Jewish grandmother and I had long conversations about the similarities of Judaism and Islam and we had a very close relationship until her death. Because of the way I grew up, I feel comfortable in a multitude of settings and dealing with people that are different than me.

My experiences growing up in a Christian and Jewish world, in a black and white world, of being a Muslim in America and then living as an expatriate for eleven years in Malaysia and Dubai, have helped me realize my role in the world, as both an American and a Muslim. Islam teaches us to operate in an environment of truth, justice, and equality. I believe that American Muslims are uniquely placed to carry these values forward into reality in America and globally, and I want to be a part of this new vision. I have started an advisory firm that develops commercial and cultural ties between the US and other nations, with an emphasis on Muslim-majority countries. I am helping create a reality where American Muslims are able to use their Islam and American heritage as points of understanding and commonality with the rest of the world, for the benefit of the world.

Yes, You Can
by Atif Moon

Atif Moon was born in 1985 with a late stage cancer of the spinal cord and had little chance of survival. Despite three surgeries at the age of one month, and four more surgeries, one lasting fourteen hours, he survived and thrived. He grew up and graduated from the University of California, Los Angeles with a Bachelor's degree in Business Economics in 2007, and received his Master's degree in Sports Management in 2011 with 4.0 GPA. He has worked for prominent organizations, including Fox Sports, NBC and the Tonight Show with Jay Leno, and the Los Angeles Clippers. In 2006, Atif also had the great honor of working for the President as a White House intern. Since his early childhood, Atif has been involved in wheelchair tennis and was ranked among the top Junior players in the nation by the United States Tennis Association (USTA). Atif was the first Muslim to receive the Ten Outstanding Young Americans award by the United States Junior Chamber in 2009. He is also the Co-founder of the Center for Global Understanding (CFGU), a non-profit educational organization to encourage under-represented minorities, including Muslim American college students, to participate in civic engagement. Atif is currently pursuing a career in Sports Marketing and lives in Southern California.

"A hero is an ordinary individual who finds the strength to persevere and endure in spite of overwhelming obstacles."—Christopher Reeve

I faced the first challenge of my life as a baby, when my survival was hanging in the balance and I had to find a way to fight for it. I was born with a fourth stage cancer known as neuroblastoma, which is a tumor of the spinal cord, and I had three surgeries when I was one-month old. At the time, doctors believed I had little chance of survival. Looking back, I believe that it was the inner-strength and perseverance I first demonstrated as an infant that has allowed me to become who I am today.

Fighting the cancer was only the beginning of the challenges I would face. As a result of my illness, I became paralyzed from the waist down. Being in a wheelchair was especially difficult for me to deal with at a young age. In elementary school I was put into special programs because of my disability, such as Adaptive Physical Education (PE), where I was separated from my classmates. This really made me feel like I did not belong, causing me to think that being physically challenged was problematic and worrying about how others perceived me. Furthermore, I had to deal with four more major back surgeries in eleven years to correct the curvature of my spine, which were mentally and physically challenging for me. I later learned that the subsequent three surgeries after the first one could have been avoided if things were done correctly, and this is something that has stayed with me to this day, causing me to fear the worst in most situations.

With these struggles, which I continue to deal with today, I have become stronger as a person. My ability to persevere through these challenges has allowed me to grow because not only have I learned that I can fight through anything, but also that I have been able to apply these learning experiences to future obstacles. For example, if I must face another surgery in the future, I know that I have what it takes mentally and physically to get through it successfully.

My illness might have been the first major obstacle I learned to overcome, but the experience that really developed my approach to struggles is the time I spent in Washington, DC as a White House intern. That period of my life will stick with me forever.

My dad had always encouraged my older brother and me to do an internship in Washington, DC. He believed that every young adult should go there for the experience of learning how our government works and also to meet other professionals, regardless of whether we had any interest in a career in politics. At first I was reluctant, because I had no desire to live in a new city 3,000 miles away from my home, friends, and family. However, with the encouragement of my dad I applied through a program at UCLA for the opportunity to intern in DC. I did not get in on the first try for the spring 2005 quarter. However, as I had learned by then, giving up on the first try is not a good idea. So I decided to re-apply and I was accepted for the fall quarter in 2006.

After I got into the fall program, the next step was to apply to different internship sites. My original plan was to apply to places such as the Department of Justice and the Department of Health and Human Services in fields related to civil rights; however, that changed when my dad said, "Why don't you apply at the White House?"

Even though I knew it would be a great opportunity to work there, I responded, "Yeah, like I have a chance…" I did not think that I would be a good fit for something like this, because I assumed being disabled was going to be an issue and I did not believe I had the right qualifications to get into the program. Essentially, I did not feel like I was good enough to be a White House intern.

Finally, I took my dad's advice and applied, because he has always taught me that I can never know the possibilities until I try. I completed the application and soon found out that I was accepted into the program. It was a feeling of elation for both myself and my parents, who could not have been happier for me. I realized that my willingness to try and my determination paid off.

The next challenge was living 3,000 miles away from home in DC for two months, which admittedly was scary, as I had never lived far away on my own for an extended period of time. I was worried about getting around Washington, DC safely. Once I moved there, I did have to face certain challenges in getting around the city and handling the weather, but they were not major issues. In fact, I enjoyed having to figure out ways to get through them. For example, it was cold and rained a lot when I was there, and I typically had to wheel over from the building I lived in to the White House office dressed in a suit. Since I was not able to use an umbrella to stay dry, I had to purchase a huge overcoat to cover my entire suit, a beanie for my head, and leather gloves to combat the cold and slipperiness of the wheels. Even though the coat was a pain to put on and take off, everything worked out well.

From getting lost in a so-called "ghetto" area in the dark and rain, to being forced to take an escalator on my own (which is clearly not safe) at the subway station, I faced my share of challenges, but I also realized how fun these moments were. I met some amazing people and made great contacts during my time there. Being a White House intern and knowing that I was working on behalf of the president was an unforgettable experience.

My experience in DC will always be with me. It was a defining moment that taught me that we must be persistent and not be afraid to try new things. I believe the fact that I was in a wheelchair and a Muslim working for a Republican president shows how accepting other people are as long as you make an effort to get yourself out there. I was just like any other American working for our country. My co-workers knew I was Muslim and it was not an issue. In fact, they wanted to learn more about my religion and I was happy to tell them more about it.

Even today my confidence level has its ups and downs. Though I know I have been able to achieve many of my goals, including being nationally ranked in the top five in Junior Wheelchair Tennis by the United States Tennis Association (USTA), receiving Bachelor's and Master's degrees, and working at prominent organizations, it has still been difficult for me to maintain a steady confidence due to fears I have carried throughout my life. What has helped me stay strong throughout is my faith in God and the knowledge that I am fortunate enough to have been given opportunities to do great things. I also credit the support of my family and friends, who have always reminded me of my accomplishments and provided words of encouragement that keep me going. People tell me that I am an inspiration to them, and it is a great feeling knowing that I am helping others by living my life.

Even though I am doing things that I enjoy by seeking a career working in the sports industry, which has always been my passion, I think about how I am having a positive impact on others, and this has encouraged me to do more good. After realizing that doctors from various backgrounds (Christians, Jews, Muslims, Hindus) worked together to save my life, I was inspired to start The Center for Global Understanding (CFGU) in 2007 with the vision of "Bringing People Together." CFGU encourages Muslim Americans and other under-represented minority students to get involved in civic engagement and help others, in hopes of bringing more unity in the world. In the future, I also hope to get more involved in motivational public speaking to encourage others that they are not alone with their struggles, and that they can achieve their goals as long as they set their minds to it and believe in themselves. I believe that people are meant to help others and feel that using my life experiences to reach out to others is my opportunity to do this.

A Call to Duty
by Basim Elkarra

Basim Elkarra is Executive Director of the Sacramento Chapter of the Council on American-Islamic Relations (CAIR). Elkarra was re-elected in 2011 to the California Democratic Party's Executive Board, and Chairs its Arab American Caucus and Affirmative Action Committee. Elkarra chairs CAIR-California's Muslim Youth Leadership Program (MYLP) Conference at the State Capitol, and appears regularly in the media as a commentator on issues of civil liberties and foreign affairs. He serves on the American Civil Liberties Union-Sacramento Chapter Board, New Leaders Council (NLC-Sacramento) Advisory Board, and Sacramento Police Multicultural Advisory Committee, and Chairs the Los Rios College Bond Oversight Committee. Elkarra, a San Francisco native, holds degrees in political science and Middle Eastern studies from the University of California, Berkeley. He is a graduate of Georgetown University and the University of Southern California's American Muslim Civic Leadership Institute (AMCLI). Elkarra is currently a senior fellow with the American Leadership Forum.

As the late Steve Jobs once said about life, "You can't connect the dots looking forward; you can only connect them looking backwards." As I look back at my life and attempt to connect the dots, everything seems to point in a certain direction. From an early age I was destined to be someone who brings understanding between people.

In the fall of 1977, a young Palestinian bride immigrated to the United States. Her broken English, bell bottoms, and headscarf made her stand out. She did not allow her obvious differences to prevent her from admiring the American dream. It was the freedom she experienced in America that would allow her, in the coming years, to practice her religion and hold on to her traditions while slowly integrating into American society. This determined young woman was my mother. Her strength and faith enabled her to make sure my four siblings and I became proud Americans while maintaining our Muslim and Arab identity.

As my siblings and I grew up, my mom wanted to ensure that we would retain the essence of spirituality that she had cherished in her youth. There were no Islamic Schools at the time, so she sent us to St. Nicholas Orthodox Church for preschool. Most of the students were of Arab Christian background and we were very welcomed there. Though we were very young, we were able to negotiate all of our identities with relative ease.

In 1984, when I was five, my younger sister was born and my parents decided to take the family to Egypt for a few years in order to learn Arabic, as well as help us preserve our Islamic faith and Arabic culture.

We came to spend the next two and a half years in Cairo. I recall my dad coming back from the US on a visit, bringing me a Rambo toy and a baseball. Having spent my early childhood in the US, the favorite American pastime was dear to us. At the time, I had no idea that few people outside the US actually played baseball. Thus, I found myself repeatedly frustrated as my attempts to play baseball with the other children were constantly foiled. It was soccer that they wanted, not baseball.

While living in Cairo, I went to St. Peter's School for kindergarten. During the summers, I would go to the local mosque to memorize the Qur'an with the other children from the neighborhood. There was something very moving and spiritual about reciting the Qur'an in Arabic; it was music for the soul. Those years in Egypt put the love of spirituality in my heart. Ramadan, as celebrated in many Muslim nations, is a month filled with delights and wonders for young children and adults alike. In Egypt, Ramadan is every child's dream. From the festive nature of the evenings and the special programming that occurs once a year during the holy month, to the late-nights in which every child in the neighborhood is outside playing, I still recall those memories fondly every year as the month of Ramadan begins. My years in Egypt instilled in me a sense of Muslim identity that I would carry with me to America.

Though I was away from the United States for a few years, I never lost track of my American identity. Upon our return to the United States, our American heritage would once again be nurtured. Our Aunt Helaine, whose family goes back to the founding fathers of this nation, took us to swimming lessons and made us listen to country music while in her car. We loved the swimming lessons, but for this urban San Francisco kid, the country music was unbearable at times. We celebrated all the holidays at her house. From coloring Easter eggs, to singing Christmas carols and opening gifts on Christmas Eve, to lighting fireworks on the Fourth of July. It was through the efforts of Aunt Helaine that our family integrated into American society.

Our parents put us in public school, but after a few weeks of barely any homework and constant fights at school, we transferred to a local Catholic school, St. Finn Barr, after a recommendation from my mother's best friend Gloria, a Maronite Christian from Lebanon.

I can still remember my first day at St. Finn Barr. I had just joined the third-grade class and was donning the school uniform—a bright turquoise sweater and navy pants. I stood out like a sore thumb. Everyone in the city knew which school we were attending as soon as they glanced at our very colorful uniforms.

Going from the public school system to a Catholic school was a world of difference. We used to hear stories of children being disciplined by Catholic nuns. Luckily for us, by the time we arrived, the days of spanking were over. Even so, those years at St. Finn Barr were marked by discipline (which I would later grow to appreciate for helping shape our character). The nuns had their spies all over the neighborhood. Not a single student dared date, knowing that the watchful eyes of the nuns' friends were ever fixed upon everyone in turquoise.

Though the nuns told our parents that we did not have to attend the religion course, our parents encouraged us to sit in, attend church, and read the Bible in hopes that we would increase our knowledge about "People of the Book" (the name given to Jews and Christians in the Qur'an). At this young age, I felt comfortable asking the tough theological questions whether they were addressed to Sr. Agnes at school or to my parents at home. With age I became very appreciative that my parents allowed my siblings and I the opportunity to learn about other religions without feeling threatened towards our Islamic faith. To my parents, knowledge was key to a mutual understanding with our fellow Americans, and this would have a profound effect on me throughout my life.

I must confess though, that while attending church, I would often tell my friends not to disclose to the priest their sins, but instead to ask God directly for forgiveness. Also at Church, the nuns would ask me to genuflect and make the sign of the cross, but I would respectfully decline, reminding them that though I loved Jesus, I did not believe in bowing before statues. Alright, I may not have stated it exactly like that, but they got the point. That said, it should be noted that millions of Muslim children attend Catholic and Christian schools worldwide, and share a very similar experience to mine—one marked with fond memories, discipline, and a deep-seated respect for our Christian brethren.

These days, when I speak at churches I always say that I would not have been a practicing Muslim if it were not for Catholic school. I get a few chuckles and a few annoyed looks at first. The latter because they assume I mean that Catholic school was so bad that I became a practicing Muslim. What I truly mean is that being placed in a spiritual environment during my formative years allowed me to maintain faith throughout my life.

In 1991, as bombs were being dropped on Baghdad, I couldn't help but watch as so many men, women, and children were being indiscriminately killed. The fact that it was a televised war, with images of the civilian bunker (filled with women and children) that was accidentally bombed, and the "Highway to Hell" (the road from Kuwait back to Iraq that was littered for miles with dead Iraqis and burned out trucks and vehicles), forced me to recognize the horrors of war at a young age. Though nobody in my family was a fan of Saddam Hussein, we were very opposed to the war. I recall attending a massive rally in San Francisco and an event at the landmark St. Mary's Cathedral, where people of all faiths were showing their opposition to the war.

But the Gulf War had another lasting impression on me. I recall one my friends wearing a shirt featuring Bart Simpson choking an Iraqi. During this period, friends began to make more jokes about Arabs, making me more conscious of my identity as an Arab-American. In 1993, during the Waco Siege, I remember Sr. Anne making a comment during class that Islam was a cult, similar to the Branch Davidians. I asked Sr. Anne, "Why is Islam a cult?" She responded, "Because often, many Muslims live together in one house." In shock, I had to explain to Sr. Anne what the definition of a cult was, in comparison to the religion of over one billion adherents. Sr. Anne apologized and stated that she would not make another comment about Islam before verifying with me first. My Arab-American and Islamic identities were being tested during the Gulf War, and this would not be the last time.

And so the years passed. Then came that fateful morning, when I awoke on September 11th, 2001, and prayed the dawn prayer with my roommates. We went back to sleep after the prayer, only to receive a call from my sister telling me to turn on the TV. I turned on the television and the first tower was in flames. I remember thinking to myself, "Oh God! Please don't let it be Muslims..." I woke up my roommates and we prayed, hoping that it was not a terrorist attack. Then the second tower was hit and we immediately knew that our lives would change forever.

Shortly thereafter, I felt a call to duty, a different kind of duty, not on the battlefield but one that spurred me to build bridges between communities. I felt that, as an Arab-American Muslim who navigated his identities with ease, it was my duty to help bridge gaps at a time when people were calling for a clash of civilizations. I knew the challenges and opportunities of my life had been leading me to this juncture—to be an advocate for mutual understanding. Looking back and connecting the dots in my life I realized that the different stages, from St. Nicholas to Egypt to Catholic school, were not mere coincidences. They were rich experiences that would help me in the battlefield for mutual respect and understanding.

Finding My Purpose
by Abid Husain

Abid Husain is a middle school math teacher who resides in Tacoma, Washington. He was born and raised in Laramie, Wyoming, and is proud of his Wyoming roots. Abid is the youngest of five children of one of the earliest known Muslim families in the sparsely populated state. He studied Civil Engineering throughout his college years, earning a Bachelor of Science degree from the University of Wyoming and a Master of Science degree from the University of California, Berkeley. He eventually made a transition to teaching in order to find a career that led to more personal fulfillment by impacting the lives of those around him. More importantly, Abid one day hopes to mold the middle school basketball team he coaches into a dynasty akin to his beloved Showtime-era Los Angeles Lakers.

Growing up as a minority and a Muslim in Wyoming gave me a strong sense of identity and purpose. From a young age I felt people were watching me closely because of my differences, and this, along with the teachings of Islam, made me want to lead a life of meaning that made a positive difference in the world. Since then, I have striven to find a profession that I enjoy, while at the same time feeling as though I am contributing positively towards society. I fondly recall what my friend's father said when we were graduating from college: "The key is whether you have left this place in better shape than it was before you were here." His advice made me think of my Hispanic friends who were marginalized by our school system and community when I was growing up. They did not dare to dream outside of our small town. They needed someone who would challenge them to think beyond the confines that had been placed on them; perhaps a certain kind of teacher could have made a difference in their lives. My goal is to be that certain kind of teacher, and to help kids who are in the same position today.

Before I began teaching, I was an engineer. However, I found no enjoyment or passion in what I was doing. I knew sitting in a cubicle doing calculations and preparing building plans was not what I was meant to do. I was not using my talents to directly help anyone. I also felt that I needed to work with young people, because working with engineers who are fairly certain they know everything was uninspiring. When I moved away from the world of engineering I started off working with an after-school program mentoring kids. It was enjoyable, refreshing, and rewarding. Eventually I decided to get into the classroom as a teacher, and I now feel like I am doing what I am here to do. I have been teaching in a low-income neighborhood for four years and I have a job I look forward to every day.

I believe that in the journey of life, each of us has our own calling. For me, it is to inspire every one of my students to do their best, and to make sure they know, without fearing failure, that they can work hard to achieve their dreams. One of the main things I like to impress upon my students is that education is a powerful route to having choices in life. I have been fortunate enough to be able to choose to become a teacher, but many of my students may not have many options, due to their environment or financial situation. So I use my experiences to influence them to stay engaged in their education in order to create a wider array of positive choices for their future. My students usually think I'm the crazy one for leaving engineering just to be a teacher, but they understand when I tell them why. Hopefully, my story is something that makes me seem more human in their eyes and helps them whenever they have difficult decisions to make.

Teaching in a low income neighborhood can be a hard and personal ordeal. While the goal is always to improve student achievement, in a school setting it is vital first to forge relationships with your students that are built on trust. This means the teacher must be willing to open up a little in order to get a true and real glimpse into the students' world. It always helps that I can play basketball and that I coach the school's basketball team; these are things that build street cred for me with my students at school. But every single school year, the subject of me being a Muslim has come up with my students. It is a dialogue that I have never been too worried about, seeing as how I have had to explain my beliefs my entire life. Up until this point I have not received any negative feedback when I discuss this aspect of my life with my students, and so the dialogue continues even though it's not the easiest subject to incorporate into my math lessons! The mutual trust developed through these talks definitely strengthens the classroom community, which, I believe, is vital for academic learning to take place.

I have found my students to be very receptive to my beliefs and a number of my African American students have had a family member or friend who has either been interested in Islam or is a Muslim. I had a student a few years ago who tried fasting during Ramadan when she found out I was fasting, and last year we had some Muslim women from the community come to the social studies classes to give presentations on Islam. Sharing our beliefs with as many people as possible helps us promote a positive perception of Islam and Muslims. It is also nice for me to have the hope that my students, who will someday be leaders in this world, might just remember me and not blindly believe all the negative stereotypes floating around. It's funny for me to think that just a few years ago when I started teaching, I would break the ice by saying, "My name is Mr. Husain, no relation to Saddam." My students would be relieved to hear this and, of course, laughter would ensue. There was extra comedy one year because the student class schedules all had me listed as Husain, S. Some of the students said their parents were more than a little concerned. This past year only a few of my students even knew who Saddam Hussein was, so it seems I need to come up with a new introductory phrase. I might try, "My name is Mr. Husain and I am not a terrorist." I may have to check for copyright infringement on that one.

An idea that teaching has cemented in me is the feeling that I have to be a good role model of a Muslim, an American, and a human being in general. This is something that got thrust upon me, growing up as a minority in small town America, and it has stuck with me to this day. It's amazing how many times people have told me I am the only Muslim they know! I feel that my colleagues and students might look at me as an example of what it means to be an American Muslim, so it is important for me to provide a positive image for them. This means that I have to treat people right, behave professionally, and be dedicated to my craft. I want to show people that we Muslims are human just like everyone else, and can even be funny, or mischievous, every now and then. So, in addition to being the co-lead for the math department this past year I may have also been involved in "decorating" our principal's and assistant principal's offices with confetti, chairs, trash cans, balloons, and other random items. Yes, I'm still waiting for their acts of revenge, but hopefully I've had the last laugh.

Think Greatness
by Preacher Moss

Preacher Moss has long been an advocate of a positive social message in the Muslim and non-Muslim communities. His ideologies on social activism and community life directly mirror that of the African American Muslim community under Imam W. D. Muhammad to the recognition of the need for indigenous and immigrant Muslim sustainable development in the United States and abroad. A Hollywood comedy writer and a successful mainstream college and comedy club circuit comedian, Moss has traversed many levels of speaking truth to power and, with God's mercy and favor, continues to do so. His principles are explained with the least amount of complexity. He begins as he ends, "Allah is God. Keep it Simple."

Often times I've joked with my audiences, especially Muslim audiences at comedy events, by challenging them to "think Black." In this I want them to be practical about the things that have happened in American history as a result of race, and to understand that if they ignore the mistakes of the past, they won't have a future that is any different. I speak to the power of remembering justice, fairness, and freedom: when people forget that all these things are from God, not the Congress, Senate, the Right, or the Left, I help them remember. In fact, I think I won't ask my audiences to "think

Black" anymore. I'll challenge them to "think greatness," because Allah is the One who gives us greatness.

As I have shared these sentiments with people over the years, I often remember my first forays into the comedy business. Back then, I was seventeen years old, confident, and principled around the idea that the world should be a better place, and I was going to impose my will to make sure it did improve. As foolhardy as it was, there was an unbridled sincerity that ran through my blood in those days. Such sincerity is strange to see in such a young person, and I often got some funny looks and stares. It didn't occur to me then that I would wind up a Muslim. I unabashedly had fun living a purposeful and transformational lifestyle called "stand up comedy." I would openly draw contempt from audiences speaking on issues of civil disobedience and the loathsome conditions for Blacks and Latinos in urban Milwaukee. My comedy morphed into civil protest as art during my college years. The fundamental question I began to ask myself in private spaces was, "Why?"

My junior year of college I lost a very good friend, Ardell. Ardell was murdered in a common street fight. Since he was close to my age, I was devastated, but what proved even more devastating was that the streets that killed him were the same streets he was trying to escape. Neither one of us were saints back then. We excelled at trying to get our respective hustles on whenever and wherever we could. The difference between the two of us was that he had a better plan. I say this because his plan involved submitting his life to Allah. My plan was admittedly a bit shortsighted, but involved serving the community. I would learn of my friend's plans only after his mother asked me, and several others, to go through and organize his personal effects. In the effort I found he had a Qur'an and some pamphlets on Islam. It was clear that he intended to convert.

In the darkness that comes in these types of scenarios, I would recall the subtle conversations I had with Ardell about the need for longevity, and what would constitute righteous living. Despite all of our talents and skills, we were essentially living unbalanced lives. As a comedian, I recognized that every time I took the stage, I was voicing the importance of moral good. In comedy you make choices about what your artistic voice is going to be, as well as its intent. Sometimes comedy is about engagement and education along with humor. Comedy became, for me, a way to talk about the world we live in. It occurred to me that the funny looks I sometimes got were people actually listening to my message, beyond the laughter. It caused me to crack a smile, because I actually loved those funny looks. It made for a higher challenge. Finally, I realized this was my purpose. I now needed to explore the concept of who and what gave me that purpose. For the answer I needed to look no further than my friend's personal effects: it was Islam, and I would be a Muslim.

I don't really remember the exact day I became Muslim. I like to think of the moment that I became enlightened. I told all of my lady friends that I was I dealing "strictly with deen." Of course, they, like my Mother, thought I was on the gay side, and in a serious relationship with a dude named "Dean." I look back now and laugh, because my relationship with "deen," not "Dean," was not a torrid one in the least. Islam cleaned up my thinking, framed my spiritual correctness, and in one fell swoop laid the infrastructure for the comedian I am today. Me and deen...who knew?

I've stood in front of comedy audiences for the last twenty-five years and stared them down like a gunslinger at high noon. But I didn't have a gun; I only had a smile and the quiet confidence that whatever the challenge, Allah was going to make me a better human being despite the outcome.

I remember doing a gig in Baraboo, Wisconsin. I took the gig because I needed work and stage time. I sensed nervousness in the bar owner's eyes when I walked through the door. He asked me if I'd consider doing the show early even though the place was empty. I went into some tirade about how I was a professional, there to do a professional show. It went in one ear and out the other. Finally he said he was canceling the show and would pay me to leave. The crowd started arriving, and he recanted, but wanted me to go up first. I declined. When I finally got on stage I was killing the crowd. Just as I was going to hit them with another line, seven Klansmen walked into the bar and sat down to watch the show.

The crowd was silent. The Klansmen decided to be a part of the show, and I obliged. The HWSIC (Head White Supremist in Charge) said that he had just come from a rally, where he had been talking about me. I responded that I just came from his sister's house, and we were doing the same thing. The crowd started laughing. He didn't laugh. He made the mistake of asking me what he and his friends looked like. I responded that all those white hoods made them look like "a pack of surrenders" (white flags signaling a truce). The Klansmen looked at each other and laughed, then the crowd laughed. The HWSIC was irritated and embarrassed. He didn't want to be embarrassed further and said he just wanted to see the show. I asked, "Do you surrender?" He responded, "Yes." To rub it in I said, "Spell it." He attempted to spell it but got stuck. The entire bar broke into fits of laughter. To be a total jerk, I proudly told him. "My Muslim name is Shamsideen." He asked, "What does it mean?" I said, "It means, 'White man that can't spell surrender.'" This was by no means a great set, but I strongly believe this was instrumental to the evolution of my Islamic identity and my comedic voice.

I realized in that moment that I wasn't scared to give a message, or stand for what I believed in. Indeed, this was a complete submission to Allah. More importantly, this was what my friend and I were looking for. We just didn't know it was called Islam.

The ironic thing about my Muslim identity is that I had it all along, but I was indeed the last one to see it. True to the realities of the Qur'an, I would become what I was looking for. Being Muslim meant a willingness to take journeys to a better self. I often think of my friend Ardell, and wonder what kind of Muslim he would have been. After all, it was his journey that led me to my own.

I have a small but intense flame that burns deep in my soul. It resurrects memories of Brother Malcolm, Frederick Douglass,

Harriet Tubman, Richard Pryor, Dick Gregory, Jesus, and Prophet Muhammad (peace be upon him). That small flame removed my doubts about who God is, and defined who I would be for God. I can say with pride and purpose, "Allah Made Me Funny." You will sense no uncertainty or ambiguity when you look me in my eyes or shake my hand. When you do these things I would also implore you to smile.

When all is said and done, I will follow the rule of the 3 B's, which means, "Be brief, brother." The enduring truth is that I have sought to achieve levels of greatness in all of my identities, as an American, an African American, and most certainly as a Muslim. In short, I have usurped, with God's blessings, the ability for people to put labels on my beliefs, my opportunities, or me. To be clear, when I speak for myself, I speak for the many of those who weren't able to speak at all. I speak to the many who have passed me by like I was invisible, and I speak from a tradition that says I am supposed to seek out excellence, because we are commanded to do so.

Parrot on My Shoulder
by Rashid Dar

Rashid recently graduated with Honors from the University of Wisconsin, Madison. He majored in global security, with certificates in both Middle East and South Asian Studies. His interest areas include geopolitical strategy, Islamic legal and political theory, and Islamist movements. The evolutions of modern Muslim identity hold are of particular interest to him—more specifically the potential impact that the development of a spirit of modern Muslim cosmopolitanism can have on global affairs, from citizenry on the ground to leaders at the highest of echelons of power. In his spare time, he enjoys reading, music, films, baking, and contact sports. What he prefers perhaps more than all of this, though, is engaged conversation with good people, preferably over hot beverages and cookies.

It sort of bruises you, an examined life. But bruising though my examined life is, I don't believe I have a choice.

As a Muslim growing up in Wisconsin, I always stuck out. Accepting life passively as it came at me was not something easily done. My difference was real and inescapable, affectionately latched onto my shoulder like a proverbial parrot. And eventually I became more or less comfortable carrying this parrot around in public.

Some days I'm thankful for it, that difference. I'd say most days I'm thankful for it. But I'm not afraid to admit there are times when I feel something not entirely unlike jealousy slithering its way through my system. A jealousy of that ability to passively accept life as it unfolds as only the majority in a society can, an almost always unrecognized privilege-curse that, I, for whatever reason, could not be similarly afforded. It is through this lens—thinking about the advantages and disadvantages of difference—that I tend to view my life, it is here that I find myself returning time and time again.

Upon meeting me for the first time, you might judge me. I certainly wouldn't blame you. It's hard to deny that I fit the profile: two-time MSA president, active in many Islamic organizations and initiatives, you know, *that* guy. That annoying guy, reminding you it's time for 'asr (the afternoon prayer). That's how a lot of people know me today, and I'll admit that I don't do too much to try and disabuse myself of the reputation. You may be surprised to know, though, for a guy like me who, on the surface, seems so sure of himself and his beliefs, how fragile things actually feel on the inside. How, for the longest time, I have been beset by thoughts and whisperings. Questions like, how much of my beliefs can be said to be truly organic, coming solely from my own convictions? If they're not coming totally because of my own choice, what then explains my apparent enthusiasm for Islam? The simple answer is usually found on the lips of beaming aunties as they pat my head: "*Ma sha' Allah, beta, Ma sha' Allah!*"—"Such is God's will, child, such is God's will!"

Simple answers like that, though, rarely suffice a young mind. Could it be that my adherence to Islam is a response to the tension of being born different, a Muslim in America? I think of my cousins in Pakistan—what if I had grown up there? Would I feel this special push to accentuate my Muslim-ness all the time? The difference-parrot yet again makes itself known. It nibbles at my hair, its talons dig into my shoulder as it ruffles its feathers and squawks loudly, causing commotion. Some people I know try and hide or otherwise downplay the fact that they're Muslim; they try and shut the parrot up whenever it makes so much as a peep. Am I any better than them if I reassure myself that having an exotic bird at my side at all times is simply how things ought to be for everyone, that I'm somehow *blessed* to be one of the lucky ones, that I *need* the parrot in my life? Both approaches allow one to live less self-consciously, don't they, so why should I think that my route to self-confidence is any better? What's even scarier is that both approaches are inherently selfish—because *I* want to be accepted, or because *I* want to mitigate that feeling of difference: is that why *I* am the way *I* am? If it's all about me, me, me, me...what happens to He?

I like to tell people that I'm sort of a "former nerd," but for those of us who know what being a nerd is like, you know I'm totally lying through my teeth when I say that. Being a nerd isn't like alcoholism, it isn't something you recover from. Ninja-like, some of us simply learn to hide it in a more socially acceptable fashion, and keep our inner Poindexter at bay. I was never the best at the whole hiding thing, though—I too easily get passionate whenever a topic of discussion I care about comes up. Just a few too many four-dollar words slip out unintentionally, and before I know it, my cover is blown, forever typecast. Nowadays, I don't try and deny what I am, but I am also tragically aware of how uncool it makes me at times. As both a teen and a Muslim, I had enough difference on my plate as it was, and when I initially realized how sorely lacking I was in social cache on top of that...it stung a little bit. I would probably go as far as to say that these feelings made me not like or appreciate who I was as a person, or the kind of life I was born into and being forced to live. These negative sentiments towards my own self touched off what became a deep-seated sense of "separateness" from others that I still have a hard time shaking. It didn't matter who you were—family, friend, Muslim, non-Muslim—there was always going to be a limit to how close I would be able to get to a person before I would feel crippled from going any further.

But how do you cultivate a sense of neediness (*faqr*) before God if you feel that your needs are being adequately met, when you actually do feel a real sense of belonging to the people around you? Is He even necessary then? I felt that it was only because the life of this world had said no to me so many times that I had finally said yes to Allah. What did that say about my *ikhlas* (sincerity)? I struggled with these feelings of separateness and pseudo-sincerity for a while, thinking things might change in college, where I would meet Muslims like me. And there I did indeed meet many young Muslims my age that had developed an attachment to their religion, but coupled this attachment with the subsequent development of an intolerant sub-culture that turned away anyone who didn't connect to God in precisely the same way they did. The irony was not lost on me: because many of us failed to find acceptance in the world we were born into, we decided to brood, become insular, and create spaces in which we had control over what behavior was to be permitted and what was not. This was our tree house, not yours. Many of these folks were my friends, but I knew I couldn't inhabit such a world. It was too spiritually flimsy, it worshipped a very narrow approach to Islam rather than The Eternal Allah, and when iman is built on a foundation other than God, it becomes very liable to collapse.

That lonely feeling returned again—but really, though, it had never left.

A thought occurs to me. I could spend my entire life worshiping God externally while never having made even one *sajdah* (prostration) to Him in my heart. I ask God everyday for many things, things both mundane and lofty, but why be granted those things if their bestowal carries with them a loss of that feeling of neediness before He who is beyond all need (*al-ghani*)? Gratitude is, unfortunately, not something ingrained in us from birth, and we are prone to forget our dependence upon God. Does He not say: *"For [thus it is:] when affliction befalls man, he cries out unto Us, whether he be lying on his side or sitting or standing; but as soon as We have freed him of his affliction, he goes on as though he had never invoked Us to save him from the affliction that befell him!"* (10:12) Is it trifling gifts—such as a sense of belonging—that I'm longing for, or is it the One sending them? The danger of this inner *shirk* (to ascribe equals to Allah: a grave sin) takes hold of me, I occasionally feel as if I could maybe be bordering on psychosis. I wonder sometimes if I ever would have even had thoughts like these had I lived a different life in a different place... maybe a place where everyone walked around with parrots on their shoulders.

So I would caution you against pegging me as that preachy Muslim guy with ironclad iman. I don't consider myself as such. God knows best. And as it turns out, the aunties were right, the only thing that can totally explain life—past, present, and future—is *masha'Allah:* that traditional Muslim refusal to assign ultimate causal responsibility to anything other than the Will of God.

There will, in all likelihood, continue to be moments of weakness, darker times, when I wonder if my meticulously maintained faith is just a cover for my own insecurities. I pray that they become less frequent. I've come to believe now that this feeling of inner estrangement is perennial—it's what every human being feels in his or her core, so long as one deceives the self into thinking that anything other than God can fill that void. *"Live in this world as a stranger,"* the Prophet is reported as saying, in effect confirming estrangement as a permanent resident of the heart's deepest chambers. To not acknowledge that is, to me, true *kufr* (disbelief, or the act of knowingly covering up the Truth); it is a denial, a "covering up" of a defining characteristic of one's humanity. Only by embracing that void do we become whole again, and then realize the literal meaning of Islam: surrender accompanied by an otherwise unattainable inner peace. I may meander off the path here and there, but the system of Islam keeps reminding me that I've been here before and that I should know better. The way out always remains the same: sitting still, and exchanging my heedlessness for His remembrance.

Towards a Compassionate and Accepting Orthodoxy
by Omar Suleiman

With his youth and dynamic style of speaking along with his unique depth and grasp on Islamic sciences, Imam Omar Suleiman is a national figure in the Muslim community and an up and coming speaker at Islamic events worldwide. For the past six years, he has served as the Imam of Masjid Abu Bakr (Jefferson Muslim Association) in New Orleans, a member of the Islamic Circle of North America Shariah Council, and a Professor of Theology, Qur'anic Exegesis, History, and Heresiology at various University level institutes including the Islamic University of North America and the Islamic Learning Foundation. He is also the outreach director of Muslims for Humanity in Louisiana and one of the founders of the East Jefferson Interfaith Clergy Association.

It was 2003. I returned home from the United Arab Emirates after rigorously immersing myself in the study of Islam for three years. Although I was born and raised in Louisiana, everything now looked and felt like an entirely different world. My plan was to enroll in university to pursue a degree in pharmacy, because "religious education" wasn't enough to make it in this world. To say that I felt out of place is an understatement.

Growing up, I was a typical New Orleans American boy. I loved basketball and aspired to make it to the NBA one day, and I enjoyed the same movies and music as my non-Muslim counterparts. Yet my life was divided between two incompatible worlds. There was the "Muslim" world at home and the "real" world at school. At home, I had an extremely loving and devout mother who was more often than not in her prayer clothes, reading the Qur'an. My father, on top of being a distinguished chemistry professor and researcher, was possibly the most respected figure in the Muslim community in Baton Rouge, and I genuinely admired him.

Yet in order to fit in at school, I had to conceal my home life as efficiently as possible while convincing my parents that I was donning my religion and heritage as proudly as they were. Eventually this took a toll on me, and I found myself drifting farther and farther away from my religion and heritage. It was just too hard to maintain. Yet as I became a teenager, I grew increasingly restless and concerned that I might be dooming myself to eternal failure. I found myself once again trying to merge my two seemingly incompatible worlds. Around this time, my best friend started to ask questions about Islam. Joshua was the only friend of mine who knew about both of my worlds. Now that he was seriously inquiring about Islam, I was forced to rediscover my own faith. Eventually, Joshua converted to Islam and I reverted to it.

All of a sudden I was taking my faith extremely seriously. I voluntarily started to join the prayers and study circles at my local mosque. But I noticed that this world wasn't very accepting either. The judgmental looks I received for wearing my jeans baggy and low with my shiny necklace and bracelet donned shamelessly are forever etched into my memory.

It was at that point in my life that I realized that in order to attain true spiritual contentment, I needed to immerse myself in an environment of faith. Still in my delicate teen years, I set out on a journey to study my faith in the United Arab Emirates. My parents were incredibly supportive. My father landed a job at the American

University of Sharjah and both of my parents left behind a community that adored them in hopes that I would grow to intimately befriend the Most High in a land where I truly had no one else. I am forever indebted to them for the enormous support that I always received.

When I first got back to the United States, post 9/11, I felt like a complete stranger. Everyone and everything looked totally different to me. But it was time to get back to the real world. I had to get a secular education, many had me believing, or else I would end up being a poor bum. My two incompatible worlds had once again begun to clash, but this time they switched roles. My real world was at home and my world of estrangement was in public. Although I was able to disguise myself now and dodge the majority of my old crew with my new beard and years of absence, I still had a good number of awkward encounters. My old female friends were shocked when I had to explain to them that I couldn't touch them anymore and my old boys wondered why I wasn't interested in the same things that I indulged in before.

I was admitted into Louisiana State University as a pre-pharmacy major. I continued to be book-smart, but was growing increasingly troubled with my major. Instead of reconnecting with my friends or making new ones, I decided to shadow the imam of the Islamic Center of Baton Rouge. I then moved on to Xavier University in New Orleans in pursuit of my degree in pharmacy. I felt empty in New Orleans, since I now had no one to be around. Slowly, I started to give a few short talks in Masjid Abu Bakr in New Orleans, along with lectures in the Islamic Center of Baton Rouge on the weekends. Anyone who knew me growing up was shocked. I was a terrible public speaker my entire life and used to dread class presentations. In fact, I used to sweat and shake with every single one of them, which usually resulted in my class rumbling with laughter before I could finish. But suddenly I felt absolutely no sense of stage fright or nervousness. I could lecture in front of five people or fifty with the same command and confidence.

When Hurricane Katrina hit, I moved back to Baton Rouge, but served diligently as a disaster relief volunteer, and later as a paid field coordinator for ICNA Relief. The experience of Hurricane Katrina taught me that God indeed has a plan for everything and everyone. Through this experience, I got a chance to shadow the imam of the Islamic Center even more, which allowed me to learn a wealth of Islamic knowledge…and to also marry his wonderful daughter. It also opened my eyes to the concept of professionalizing your passion, and I realized that showing compassion to my neighbors and being a source of comfort to people of all faiths in need is not just an aspect of my faith, it's the heart of it.

After this experience, I moved back to New Orleans, where yet another veiled blessing of Katrina was made apparent when I was appointed as the Imam of Masjid Abu Bakr, also known as the Jefferson Muslim Association. This position, combined with my post with ICNA Relief, has allowed me to connect with thousands of Muslim youth both locally and nationally. It has given me the liberty to do what I love for a living. As imam, I've continued to try to reach out to other audiences by often joining and even initiating interfaith and social justice work here in New Orleans. In 2009, I was able to be a part of the founding of the East Jefferson Clergy Interfaith Association, which has become the source of much good to the area of Greater New Orleans. My primary goal, however, has not been to just reach out to non-Muslim audiences, but to reach the plethora of young American Muslims who often feel unwelcome in Islamic settings and alienated from their faith as I once was.

I reflect often on the approaches in mosques that were used to "save" me when I was falling. One approach was to shun me and make me feel ashamed of myself for the way I looked and acted. The other way seemed to water down the faith so that it could appeal more to me. Needless to say, both of those approaches failed miserably. Therefore, as imam, I have tried to seek a balanced approach that accommodates the "sinner" while not blurring the faith's stance on the "sin."

The narration in the collection of Imam Ahmad of the Prophet Muhammad, which always shakes me to the core, is that of a young man who found himself overwhelmed by his sexual desires. The young man paced around impatiently in the mosque until he finally approached the Prophet asking him flat out for permission to fornicate. The companions of the Prophet were appalled and infuriated by the young man's audacity to ask for such a thing. The Prophet did not shun him, nor did he give him permission to commit the forbidden action. Rather he came down to the young man's level and reasoned with him by asking in a soft voice, "Would you like that for your mother? How about your daughter? How about your sister? How about your aunt?" When the young man responded in the negative each time, the Prophet then simply said, "That's how everyone else is, too." He then put his hand on the chest of the young man and prayed for him, which, according to the narration, left the young man content and free from the pressure he faced before.

The facet of this incident that strikes me most is not that the Prophet was loving enough to come down to the young man's level and help him, but rather the fact that the young man felt like he could approach the Prophet with his problem and not be chastised or reprimanded. To me, this incident represents the perfect implementation of "hate the sin, but love the sinner."

Over the past few years, my goal has been to make the mosque more youth-oriented by catering programs specifically to them, and also being there for them in their times of need. The challenge is always to generate a sense of approachability without changing the faith itself to accommodate those struggling with it. The program in the mosque that has been most successful is the "Youthtube" halaqa (Islamic gathering which serves as an occasion of learning and the remembrance of God), which is a no-holds-barred gathering for youth every Friday night that addresses the real issues they face with a blend of compassion, urgency, and reality checks. The halaqa starts off with a video of some sort of Islamic nasheed (song in praise of God), poem, recitation of Qur'an, etc.—hence the name "Youthtube."

Through this group, I've been able to build a healthy relationship with many of the attendees on an individual basis. Interestingly enough, many of them refer to me as "Omar," which is what I've always preferred, while their parents feel obliged to call me "Imam Omar." We play sports together, watch games, go on retreats, and try to stay as close as possible. I strive to avoid being judgmental and condescending towards them as the "religious" crowd was to me when I was in their shoes. Many Muslims are downright oblivious to the nature of the challenges that young Muslim Americans face in this society. The "uncles" in the mosque often angrily point out the minor outward displays of the struggle of the youth and focus too much on preserving the image of religiosity. My response to the complaint of "he dresses un-islamically" has always been and will always be, God willing, "I'll work on his heart for now, and he'll change the way he dresses himself."

There is no doubt that striking the perfect balance between tough love and gentleness is no easy task. I often wonder if it would have been better for me to grow up sheltered in a conservative society with limited access to the things that once derailed me as a young man. On one hand, I'm certainly remorseful of the sins I committed. On the other hand, however, I know that I wouldn't be able to understand what young American Muslims go through today had I not once treaded their path. With changing times and trends, I know that there will certainly be instances in which my approach may not generate the desired results. But as long as these young men and women recognize that I'm there to help and not judge them, then I've done my part. My only hope is that I may be used as a medium to inspire struggling Muslim youth with the prophetic message that they are greater than their sins, and not vice versa.

Veering off the Roadmap
by Humza Ilyas

Humza Ilyas is a native of Pittsburgh, Pennsylvania. He attended Penn State University before pursuing his medical education at Jefferson Medical College in Philadelphia.. After concluding his post-graduate training in New York and Wisconsin, Humza moved to the Atlanta area where he is a practicing dermatologist and Mohs surgeon (for the treatment of skin cancer). Humza is an active participant with several interfaith groups, both in his native Pittsburgh as well as in Georgia. He enjoys reading, traveling, and spending time with family. He resides in Atlanta with his wife and daughter.

The classic roadmap for being a first generation Pakistani American boy raised in the United States follows a fairly simple and not altogether unpredictable route. It goes something like this:

Do well in school
Get into a good college (extra points for Ivy League)
Go to medical school
Pursue a career in a desirable medical specialty
Get married to a nice Pakistani girl (extra points if she hails
from the same part of Pakistan)
Settle down and have kids
Raise said kids using the same roadmap

It's a tried and tested plan with many a success story to bear out its value. While we often may have rolled our eyes when our parents made these suggestions over the years, the benefits of a strong education, a stable and financially sound career devoted to helping others, and building a family with a spouse of the same background are all self-apparent. What this formula may lack in originality, it more than makes up for in gratification. Wanting nothing but the best for their children, our parents' generation threw down the gauntlet of this Desi Triple Crown to us.

So it was that I began my chase. The initial phases of this plan passed fairly smoothly. With the guidance and support of my parents and older siblings, I navigated the waters of my pre-professional and medical education successfully. By the time I neared the conclusion of my residency training, the steady drumbeat building around me surrounded the question of finding a spouse—the ever-elusive third leg of the Triple Crown.

As is often the case, well-meaning friends and family suggested possible matches. The commentary surrounding these proposals was equal parts amusing and terrifying: She's a doctor! She comes from a good family! She's very fair! She's tall! I felt as though I were involved in some kind of bizarro *Weird Science* remake. Of course, the one descriptor that went unsaid—she's Pakistani!—remained so because, well, we all just assumed that was understood. And despite meeting some very nice people, I hadn't found anyone compatible enough to ask for her hand in marriage. Then one day, as it is wont to do, life led me to a girl named Yasamin, who seemed to meet every criterion I could ever dream up in a life partner. And she just happened to be Iraqi.

I grew up in a home in which my parents were very actively involved in the Muslim community as well as the interfaith community. They counted among their closest friends people from a tremendously diverse group of ethnic backgrounds, both Muslim and non-Muslim. We entertained friends at our house who were everything from Egyptian to Bosnian, Italian to Iranian, Turkish to

Greek. Unity, tolerance, and building bonds of brotherhood and sisterhood with the members of our community were life lessons I was taught at a young age. That said, the distance from having close friends of another culture to having a spouse of another culture seemed about as far as the distance from Lahore to Baghdad. After all, the issues related to a cross-cultural marriage extend far beyond whether one prefers to break the fast with *dolma* (a traditional Middle Eastern appetizer consisting of grape leaves stuffed with rice and meat) or *samosa* (a traditional Pakistani appetizer composed of a fried dumpling stuffed with potatoes, peas and spices).

There are multiple motives behind marrying within one's culture. Commonalities in customs, cultural mores, language, and cuisine (not to be overlooked), among others, are commonly cited reasons for doing so. My three older siblings each followed this trend and married Pakistanis. Nevertheless, I was both comfortable with and optimistic about pursuing Yasamin's hand in marriage for a variety of reasons. First and foremost, I was comforted by a verse of the Qur'an that anyone who has been invited to a Muslim wedding has likely seen gracing the invitation:

> O mankind! We have created you male and female, and have made you into nations and tribes so that you may know each other (not that you may despise each other). Verily the most honoured of you in the sight of Allah is (he who is) the most righteous of you. And Allah has full knowledge and is well acquainted (with all things). (49:13, Surah Al-Hujurat)

When I re-read that verse after Yasamin came into my life, it took on an even more powerful tone. The beauty behind the idea that God has molded mankind into so many distinct and varied groups scattered all over the world as opposed to a repetitive monolith really struck a chord with me. He exhorts us to "know each other"; to build bridges between communities, and seek opportunities for mutual understanding and growth. Further, He provides us with the idea that the most important barometer of a person's worth is his or her righteousness, and not his cultural, racial, or religious affiliation. Truly, God guides away from narrow-mindedness and provincialism and guides towards right action and good conduct.

On a practical level, Muslims of all ethnic backgrounds growing up in the US have far more in common with each other than with their counterparts in their respective native countries. I certainly have less in common with a Punjabi Pakistani born and raised in Islamabad than with Arab American friends I grew up with in Pittsburgh. Our shared Islam forms the foundation of a great many friendships and relationships as we address the challenges and enjoy the successes of our communities. As immigrants of all stripes embrace the melting pot phenomenon of America, we come to enjoy and accentuate the similarities we all have, while cherishing and honoring our respective cultural traditions.

Ultimately, while it may have been an unexpected twist, I was confident that my family would be open to the idea of my marrying someone who was not Pakistani. Their response surpassed my expectations. After meeting Yasamin and her family, my parents were very excited about the prospect of marriage bringing our two families together. Whatever minor reservations existed were entirely the product of a lack of familiarity with certain elements of a foreign culture. As our families got to know each other better, those reservations quickly abated. Shortly thereafter, we were married (yes, the above verse was on the wedding invitation), and the wedding served as our first celebration of the union of two different cultures under the shared umbrella of Islam. After all, under what other circumstances would one attend a wedding featuring a dance floor transitioning seamlessly from *bhangra* (a Pakistani/Indian folk dance) to *debka* (a traditional Arab folk dance) and back?

These days interracial marriage barely raises an eyebrow across a great many communities, cultures, and religious groups around our nation. Amongst American Muslims, stories like Yasamin's and mine are becoming ever more prevalent. As our immigrant communities follow the examples of those that preceded us here, it is increasingly likely that we will continue to become more integrated into one unified fabric with lines of distinction being increasingly blurred.

Just as so many in our generation have proven the value of pursuing careers in fields ranging from journalism to law to teaching to politics to business and beyond, so too are increasing numbers of Muslim Americans discovering the value and rewards of interracial marriage. As Yasamin and I eagerly anticipate the arrival of our first baby, God-willing, we look forward to raising her in a pluralistic society that celebrates our cultural differences as well as our many commonalities. We hope to raise her with a strong sense of self, emanating fundamentally from the strong morals that Islam teaches us while being enhanced by both her Pakistani and Iraqi heritage.

In the meantime, I can be found snacking on *hummus* (an Arabic spread/dip) and *pakoras* (a fried South Asian snack), and patiently saving money to put her through medical school (some dreams die hard).

From Islam to Islam
by Michael Muhammad Knight

Michael Muhammad Knight is the author of eight books of fiction and nonfiction, including the novel, *The Taqwacores*, and his hajj narrative, *Journey to the End of Islam*. His work has been translated into multiple languages and taught in numerous college and university courses. He earned an MTS (Master of Theological Studies) degree from Harvard University, and is presently a Ph.D. student in Islamic studies at the University of North Carolina at Chapel Hill.

When I told my father that I was becoming Muslim, he looked at me and asked, "You don't like niggers, do you?" I was fifteen years old and had known him for less than an hour. Dad explained that he was a racial separatist, claiming that races were divided by profound psychological differences that prevented them from ever living together in harmony.

My father couldn't have known this on the day that we met, but his reaction only provided fuel to my developing personal mythology. I did not have the self-awareness to see it at the time, but much of what I wanted from Islam was a divorce from white people. As an angst-ridden sophomore at a Catholic high school, I saw Islam as the answer to everything wrong that I saw in the world—and also within my own family. Islam, I believed, was not only the antidote to racism and imperialism, but also to the kind of familial chaos that would lead a boy to first meet his neo-Nazi biker dad at fifteen. I sought Islam to fix what was broken.

I don't know if any religious conversion is entirely about "religion." At least mine wasn't. Long before I took an interest in theology, Islam spoke to other needs that I was trying to meet as a teenager: the needs to define and mark myself, create my own identity, and find a place in the world. Islam did all of that before I thought about God or the fate of my soul. My first exposure to Islam came through Malcolm X, whose interest in religion seeemed to give privilege to social and political consequences over inner spirituality. Even in Malcolm's highly confessional account of his second conversion to Islam, during his pilgrimage to Mecca, his rebirth has less to do with the sacred realms of God, soul, and spirit than what he sees Islam achieving on the ground: the changes in how human beings relate to one another.

For Islam to have been my rebellious pose does not mean that I was insincere. Inspired by *The Autobiography of Malcolm X,* I hoped that Islam could transform my life as it had for Malcolm. Granted, my lows weren't as low as what Malcolm had experienced, but I was a fairly messed-up kid. Around the time that I discovered Malcolm, I was also writing letters to Charles Manson (and Charlie did write me back). Between Malcolm and Charlie, I had a choice to make. I chose the path of Malcolm.

My encounter with Islam's spiritual dimension did not occur as a single, definitive "born again" moment like that of Malcolm's rebirths in prison and at Mecca. Faith eased its way into my heart slowly, with the ingestion of more books and my learning the prayers in Arabic. Before coming to Islam, I had called myself an atheist; the god of my mother's Catholicism seemed too small for me, too human and too limited. Islam's concept of tawhid struck me as a cleaner monotheism, and allowed my heart to open up to God in ways that it could not while in the church. Islam became more than a way of redrawing my relationship to white America; it began to mark my heart.

My mother supported my conversion. She even drove me to the nearest mosque and witnessed as I performed shahadah. Until that day, I had never even met a Muslim in real life. Over the next few months, I developed a genuine, community-based relationship with Islam. Through connections at the mosque, I also received an invitation to spend two months of my senior year at Faisal Mosque in Islamabad, Pakistan, where I would participate in an educational program specifically designed for new Muslim converts. Only seventeen years old, I was the program's youngest participant ever.

I loved Pakistan; the madrassa was at least everything that I needed at that particular time. It felt like a Muslim fantasy camp; we spent all day hearing that we owned the ultimate and absolute truth, the singular truth that could end all suffering and injustice on this planet and secure eternal salvation. The power of this truth, we were taught, had already been proven once, in the Golden Age established by the Prophet and the early generations of Muslims. Islam, *real* Islam, was perfect and pure; problems only arose when people tried to deviate from this real Islam and follow their own desires.

They told such a beautiful story at that place, and I believed every word. When the camp was over, I went back home and finished high school. Going from my Muslim paradise in Islamabad to my dumpy small town filled with promiscuous drunken teenagers was hard to bear. Desperate to hold onto my experience of Pakistan, I took to wearing my robes and kufis and sleeping in the mosque. At one point, I decided to wear a gigantic black turban that made me look like an Iranian ayatollah.

I kept reading, and eventually I encountered books from the Shi'a perspective. Nothing in my lectures at Faisal Mosque had prepared me for this; we had been taught to believe in that early Golden Age of Muslim unity, with four rightly-guided caliphs and such. In the Shi'a books, I learned that this Golden Age never existed; Muslims were fighting and oppressing each other from the day that the Prophet died.

It destroyed me to learn that human beings are always human.

In Pakistan, I had had been taught a declining view of history; that as a species, we reached our pinnacle of justice, equality, and ethical development during the lifetime of the Prophet, and that after his death we would only regress—each generation worse than the one before it—until at last humanity reached a state of total ignorance. The Prophet's companions were supposed to be superheroes of whom imitation was both required and impossible. I found this image challenged, however, as I began to read books from the Shi'a perspective. Exploring another version of our history put some cracks in the Islam that I knew, the Islam of mythical Golden Ages, and it broke my heart. If the earliest Muslims were the greatest, why did they allow petty politics to divide their community forever? If every generation was another degree of separation from the Prophet, and Muslims from that Golden Age were willing to butcher the Prophet's grandson, what kind of Muslims could we be? The Prophet's companions had been the foundation for my Islam. Once it became possible to question them, the whole construction of Islam fell apart for me.

I would still make night visits to the mosque, but I gave up the days. I only felt at peace with the mosque when no one else was there and I didn't have to feel like a hypocrite. Eventually, the tough questions pushed me out of the mosque altogether. I began to consider that I might be an apostate. As the only Islam that I had known called for the execution of apostates, this made things difficult.

I did not know where I belonged; I wasn't necessarily a Muslim, but I wasn't anything other than Muslim, and could never be. By this point, Islam was too deep in me to ever find its way out. Even as an apostate, I loved God, and I could only express my love with the gestures that I had learned in the mosque.

Being Muslim or non-Muslim depended on the idea that Islam had clear borders that everyone could see and recognize. But as I kept reading, the border became sloppy. Sometimes I couldn't see it. Everything that I had taken for granted as essential to an un-compromising and unchanging "Islam" was actually the result of human power struggles. The border has never stayed in one place, and "orthodoxy" has continually readjusted itself.

No matter how Muslims defined orthodoxy in a given historical moment, there were Muslims outside those bounds: philosophers, mystics, and members of unpopular movements who found themselves at odds with the Islam of their day. Islam has always had rebels; they comprise their own tradition. Within Islam, I found a heritage. There are voices that justify my place. My Islam is Avicenna who loved wine and denied the bodily resurrection, Ibn 'Arabi having sex with the letters of the Arabic alphabet, and al-Hallaj building a Ka'ba in his yard. Whether or not I would agree with everything that they said or did, or even if the sum total of Islam's rebels and heretics could add up to any coherent message didn't matter. The point is that the borders opened up for me and my own confusion.

The more I read and the greater diversity of Muslim voices I al-low into the mosque of my own head, the less I can speak with any confidence on what's authentically "Islamic." I don't think of this as disbelief, because it has brought me back into the mosque. It allows me to cry for the Prophet, return to the Qur'an, perform hajj, and marry into a Muslim family; it allows me to join Muslims in prayer, even if I don't yet have all the answers, without feeling insincere. If any particular version of Islam attempts to squeeze too tightly, I'm out; but these days I travel among numerous Islams, taking the best that I can from each one. I pray like a Sunni, but also join in Shi'a observations of Muharram. I have received initiation in an Iranian Sufi order. I consider myself a friend to the Nation of Islam and have no issue whatsoever with calling them Muslims. I am also a friend to queer Muslims, and embrace the feminist heresies of Pro-gressive Islam. In 2005, I took part in the historic congregation of women and men standing together, shoulder-to-shoulder, feet-to-feet, praying as one body behind a female imam, Dr. Amina Wadud.

I'm confused and I will always be confused, and it has to be this way, because I am not the Creator of the universe. I can see my religion as having integrity only when I don't pretend to know the answers. This is my submission, my peace in Islam. I love God, I love the Prophet, and I submit to my smallness—the smallness of my human brain, my numerous failures, the smallness of this moment in history, the limits of my own path to Mecca. I submit, I submit, I am of those who have surrendered, and I have found peace in my confusion. It took a lot of fucking around to get here, but I'm here.

Glossary

Alhamdolillah. "Praise be to God." A term often used by Muslims to express thanks to God.

assalaam alaykum. Arabic greeting, "peace be upon you."

ayah. Literally, a sign or evidence. A reference to verses from the Qur'an.

azadari. Mourning congregations, lamentations, chest beating, and all such actions which express the emotions of grief and solidarity with the Imam Hussein.

dawa. Inviting others to Islam.

deen. Faith or religion.

dhikr. Literally, "remembrance." Devotional chanting of short phrases or sacred words from the Qur'an.

dhuhr. Mid-day, time for afternoon prayers.

Eid al Fitr. The Islamic holiday that marks the end of Ramadan, the month of fasting.

fatwas. Religious rulings issued by Muslim scholars.

fiqh. The practice of Islamic jurisprudence. *Fiqh* is an expansion of the code of conduct (*shariah*) expounded in the Qur'an and supplemented by tradition (*sunnah*) as set out in interpretations of Muslim scholar-clerics.

fitra. One's natural state or inherent nature.

ghazals. A poetic form consisting of rhyming couplets and a refrain, with each line sharing the same meter. Very popular style of Persian and Sufi poetry.

hadith. Sayings and acts of the Prophet Muhammad and his companions collected after his death that serve as guidance for understanding the Qur'an and Islamic law.

hajj. The pilgrimage to Islam's birthplace, the holy city of Mecca. This spiritual journey is the fifth pillar of Islam, a requirement of every Muslim to perform, if within their means, at least once in their lifetime.

halal. Refers to Islamic dietary laws or, more specifically, meat that has been slaughtered in a prescribed way. Can also refer to anything proper or legitimate and according to Islamic law.

halaqa. A spiritual gathering that serves as an occasion of learning and participating in dhikr chanting and prayer.

hijar. White drawstring pants.

iftaar. The evening meal that breaks the fast during the month of Ramadan.

imamah. In Shi'ism, the line of divinely ordained guides descended from Ali and Fatimah.

iman. Faith.

jihad. The Arabic term for "struggle in the path of God." The Qur'an speaks of the greater and lesser jihads. The greater jihad is the personal struggle to overcome one's own imperfections and shortcomings, the effort by Muslims to perfect their submission (*islam*) and their faith (*iman*). The lesser jihad is the battle against the enemies of Islam as regulated by the *shariah*, as in defensive war.

jummah. Friday congregational prayer held just after noon.

keffiyeh. Traditional Arab headdress for men.

khameez. Long shirt or tunic.

kufi. Traditional Muslim skull cap for males.

kufr. Disbelief.

kurtah. Long white shirt.

maghrib. Literally, "the west," also refers to sunset and time for evening prayer.

masha'Allah. "God has willed it." A phrase used to express thankfulness and appreciation.

masjid. Also referred to as a mosque, a place of prayer and worship.

massalla. A prayer-mat.

nasheed. A song in praise of God.

namaaz. Persian term for the five daily prayers said by Muslims.

nubuwwah. The term for all the prophets of the Abrahamic faiths of Judaism, Christianity, and Islam.

raka'ah. The prescribed movements and words followed by Muslims during salaat prayers.

Ramadan. The month of fasting for Muslims.

Ramadan Mubarak and *Ramadan Kareem.* A greeting and response said during the fasting month. Literally, Blessed (Mubarak) Ramadan and Generous (Kareem) Ramadan.

qibla. The direction of the Kaaba in Mecca toward which Muslims face during prayers.

Sajdah. Prostration made during prayers.

Shalwar. Loose pajama-like trousers.

shariah. Islamic law. There are two primary source of Islamic law: the precepts set forth in the Qur'an and the example set by the Prophet Muhammad in the sunnah.

salaat. The five daily prayers said by Muslims.

sunnah. The body of Islamic custom and practice based on Muhammad's words and deeds as recorded in the Qur'an and hadith collections.

taqwa. Self awareness, God-consciousness.

tawhid. The oneness or unity of God.

topi. The traditional Islamic cap worn by men.

TUS. Abbreviation of the phrase *tawul umur sharif* "may his life be lengthened," in the Arabicized Gujarathi language specific to Dawoodi Bohras.

ummah. The Muslim community.

umrah. A pilgrimage to Mecca at any time of the year, i.e. outside the hajj period.

wahdah. The concept of unity, related to the term tawhid.

Wahhabism. An eighteenth century theological movement that aims to purge Islam of perceived innovations and corruption. It has become the dominant form of Islam in Saudi Arabia.

wudu. Ablutions performed as part of the daily prayers.

Questions for Discussion

1. What is religion? What is the purpose of religion? What is the difference between religious doctrine and what people of faith do in practice?

2. What is culture? How is it intertwined with religion? Is it so intertwined in the United States compared to other countries?

3. How do the men in *All-American* address the act of balancing their faith with their American identity?

4. What was your perception of Islam before reading *All-American* and has it been changed or confirmed after reading the book? In what ways, if any, has it changed?

5. What information or argument or perspective in the book did you find especially surprising or compelling? And furthermore, with whose story did you identify most strongly?

6. Did this book inspire you to read more about the history of Islam and Muslims?

7. Some writers insist that a "clash of civilizations" is inevitable. Others have claimed that a person cannot be both a faithful Muslim and a loyal American citizen. What do you think?

8. Do you adhere to a religion that has a sacred scripture? Do you know what every word in scripture means? Do you take every word literally? If not, why not?

9. Are the words "objective," and "biased" appropriate to a discussion of religion? How are they used in the public discourse? Is there an objective view or only different points of view?

10. There has been a rise in attacks on Muslims and mosques in the United States. Has Islamophobia effected your community? How do you respond to Islamophobia?

11. What is the role of religion in politics? How does religion impact our public discourse on where we are going politically or culturally as a nation?

12. What would you like to investigate further after reading this book?

About the Editors

WAJAHAT M. ALI is a playwright, attorney, essayist, and humorist. *The Domestic Crusaders* is his first full-length play published by McSweeney's in January 2011. Ali's essays and interviews on contemporary affairs, politics, the media, popular culture and religion frequently appear in a variety of publications. He is the associate editor of Altmuslim.com and contributing editor to the award winning *Illume Magazine*. Ali is a frequent consultant on Islam and Muslims, post 9/11 Muslim American identity and politics, multicultural art and activism, and New Media Journalism. In 2011, he was the lead author and researcher of *Fear Inc., The Roots of the Islamophobia Network in America* published by The Center for American Progress. Ali lives in the San Francisco Bay area.

ZAHRA T. SURATWALA is an author and editor. As President/CEO of Zahra Ink, Incorporated and Co-Founder of the *I Speak for Myself* book series, she has found a way to combine her love of writing with her desire to pursue projects that can truly affect change. Zahra's articles have appeared in various publications including Patheos, Elan Magazine, AltMuslimah and Feminist.com. She obtained her Master's of Arts degree in English Literature from Loyola University in 2003. She has lived in Egypt and Thailand but will always call Chicago home: she loves its beauty and its very fickle weather. When she is not writing, Zahra can be found causing a ruckus with her husband, son, and daughter. If home is where the heart is, her home is firmly placed in their hands.

Acclaimed Books on Islam from White Cloud Press

I SPEAK FOR MYSELF *American Women on Being Muslim*

edited by Maria Ebrahimji & Zahra Suratwala

Selected as a Huffington Post "Top Religion Book for 2011"!

$16.95 / Islam / ISBN: 978-1-935952-00-8

"These are the voices of mothers, daughters, sisters and neighbors we can all identify with representing an honest effort to allow American-born Muslim women to change the narrative of American Islam—in their own words." DEEPAK CHOPRA, AUTHOR OF *MUHAMMAD*

DEMANDING DIGNITY *Young Voices from the Arab Revolutions*

edited by Maytha Alhassen & Ahmed Shihab-Eldin

$16.95 / Islam / ISBN: 978-1-935952-71-8

AVAILABLE FALL 2012

A collection of 20 essays written by Arab youth who have directly inspired and sparked a revolutionary spirit that toppled governments. Each story captures the changes revolutionizing the region. Their journeys point to a vision of pan-Arab identity as seen in these connected struggles.

THE MUSLIM NEXT DOOR *The Qur'an, the Media, and that Veil Thing*

by Sumbul Ali-Karamali

$16.95 / Islam / ISBN: 978-0-9745245-6-6

"A beautiful book. For anyone who truly wants to know what Muslims believe, this is the perfect book." REZA ASLAN AUTHOR *NO GOD BUT GOD: THE ORIGINS, EVOLUTION, AND FUTURE OF ISLAM*

APPROACHING THE QUR'AN *The Early Revelations*

by Professor Michael Sells

$21.95 / Islam / ISBN: 978-1-883991-69-2

"The best version of Muslim scriptures available in English ... An important and illuminating work, one that will be welcomed by scholars, students, believers, and all who seek to better understand Islam and its sacred scripture." CARL ERNST, PROFESSOR OF ISLAMIC STUDIES, UNIVERSITY OF NORTH CAROLINA, AND AUTHOR OF *THE SHAMBHALA GUIDE TO SUFISM*

WHITE CLOUD PRESS
www.whitecloudpress.com   800-380-8286